THE TWELVE HIERARCHIES OF EARTH

Trace your spiritual family and find your place of belonging

AMANDA GUGGENHEIMER

Arcadia Press

The Twelve Hierarchies of Earth

Published 2018

ISBN 978-0-6483772-1-4

For more information
www.amandaguggenheimer.com

Published by Arcadia Press
www.arcadiapress.com.au

Country of publication: Australia

For my son Raphael

May there be no further need for you to forget as you put aside the veils that we have worn and glimpse the Oneness beyond. May you re-awaken the knowledge within so that in all situations you may remember who you truly are and your divine origins.

Other books by Amanda Guggenheimer

The Light-Worker's Companion

The Channel's Companion

Tobias and the People of the Sky Realms

ACKNOWLEDGEMENTS

Thank you to Kay Jones who also wears the cloak of Lady Leto and with her sword of discrimination has throughout this assignment been a chaperone and true companion of the highest order, as always. Thank you, Kay, whom I wish to acknowledge not only as Editor of the manuscript, but also as a contributor. In particular, Kay's relationship with the Saints, and her insight into the Mer people and the Lady of the Sacred Waters of Life provide the work with a depth that otherwise would not be available. I wish to express my heartfelt gratitude for her mentorship over many years.

Thank you to Shannon, who twenty-two years ago allowed me to live in her mountain retreat as her apprentice for four years. She laid an important foundation for what has become my vocation, but also held the energy and space for this book to first reveal itself to me. Shannon's tireless service set a high example of commitment to one's Earth assignment.

Thank you dearly to Paul Guggenheimer for reading the book and sharing his thoughts, which improved the manuscript immensely, and for giving me my first copy of the *Tao Te Ching* all those years ago. Thank you to Dr Leanne Hao who provides me with tremendous spiritual support. Thank you to Bill and Jennifer Bennett for including my work in their film *PGS - Intuition is your Personal Guidance System.*

Thank you to my clients, readers and those who have attended my workshops. I have grown as a channel and as a human being through the privilege of being of service to you.

Contents

Foreword

The concept of the Hierarchy has existed since the beginning of time, among all humans who intuitively grasped the concept of inclusivity as a blueprint of the cosmos and the inter-relationship of all within it. This understanding resided in humanity as an impulse or spark, fanned by the realisation that the prospects of survival were enhanced by communion with all beings (human and non-human), in a vast network wherein each one had a part to play but which also extended beyond themselves. They might not have been able to articulate it in so many words, but an awareness of the divine principle flowing through individual souls and forming Earth itself was seeded with the birth of humanity and continued to grow. The capacity to recognise a universal and unifying force is in fact our birthright; to acknowledge - in however rudimentary a manner - the Spiritual Hierarchy of Earth that sits at the core of creation.

Over the ensuing thousands of years, with the evolution of humankind, as civilisation spread and different races settled in different parts of the world, as societies developed with different religions, beliefs and practices that brought diversification on so many levels and the pooling of power, the collective mind then fragmented into a myriad of strands - and the notion that we are all held together by an overarching Hierarchy was replaced by a hierarchical view of a different order: one that pitted race against race, religion against religion, tribe against tribe, person against person. Paradoxically as society became more hierarchical, the old notion of hierarchy as a cohesive factor was obliterated and divisiveness became the new keyword. Slowly, inexorably, a unified world view that had encompassed all creation and all life forms was dismantled.

At the same time, innate understanding of the workings of the cosmos was dismissed in favour of outer systems of information and access to learning was restricted. Knowledge itself became a commodity, concentrated in the hands of a few and subject to tight control as those in authority realised its inherent power and used it as a tool of oppression to suppress conflicting views.

Yet the flame still flickered in the heart of humanity, men and women from all backgrounds yearning to explore the manifold realms of the universe - seen and unseen, and to find their place in it. Among those, some quiet souls watched from the sidelines, silent witness to the abuse of power and manipulation of knowledge; ones who felt keenly the loss of old ways and inner knowing. Gradually these ones withdrew from the outer world, moving in secret to preserve their sacred texts and protect them from further plunder and misinterpretation. Their treasure-house of ancient knowledge would furnish the new mystery schools with volumes of wisdom accrued in centuries of contemplation and questing. However even as they redirected their learning into underground streams of spirituality, they did so with the pure and clear intention that the material would one day be returned to the Light in the right conditions.

Indeed, in more recent times, some information has been disseminated, yet often presented in language so dense that its message is obscured. As a result, it seems to exclude access to all but the privileged few, the cognoscenti who by virtue of their special knowledge are able to absorb the complex material. No judgment of writing style is intended here; as we have seen, at certain times in history, that would have been an appropriate approach, and any who subsequently submitted such manuscripts are likely to be well attuned to the difficulties faced by their forebears and the severe consequences for holding views other than the prevailing one. Such experiences are carried deep in the memory cells, submerged but not forgotten, resurfacing with those brave souls as they stepped forward, clouding their expression as they sought to bring forth information so long concealed. No matter their manner of delivery or transmission, they are to be thanked for their contribution: for accepting their assignment and paving the way.

However in the New Age, as the veil is lifted, the collective consciousness readies itself to receive the keys anew and raise the vibration of all humanity. In a sense, the volume in your hands closes the circle and opens the door to a new - or another - round of being that is anchored in the past and yet extends into eternity around a central hub that is the unifying force of all creation. Both a synthesis and a prototype, it transcends the old divisions and accommodates all in a wondrous web of interconnectedness. For it is a simple truth that we are all one: that the Universe and all within it, material and non-material - every human being, beast, bird, river, lake, rock, leaf, belief, breath and transient thought - comes from and returns to the one source that is itself in a continuous spiral of co-creation. It has always been so, it will forever be thus, and it is the purpose of this book to help people re-discover that source, once more to tap into the wellspring from which all streams flow and surrender to its energy and feel again the power of its current.

This is a great work of restoration. It reconnects humanity with a body of knowledge and a universal model of belonging that had been lost. By comparison to older tomes, it is both transparent and non-technical. *The Twelve Hierarchies of Earth* is open to esoteric students and everyday seekers alike and as such, it is a rare achievement and a welcome addition to any library. Thus may this book direct your steps Home to your Hierarchy, and with a renewed sense of awe and oneness, may you be inspired to serve your Hierarchy in ways that will fill you with joy and benefit every other Hierarchy, all within the embrace of the Spiritual Hierarchy for Earth.

Lady Leto
21 June 2018
Winter Solstice

Preface

In my first book *The Light-Worker's Companion - A gateway into higher realms and the dimensions of consciousness,* I set out to assist readers in their spiritual quest, to help them heal and re-awaken and discover their divine plan and purpose by reconnecting with the Higher Self and Hierarchy. The material it contained was presented for a wide audience: new seekers, those already on the path, and those ready to explore different systems and practices to accelerate their journey. As wide as the intended scope may have been, the information was pitched very much at the personal, at individual humans wishing to expand their self-knowledge so as to enable them to find their true purpose and thus live more soul satisfying and meaningful lives.

During the process of drafting the book, I felt strongly that it foreshadowed another body of work which would not only deepen personal levels of awareness, but also provide a much wider perspective in terms of the individual's place in the universal scheme of things. If that first book was a gateway, it was also leading elsewhere, a conduit to other worlds and other pathways progressing from the personal to the collective. At the time, however, that passage was blocked, the knowledge was beyond my grasp and not accessible to me. Yet throughout all I had an unerring sense that what beckoned, though beyond retrieval, was a vast body of material related to the spiritual hierarchies, in particular the notion of twelve hierarchies known collectively as the Spiritual Hierarchy for Earth - the supreme and over arching structure that underpins the evolution of our planet and its galaxies, inextricably linked with the evolution and ascension of the human soul. As this information surfaced, so did my role emerge: to provide a profile of each of the twelve hierarchies in a way that would guide people home to their hierarchy of origin - for indeed we all belong to one, and thence to help them discover who they truly are and how they might lead a life of joyful purpose that serves the highest good of all.

Although the many individuals who possessed the important activators to this knowledge may have had access to them for their own use, they had not yet been distributed into our collective mind - the shared consciousness of our Earth-based spiritual family across the various hierarchies. Now, after thousands of years of relative dormancy, these keys are activating. Their caretakers - the human Initiates who represent their respective hierarchies - have awakened to bring the knowledge forward for the benefit of all. It is my assignment in this undertaking to seek out and illuminate the hidden parallels between the evolution of Earth and its ancillary bodies, with the ascension of the human soul and all its facets - all its multidimensional aspects - as they journey together, mirroring one another, from their shared origin to the point of divine re-union; to shed light on Earth evolving as it dances in unison with each individual soul and humanity at large as they ascend together, all within the encompassing arms of the Spiritual Hierarchy of Earth.

Though the term 'hierarchy' and its meaning will be defined in detail in subsequent chapters, it is important to note at the outset that although it might not have garnered that particular title, the hierarchy has in some way or another been recognised since antiquity, from the earliest people who revered Nature and Mother Earth, through to the various streams of spirituality that have evolved over time in the four corners of the world, from indigenous cultures to the more formalised religions. While the hierarchy and the different structures that support it are here given specific terms and definitions, their acknowledgement in no way replaces or supplants other spiritual approaches or traditional practices.

This text is thus offered to anchor an understanding that

others may have glimpsed, but have not quite articulated in their quest to find purpose and how best to fulfil it. For some, then, this book might serve to complement their original system of beliefs. For others, it will resonate instantly and provide a guide throughout their journey Home. In another group, the contents - at the same time, both strange and vaguely familiar - will release keys to help them remember their true Self. There may well be a fourth group: those who have been lost, searching for they know not what, but who within these pages will find answers to questions they have for so long been trying to formulate. Whatever your circumstances, may this book open a new chapter in the ongoing story of your Soul.

If this serves as the primary aim of the book, my second motivation for presenting the material has been to celebrate the persistence and consistent presence of the Spiritual Hierarchy for Earth over the thousands of years of human incarnation on this planet. Throughout the ages, the Hierarchy has remained committed to our ascension, sending its members (the highest levels of us all) into our cultures and civilisations to light the way when we have forgotten our purpose and our true origins.

There have been many instances of the representatives from the Spiritual Hierarchy for Earth fulfilling this role. In the Indian, Tibetan and Chinese cultures, the regular presence of awakened men, women and enlightened masters has always served to inspire the community and there is a natural, easy acceptance of their purpose and validity. Western society has been more reluctant to extend this acceptance, although we can find many early records of individuals connecting with the Spiritual Hierarchy and serving as its messengers many times - even if such interactions might not always have been expressed in those terms. Both the Old Testament and the New Testament contain such narratives; in the former, God appears to Moses in the burning bush instructing him to lead his people out of Egypt, while in the latter the voice of Christ is instrumental in the conversion of Saint Paul on the road to Damascus and his emergence as a religious figure. Beyond these striking examples, the Bible informs us of a human's capacity to speak with God and throughout its pages are accounts of exchanges with divine agents who advise on elements within everyday earthly life. The presence of these messengers is understood as a normal, expected occurrence, as are the clairvoyant and clairaudient abilities of humans.

A little later in our history, the remarkable German Benedictine abbess and cosmologist, Hildegard of Bingen, received direct instructions from God, some of which are recorded in *Scivias*, an illustrated work of the visions she experienced during the mid twelfth century. In addition she was a herbalist who dispensed natural remedies and while the medical insights she received were applicable to her time, almost ten centuries later the spirit of her work continues to flourish and inspire healers across a broad spectrum. In other areas she developed the notion of Viriditas, the 'greening power' or divine life force infusing all creation, a view that has particular relevance for the challenges of climate change and sustainable development today.

Other saints who reported visions include Saint Francis Assisi (c.1181-1226), preacher and founder of the Franciscan Order, who was propelled to renounce his ways and pursue the course for which he is now so venerated, especially his advocacy for all creatures of creation. English anchoress Julian of Norwich was another who received visions which she wrote about in her book *Revelations of Divine Love*, itself a notable achievement for a woman in the late fourteenth/early fifteenth century. In the case of the Spanish mystic and Doctor of the Church, Saint Teresa of Avila, visions changed her life and informed her writing of *The Interior Castle* (published 1588), a classic text on Christian mysticism which charted the soul's journey home through the seven stages or mansions to union with the Beloved.

In this context, the life of Joan of Arc is relevant from the fifteen century when the higher realms, including Saint Michael and Saint Catherine of Alexandria, communicated with her as she worked to fulfil her heroic assignment. At her interrogation, Joan of Arc declared her intimate relationship with the higher realms: "I have never had need of them without having them (come)." One might argue that it was her higher council that led to her death. Here, we do well to remember that we choose our assignments, as tough as this seems, and often it isn't until after our awakening that we realise the purpose of our choices. In the case of Saint Joan, her purpose was not to live a prolonged life, but to make as great an impact within the shortest amount of time, and for her message to be remembered throughout time. As she in her spirit form lives on, her passionate example of faith and commitment to her assignment, as well as the very notion of a higher purpose, have endured as a guiding torch for many light-workers.

It is easy to assume such visitations are a thing of the past or occurred only among people of power or piety in the community or cloister. But this is not so, as events in our more recent history indicate. In what are known as the Marian apparitions, the Blessed Virgin Mary appeared before Saint Bernadette, a young girl of humble origins at Lourdes in France (1858), and again before three shepherd children in Fatima in Portugal (1917) with messages for humanity.

Thus such visits from the Divine can happen to anyone, anytime - they are not reserved for those with a high profile - and they can be experienced directly, or indirectly through an angelic or human presence. We only need to open the topic among our friends and family and it seems that nearly everyone has a little story to tell about being divinely assisted in some way through an unusual or unexpected occurrence, sometimes bordering on the mysterious or miraculous. I vividly recall an event that occurred when I was a nine-year-old child in an airport in China. I had been afflicted by a sudden, but temporary illness and my parents were very worried that the airline authorities would not allow me to fly. An elderly Chinese woman approached me in the restrooms. She lightly touched some points on my body and gave me a tiny vial of liquid to drink. My mother, who always said not to take anything offered by strangers, permitted me to drink the contents. Although the woman did not speak any words I could understand, her caring and confident manner was reassuring.

Within moments of this encounter I felt better and within a short time I had made a complete recovery. Since then I have trusted the qi, (chi), or healing force that can be transmitted through a true master's hands as well as the power of love, compassion and genuine kindness. While seemingly small, this simple encounter was significant in opening my eyes to other possibilities, shaping my beliefs and setting me on the pathway that has led to the work you now hold in your hands.

Truly, the healers and masters of the Spiritual Hierarchy have never abandoned us, but we must train ourselves to be receptive to their guidance. Through opening ourselves to our wise counsel (and council) we have the potential to make things easier for ourselves. However, left to our own devices and operating from our lower, pained aspects, we very often make things harder than they need to be. In the modern world, as no doubt it has been throughout the ages, it can appear easier to allow ourselves to be diverted from our true nature and that which supports us to return to this state of centredness. Here, connection to our higher self, hierarchy and the Spiritual Hierarchy for Earth helps us to 'fine tune' our navigation and remain on the path that serves our highest good.

With the acceptance of keys received through meditation, contemplation and direct transmission, I have endeavoured to answer the calling within me to champion the Spiritual Hierarchy for Earth and demonstrate its devotion to humanity, to our highest good, although such an ancient body scarcely needs championing by an earthling. In this, it has been essential also to demonstrate how we are all part of this grand structure and crucially, how we serve each other through the medium that is the Hierarchy.

Therefore it has thus been important to provide some parameters at the outset, some pointers to guide your search and propel your steps through these initial stages. For the Spiritual Hierarchy for Earth is indeed vast: a massive structure of sound, colour, light and frequency that houses the human race and all other realms and species that are the true inheritors of planet Earth. It consists of twelve founding hierarchies that have worked together since the formation of the blueprint for planet Earth. These twelve hierarchies which are also part of the same spiritual family are named thus:

Central Sun Hierarchy

Jerusalem Hierarchy

Mu Hierarchy

Israel Hierarchy

Tansafarie Hierarchy

Bethlehem Hierarchy

Ishtar Hierarchy

Gaia Hierarchy

Shiva Hierarchy

Pan Hierarchy

Lemuria Hierarchy

Atlantis Hierarchy

While the Spiritual Hierarchy for Earth encompasses the twelve aforementioned, in the process it becomes an entity in its own right, an organised whole or structure that in some ways is greater than the sum of its parts. Although its core governing body sits in the fifth dimension, it has the ability to hold its presence in all dimensions. In the pages that follow, we will explore in detail the overall structure, the numerous offices and councils within it, and the framework that holds it all together allowing us to find our place within it.

I am of course aware that this volume is an incomplete explanation, for one can only know the level one has reached. Until one surpasses that level, one remains ignorant of the level above it. Within time, I will come to know another level and although it will not render this material redundant, it will demonstrate further gaps to fill. If I am granted the opportunity to add the next set of stepping stones in a further volume, I would welcome it fully.

For fellow Initiates whose memory banks are activated upon reading the information contained within, hopefully it will lead you also to contribute to the overall picture of the hierarchies through producing written material and images, and sharing these by your own publications. Through our combined efforts we reinforce the bridge between the earthly plane and the higher planes of consciousness, making the journey home easier for everyone. We also release vital keys that flood the consciousness of humanity with the truth of who we are.

How to use this book

Keys are easier to access once you are consciously reconnected to your own hierarchy, in whichever way you experience this connection. Though the twelve hierarchies gather under the umbrella of the Spiritual Hierarchy for Earth, you and all your aspects belong for all eternity to one particular hierarchy and together we will explore ways to discover and work with it. The direct and personal experience of your hierarchy assists you to obtain the most you can from this book and locate your own keys to share with our esoteric community.

However, before we try to identify your particular hierarchy, in Chapter One we begin by finding out a little about the hierarchy in general and how it functions in the dimensions, as a foundation for your process of enquiry. The information offered is an abridged version of relevant sections brought across from my earlier work, *The Light-Worker's Companion - A gateway into higher realms and the dimensions of consciousness*. Thus while for many it may be a form of revision or repetition, the material in this opening chapter has been incorporated to reinforce your understanding and to allow the book to function as a stand-alone text.

In Chapter Two, we provide some background to the formation of the twelve hierarchies and an overview of each one. This chapter introduces substantially new material as we probe the essence of the book, which is to discover your hierarchy.

Chapters Three to Fourteen give a full description of each hierarchy, as well as a listing of known members, in as thorough an explanation currently available of the twelve hierarchies. Naturally through your explorations, you will discover to which of the twelve you belong and then, through working with your hierarchy directly, you will expand upon the information gathered here. Your hierarchy will reveal to you its own mysteries.

Although you may know in your heart to which hierarchy you belong after your first encounter with the information contained herein, Chapter Fifteen is designed to help reveal or confirm your connection, by providing more specific pointers for identifying your hierarchy of origin, along with a meditation guide for connecting with it

Once you have learned the hierarchy of your origin, Chapters Sixteen to Twenty are devoted to fuller descriptions of the functions, roles and offices at various levels throughout the vast Spiritual Hierarchy for Earth. We begin our discovery of the roles your hierarchy plays within the larger framework of the Spiritual Hierarchy for Earth. This allows you to identify the work of your hierarchy across the history of the Earth. It may also serve to explain your work in this lifetime. We also embark upon an exploration of the shared offices within the Spiritual Hierarchy for Earth - how each hierarchy works with other hierarchies to facilitate multiple functions within the organisation of the Earth, her realms, and various other realms, civilisations and species beyond Earth.

As with Chapter One, the information in Chapters Sixteen and Seventeen is divided into sections - earth/physical, etheric and galactic, so that the various levels of the Hierarchy are easier to navigate. These chapters provide you with a greater understanding of your hierarchy in relation to the work it does with others within the third and fourth dimensions on Earth, namely, the Nature and Elemental Kingdoms.

Chapter Eighteen explores the fifth dimensional levels of the Spiritual Hierarchy for Earth, while Chapter Nineteen outlines the seven structures that collaborate with the Hierarchy. It is here you may discover that you have a role within the High Council of Healers, or that you have aspects volunteering their services in other structures in addition to your own hierarchy, such as the Angelic family or the Elven family. Chapter Twenty discusses the Spiritual Hierarchy for Earth as it functions from the seventh to the twelfth dimensions.

Chapter Twenty-One discusses incarnation - how and why your hierarchy decided to send you to Earth, and also the wider role your hierarchy plays in supporting humankind's ascension through Earth-based incarnation.

Chapter Twenty-Two explores more fully your hierarchy at the twelfth dimensional level. It is only through gaining an understanding of this level that the full power and majesty of the Spiritual Hierarchy for Earth can be fully grasped. Through this, ideally, *your* full power and majesty are also revealed. With this knowledge, may we walk towards our greatest potential, gracefully confident in the awareness of who we truly are.

Use of the Term 'Hierarchy'

When the word 'hierarchy' is used, hackles are raised. In the usual sense, it denotes a system of ranking or a pecking order wherein members are seen as occupying positions of greater or lesser status, authority and access to riches - often without merit and regardless of effort. Hence the term evokes adverse reactions - and understandably so, as many human beings have been subjected to the lower ends of hierarchical systems on Earth and have left their incarnations feeling powerless, resentful and enslaved. Many earthly and man-made hierarchies work in a way that isolates, subjugates and draws lines of separation between human beings, relegating some to lower positions and elevating others into higher ones.

Such hierarchies in which every human plays a part, these earth-based structures that govern the economic condition of every human, are vastly different in philosophy and practical application from the Spiritual Hierarchy for Earth. We do not apologise for using the term 'hierarchy', for the concept was in existence long before human beings populated Earth's surface. The original idea and function of the 'hierarchy' was brought to Earth and readjusted by humankind in ways that have adulterated its name and purpose, and yet fragments of the original 'hierarchy' still remain in examples where human beings are able to structure themselves and resources in a way that serves the common good.

This is the original function of 'hierarchy'; a structure that allows for exceptional economy and efficiency in the organisation of species, beings and resources in ways that allow for divine co-creation - manifestations that deliver the highest benefit for all. The levels within the Spiritual Hierarchy for Earth allow each being and creation to choose the vibrational frequency it wishes to experience. These levels are not used to manipulate or determine ranking as they are on Earth. Nor do they function as levels of command such as a higher level having control or authority over a lower level.

The levels exist as a natural categorisation that occurs when like-frequencies harmonise and 'cluster together' through a shared vibratory rate. Take, as an example, a musical symphony. The notes harmonise, each different, but compatible or contributing to the whole. When they 'dance' together, a symphony is created. It is not that this note is better than that one. Rather, they complement and require each other equally, and yet they stand alone too, in their individual perfection. Such a symphony of sounds we can liken to a cluster of frequencies that come together to form a level, a dimension, an office, a council or a realm within the Spiritual Hierarchy for Earth.

It is most likely, given your interest in this work, that you are a member of the Spiritual Hierarchy for Earth who already contributes a great deal through participating in its councils and offices. Many human incarnates do this, and yet those humans who have not yet awakened have no conscious awareness of this fact. As a Light-Worker, a consciously functioning member of the Spiritual Hierarchy for Earth, you agreed to remember your presence in this great structure of light before many others did. You agreed to shepherd them through days of uncertainty, but most importantly, you agreed to turn on your light. As you walk the long path home to the highest levels of who you are, your light illuminates the path home for others to follow when they too are ready to remember and ascend; that is, to raise the vibrational frequency of their energy fields and physicality.

(As a point of clarification for readers, throughout the text the term, 'the hierarchy' is used and usually refers to your individual hierarchy, whereas capitalisation of 'the Hierarchy' relates to the Spiritual Hierarchy for Earth.)

Preparing to receive the keys proffered herein

As this book is intended as an introduction to the Spiritual Hierarchy for Earth and your role within it through identifying and participating in your individual hierarchy, as you prepare to read through the text we encourage you to ask: To which hierarchy out of the twelve do I belong? The very act of asking grants the higher realms permission to begin the process of uplifting you so that you may receive the answer. Once you know your hierarchy, ask: What is my personal assignment in relation to my hierarchy on Earth? Knowing this often brings contentment and peace, once you have accepted yourself and your purpose fully, and made a commitment to action.

The hierarchy structures and their related assignments are more elaborate and entwined than what can be realistically recorded by any human scribe. A complete picture requires a map of every human on Earth and every being in the universe, each with his or her individual experience. The result is a chart so interlaced and interwoven that humans are currently unable to produce it. And so, in the absence of such fine details we cannot come close to capturing the intricacies of the Spiritual Hierarchy for Earth. Yet this picture is painted not to confound you, but to give you an idea of the complexity and uniqueness of your being.

It is with this explanation, placed upfront for all to see, that we begin anchoring information about the hierarchies. In no way can any one person or book convey their full breadth or depth. We offer the explanations contained within this work so that they might awaken your own memories and begin for you a new level of exploration - to discover your own place in the Spiritual Hierarchy for Earth, for you certainly do have one, that is yours, set aside especially for you, that no other person or thing can occupy or replace. Now is the time to remember who you are, your contribution to Earth through your hierarchy's role within the Spiritual Hierarchy for Earth and the next phase of your earthly mission. For it is the function of this text to inform, to trigger memory banks lying dormant in human Initiates on Earth, and assist all individuals to ascend individually and collectively as one vast spiritual family.

Regardless of background, *The Twelve Hierarchies of Earth* is thus offered to all those who answer the call to live according to their highest purpose and fulfil their spiritual mission on Earth, in a way that brings joy to themselves and to others, thereby contributing to the Soul of the World and raising the vibration of each and all within.

CHAPTER ONE

An Overview of Your Hierarchy

As mentioned, the first chapter of this book contains an explanation of your hierarchy that has been adapted from the author's earlier volume, The Light-Worker's Companion. *The explanation offered here can be used for either familiarisation or revision.*

Many humans walk Earth with a very limited awareness of anything beyond their immediate experience. They are aware when they are hungry, tired, thirsty or in pain. Most people go beyond this and are aware when they are stressed, anxious, angry, happy or sad. Some people extend further to being aware of how others are feeling and they are sensitive to general emotional environments. Then there are others who know that there is more to life than what is seen or felt in the physical world. They dare to explore beyond that which is known and begin to investigate energetic realities. They may investigate the possibility of spiritual realms, afterlife, guides, angels and healing that cannot be logically explained.

You are reading a book about the spiritual realm and so it is safe to say that you are one of these people. You, like them, have stumbled upon your Higher Self, psychic abilities, intuition and meditation. You have begun to use these tools to bring peace into your life and greater awareness. You have a sense that there is more to you than what you have been told to believe. This chapter will introduce you to a basic understanding of your own hierarchy and open the door to your discovering what this is. Through your hierarchy you have access to tools that will assist you to attain higher awareness and experience.

Although your hierarchy system of light is very complex, it is also very accessible and there is an underlying simplicity in it. You will discover the multidimensionality of it through the explorations you undertake on your own. Meditation provides a good medium in which to explore your hierarchy (you will find one in Chapter Fifteen, which may assist you). Do not be concerned if you do not understand your hierarchy straight away. The real understanding comes through experiencing it yourself and certain forms of meditation will give you that opportunity. Meditation may help you open your channels - your ability to communicate with your higher councils and higher self, which in turn strengthens your relationship with your hierarchy.

Because your hierarchy exists across all dimensions and levels, it allows for your Soul to experience itself within all dimensions, planetary worlds and realms. Your Soul is your eternal, Original Self from which your hierarchy extends. Contained within your Soul is your signature frequency, your indestructible essence - your quintessence that cannot be tainted or altered or removed from the Oneness.

Your Soul sends particles of itself down into the hierarchy structure. These particles choose to incarnate into various forms such as human bodies, animals or energetic beings sometimes, all at the same time. Your Soul can be seen as a sun that sends rays of sunlight down towards Earth and other planetary worlds. The sun ray is the spirit that fills a physical form such as a human body.

These shards of light from your Soul may also volunteer themselves to be light energies that make up the consciousness and may become energetic beings such as angelic beings, and nature spirits. Some Souls prefer to manifest parts of themselves to become different planetary worlds. They may be the essence of that which is the air, the daffodil, or the willow tree. We all have so many wonderful choices of how we can experience ourselves over an endless period of time and in a variety of different yet simultaneous expressions.

Souls benefit from manifesting a shard of their light as a human on Earth. It is an opportunity to develop less evolved aspects of the Soul's hierarchy and contribute to the evolution of humanity. This process has the ability to evolve the whole Soul in a way that brings experience and knowledge. Many people choose to incarnate themselves over and over again in an effort to fulfil the very difficult and challenging goal of awakening to the sacred divine light within, amongst all of the divine earthly diversions. The important thing to remember is that all earthly experiences are transmutable and can always be evolved in a way that brings spiritual evolution to the Soul.

Key Points About Your Hierarchy

Throughout all of your incarnations, you have always belonged to the same hierarchy as it is an extension of and part of your Soul. You may have experiences, relationships etc with other hierarchies, but you always belong to your original hierarchy.

You can never be separate from your Soul, or change Souls.

Your hierarchy is constructed of geometrical light designs.

It is made up of colour, sound and light.

It is balanced within its Masculine and Feminine energies.

Even though you are on Earth, you are contained within your hierarchy.

Every person on Earth is an aspect of a hierarchy.

Your hierarchy is connected to the Spiritual Hierarchy of Earth.

Your Hierarchy Diagram

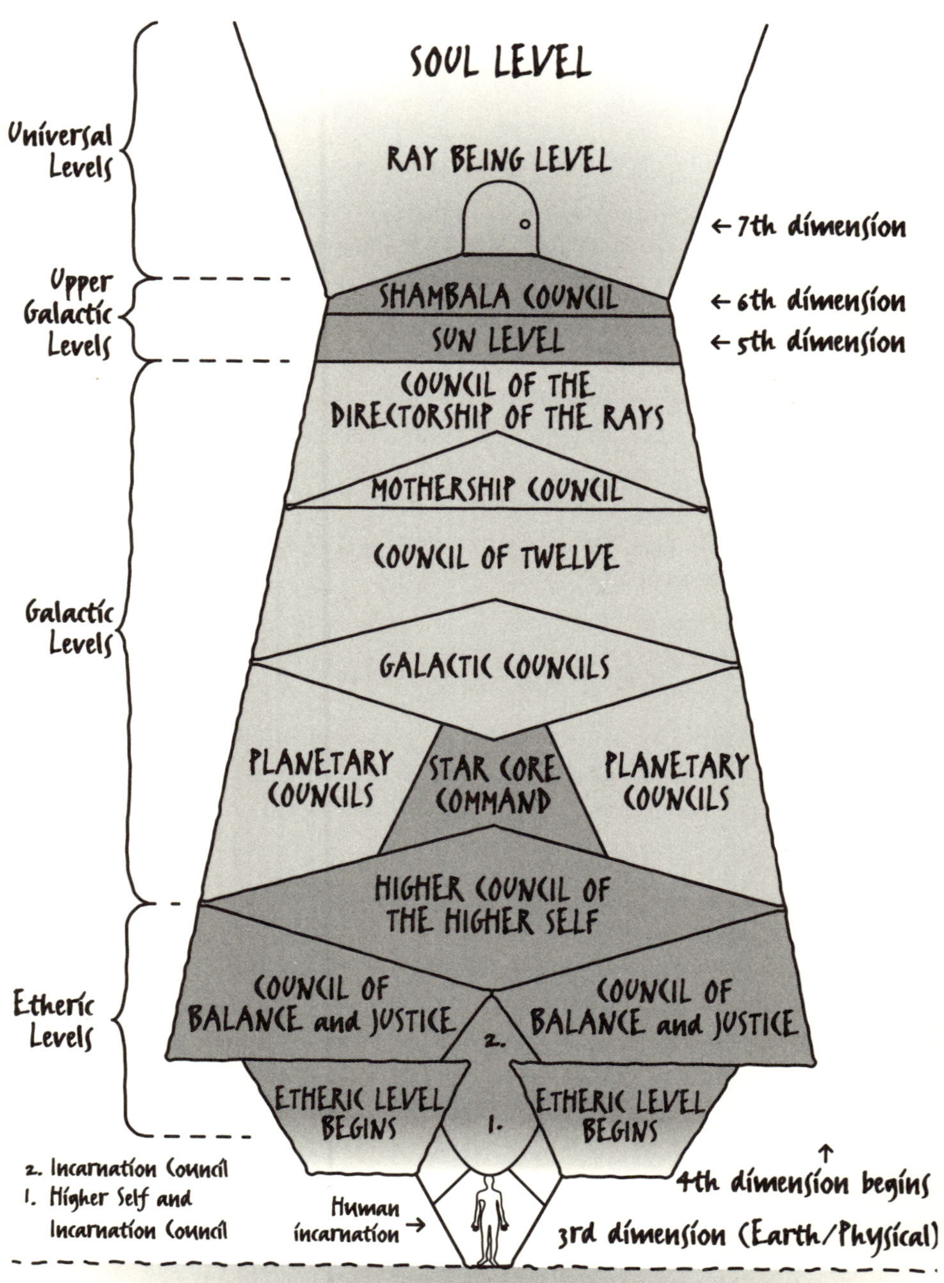

The Earth/Physical Levels of Your Hierarchy

There are many levels to the structure of your hierarchy, more levels than the ones written on the structure diagram. The ones that have been recorded are major levels that have a big impact on your long-term spiritual understanding and development. **The earth/physical** level of your hierarchy is found within the **first, second and third dimensions**. The **etheric levels** of your hierarchy are **fourth dimensional, where you will also find the current home of the Human Kingdom**. Humans have the ability to tap into and integrate the etheric levels of their hierarchy so that they experience an upper fourth and eventually fifth dimensional state whilst living in the third dimensional, earthly reality.

First Dimension

The first dimension is home to the mineral kingdom. Creation begins at the embryonic stage and gradually develops into form. All creation in this dimension has consciousness and is connected to and part of the Divine Source. It is very much connected to the Source having just been born from the Divine Womb.

Having been born from the Divine Womb of the feminine realms of the void, creation in the first kingdom enters into the light of the formed reality being the masculine realms. Thus all creation in the first dimension begins life in the balance of feminine and masculine energies. Being born **from** the womb of the Mother it knows the darkness, the feminine, and **into** the world of the Father it knows the light, the manifestation of the masculine. In the womb where there is the nothingness, creation **knows** itself. In the masculine realms that are light where there is geometric structure, colour, sound and manifested frequencies, creation **experiences** itself.

Second Dimension

The second dimension is home to the plant/vegetable kingdom. In the second dimension creation enters the next level of development. It begins to take its first steps on the path of experiencing itself by entering into the cycles of living: birth, death and rebirth. It realises its presence has an effect on the world as it makes itself recognised and experienced by other forms of creation. It belongs to a community of other forms of creation and can experience itself in relation to this.

Third Dimension

The third dimension can easily be understood as the animal kingdom. The third dimension develops consciousness further into a level of self consciousness. Creation develops an attachment to its life and thus develops the Will to Survive. Such attachment creates awareness of that which may damage or end life and thus fear is born.

The creation teaches itself to experience the duality of safety and fear in an effort to survive and will learn to instinctively sense and feel. To do this it allocates a section of its consciousness to form a survival based intelligence. This section develops a system where information may be filed in order to be recalled in an effort to keep the creation in safety. The information filed is its own past experience or the witnessed experience of other creations. A creature will create this information bank in the early stages of its life, drawing on its own experience, and the lessons from its elders or community. This type of intelligence is developed for the purpose of serving the objectives of the Will to Survive.

Humans exist in the third dimension or lower levels of the fourth dimension until they evolve themselves beyond their primary focus on survival and desire to survive, to the more spiritual aspirations of the upper fourth dimension.

The purpose of the earth/physical level of your hierarchy is to house the first, second and third dimensions thus creating a foundation for the hierarchy to evolve aspects of itself, for example, a human Initiate, into higher states of consciousness. Once a hierarchy stabilises itself within these dimensions it will then prepare to incarnate a human being onto Earth to begin the next level of its evolution.

It is important to note that although the third dimension is home to the more animalistic aspect of human nature, it is not a 'negative' or 'bad' dimension. Humans are designed to live in the upper levels of the fourth dimension and above, where the human kingdom begins - this is their true state. Species and beings for whom the third dimension is their proper home base, are not lesser or 'negative' either, they provide an essential service of grounding the higher and finer frequencies into the physical plane. Without this service, human beings would not be able to incarnate, and the beautiful physical Earth filled with the majesty of the nature realms would not exist. The offices and councils that bring about this majesty and the hierarchies they are part of are discussed in detail in Chapters Sixteen and Seventeen.

The Beginning of the Etheric Level and Galactic Level of Your Hierarchy

Fourth Dimension

The fourth dimension is home to the development of consciousness beyond the Will to Survive into more subtle aspects of living and being. It is in this dimension that creation awakens to levels of awareness that pose questions such as "Who am I?", "Where do I come from spiritually?", "Who, What, Where is my Creator?" and "What is my purpose?"

In the fourth dimension, creation seeks to reconnect to and reclaim its higher self and its relationship with the divine. The human incarnate begins a program initiated by higher beings of light that is designed to assist him to awaken to his higher self. The human incarnate may not initially be aware of the higher beings of light assisting him.

When the incarnate passes these initial awakening training procedures he is then introduced into a series of initiations to shed the foundation of fear established in the third dimension. In the higher levels of the fourth dimension, he is trained to hold the frequencies of the fifth dimension in order to gain entry into the realm of complete Christ Consciousness, that is, aligning one's will completely to the Divine Will.

The Upper Galactic Level of Your Hierarchy

Fifth Dimension

Where the fourth dimension has housed the Human Kingdom and has been a workshop, as it were, for human incarnates to resolve their issues and reconnect to their spiritual selves, the fifth dimension is the Spiritual Kingdom. By the time Initiates reach this kingdom, they are already well aware of the purpose of their incarnation and the meaning of their lives.

The doorway to Christ Consciousness, the fifth dimension is the home base of love. It is a dimension that does not carry the duality of love and fear as the fourth dimension does. It is founded on love and light and as a result many Initiates in the upper levels of the fourth dimension aspire to attain fifth dimensional consciousness. Although Christ Consciousness is obviously deeply entwined with Christianity, in this text it is not confined to that understanding nor is it associated with religion. Here, the term is used to categorise all those who align their will with the Divine Will in service to the highest good for all. That is, the term 'Christ' refers to the divine essence dwelling within each human and the aspiration to activate its potential to greater effect.

Sixth Dimension

In the sixth dimension, the Initiate leaves behind what remains of his understanding of separateness and prepares to immerse himself in the Source. He surrenders his limitations about how he perceives himself and he moves into the realm of unlimited possibility. It is here that he ceases to know himself as the physical incarnated self and comes to know himself as the All That Is. It is here he attains the complete surrender of the limited self into the

All That Is. He becomes all things from the rocks to the birds to the stars and planets. He attains God/Source Consciousness.

The Universal Level of Your Hierarchy

Seventh Dimension

Referred to as 'Seventh Heaven', the seventh dimension is home to many angelic and celestial beings as well as the Universal Levels of the hierarchy.

Once the Master has surrendered to the releasing of himself into the All That Is of the sixth dimension, he may elect to gather himself again into a form of his choosing and rejoin the community of light within the seventh dimension. As he reaches the seventh dimension, many options are presented to him. He may choose to be of service to Earth and humanity or may work on other planetary worlds and realms different to Earth. He is given the option to manifest himself within the many different forms of his hierarchy and can shape-shift to appear as he wishes to. He may choose to manifest at any given time as the wind, the rain, the water, a bird, animal or fish. This shape-shifting is always done with the permission of others involved. He may also choose to manifest himself as a Ray Being, one possible manifestation of his Universal Self.

If he chooses to come back and work for the Spiritual Hierarchy for Earth, he is aligned to an assignment. This assignment is designed by himself and the overseeing board of the Spiritual Hierarchy for Earth.

In the seventh dimension the Master has access to her full co-creational self. The Master has the ability to connect to a new level of initiation whereby she undertakes awakening into her full Goddess self. She comes to realise herself not only as All Things but as an aspect of the Creator of All Things. As she comes to understand this she begins to manifest herself as the Creatrix and takes her place within her Creator Office. This sees her training as an aspect of the Creator and here she undergoes initiation to take this Mantle of Light, Greatness and Wisdom. She takes her seat at the round table in the Office of Creators.

CHAPTER TWO

Introduction to the Twelve Hierarchies

There in the body of the God of gods, Arjuna saw the manifold universe in its entirety with its many levels and divisions, all resting in their essential oneness.

Bhagavad Gita

We each belong to a particular hierarchy. The hierarchies that are connected to the Earth assignment, come together to create the Spiritual Hierarchy for Earth. Because we are humans in this incarnation, we are automatically part of the Human Hierarchy, just as an angel is part of the Angelic Hierarchy. Our own particular hierarchy is connected to the Human Hierarchy as well as the Spiritual Hierarchy for Earth. The same applies in the case of an angel, who has its own hierarchy, which is then connected to the Angelic Hierarchy and then to the Spiritual Hierarchy for Earth. I may belong to a hierarchy different from my neighbour, however, a hierarchy can send more than one incarnated aspect to Earth, so I may share my hierarchy with millions of other people

Multiple Hierarchies Diagram

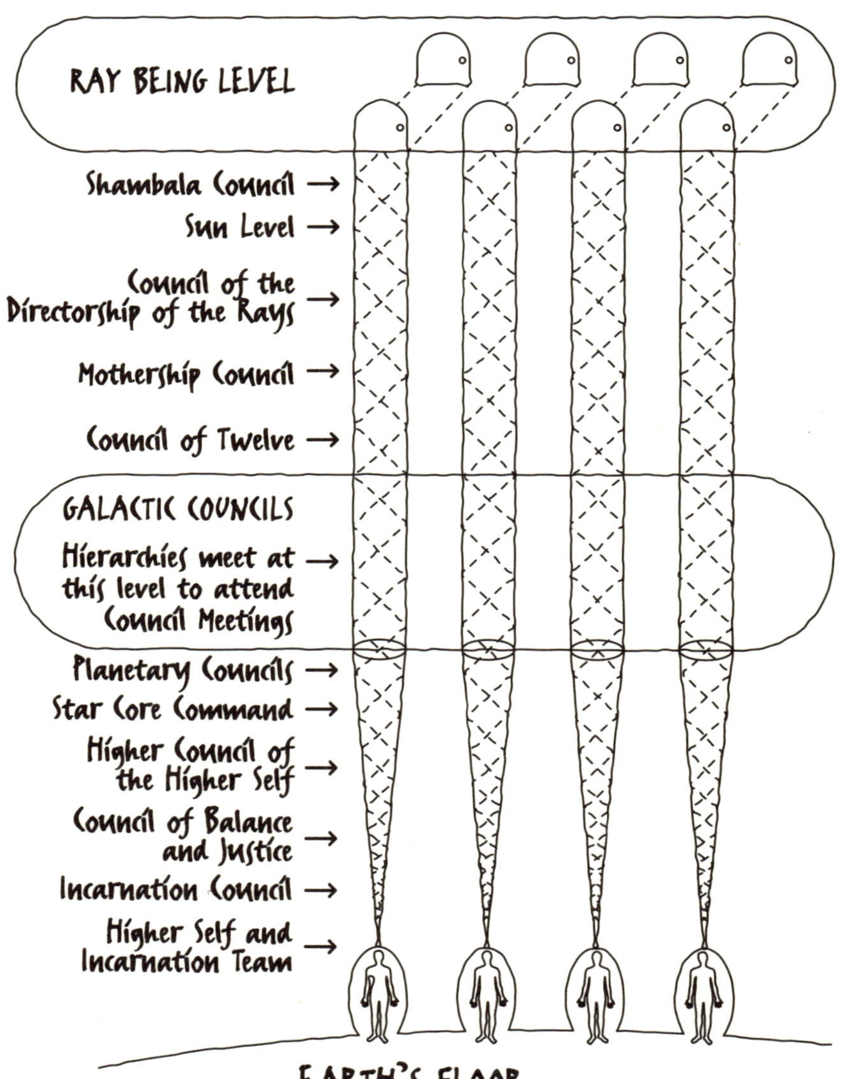

on Earth at the moment, as might you. (Please refer to the diagram for an example of four different hierarchies existing on Earth simultaneously).

Every hierarchy is equal to another, is a self-sovereign, individual organisation in its own right and is connected to the Divine Source of All That Is. Every member in its own hierarchy is considered equal to other members, and although the hierarchy is divided into levels, this is because of the different functions of each level and not because one is superior or inferior to another.

Like a diamond, the Spiritual Family (a broad term to embrace all beings in our universal Family of Light) is multifaceted. The great Cosmic Hierarchy has many levels and exists through all realms and dimensions; it is the manifested form of the All That Is. From this great Cosmic Hierarchy there are many hierarchies, like branches on a tree. The Spiritual Hierarchy for Earth is one branch. Within this one branch there are twelve sub branches or what we now refer to as the twelve hierarchies, including yours and mine, which all come together to form the Spiritual Hierarchy for Earth. In *Initiation – Human and Solar,* Alice Bailey writes: "The twelve creative Hierarchies are themselves but subsidiary branches of the one cosmic Hierarchy. They form but one chord in the cosmic symphony..." (Lucis Publishing Company, glossary, page 4).

At the top or ascension point of each individual hierarchy are the Divine Mothers and Divine Fathers of each hierarchy and from which each hierarchy extends. They gather with the Divine Mothers and Divine Fathers of the other hierarchies. This is a twelfth dimensional level, and it is here, where they meet, that the hierarchical form ceases to exist and all become one.

People have always known that there are higher sources of wisdom, whether or not they call them 'Spiritual Hierarchies', but have not always had access to empowering frameworks in which to understand their workings or the fundamental universal principles that govern the higher realms and life on Earth alike. Thus there has been through time great fear around spirituality, with the few people who claim to be the bridge between the people and the Divine holding all the power. Man's rules and beliefs have been projected onto the Divine, and the people have believed that the higher realms must think the same fearful, judgemental and condemning thoughts as humans do.

Every person is capable of creating a strong relationship with the Higher Realms and their own hierarchy and we currently live in an age where more and more people are committed to seeking greater connection with the Divine.

Consciously connecting with your own hierarchy doesn't mean that you must reject elements of your traditional religious upbringing, but it does provide you with a vast framework in which to pose questions and receive answers in the search for meaning.

Some of the benefits in understanding the hierarchy are less tangible than receiving answers to day-to-day questions. Understanding the hierarchy can act as a foundation for understanding the geometry and nature of reality - what's 'out there' and what's within. This may dispel many fears of the unknown; about the metaphysical structures governing Earth, such as what happens when we die, spirits and beings, how did we come to be here, and what is the purpose of our past incarnations and current life.

•••

The introduction briefly discussed the twelve hierarchies who founded the Spiritual Hierarchy for Earth: Central Sun, Jerusalem, Mu, Israel, Tansafarie, Bethlehem, Ishtar, Gaia, Shiva, Pan, Lemuria, and Atlantis. In existence well before Earth's physical birth, the Spiritual Hierarchy for Earth was formed to be Earth's governing body by seven 'elder' hierarchies: Central Sun, Jerusalem, Mu, Israel, Tansafarie, Bethlehem, and Ishtar. This was done at the blueprint stage of the planet's creation. During this stage, the Children of the Earth hierarchies were born. Yet, although they were 'born' as hierarchies at this stage, their essences already existed. These hierarchies are known as Gaia, Shiva, Pan, Lemuria and Atlantis. Thus, the Spiritual Hierarchy for Earth consists of these twelve founding hierarchies, at the same time it and its component hierarchies form part of a wider structure or complex called the Ancient Spiritual Family. As Earth developed, interest in her grew attracting other members from different parts of the galaxy. However, the founding twelve members remain unchanged and are the core of the governing body.

The twelve hierarchies are named by using titles that best reflect the frequencies held by them. These names are in no way complete representations of the purpose, identity or intention of each hierarchy. As Initiates connect with their own hierarchies, they may receive additional information that may serve to explain the multidimensionality and scope of their hierarchy. This information may be conveyed through the hierarchy issuing other names or titles to the Initiate. Hierarchies use different names depending upon the vibrational frequency that they are operating in. However, for ease of understanding, the Higher Realms have provided us with names deemed the most appropriate for Earth's vibrational frequency at this time. The Higher Realms urge us not to become too preoccupied with the names for these shift and change, and such changes are dependent upon multiple factors.

By not becoming too attached to the names provided to label each hierarchy, you are better able to feel into the unique offering each hierarchy shares with the All That Is. Each hierarchy is a celebration of its Divine Mother and Divine Father, and cannot be truly understood by a human incarnate until that human Initiate achieves full reunion with the Divine Mother and the Divine Father. This is particularly relevant where a human being may believe he knows or understands another person because he has discovered to which hierarchy the person belongs. One cannot fully understand another person just through knowing the hierarchy from which they originate. There are multiple reasons for this, one being that there are facets to all hierarchies that have not been revealed here or elsewhere on Earth at this time.

However, much insight into another's spiritual history can be gained. Use this insight to develop greater love and respect for the other. Understand also that there are levels to every person that exist well beyond the hierarchy structure that only they can know. A person's hierarchy of origin is personal information. It is not beneficial to pry into a person's spiritual history or information, nor ask them for it - it is more appropriate to wait until they are ready to share the information freely.

It is also important not to allow your awareness of the hierarchy structure to limit your spiritual exploration, for you can travel to the realms beyond the twelve hierarchies and reach your ultimate place of residence. It is also essential that you do not allow the ego mind to employ the hierarchy as a device to separate you from others. Remember that the manifestations that are the hierarchies is the exhalation of the One. Upon the inhalation, all returns to the One. The One, like the sun, sends out rays of itself, but although the rays appear individual, ultimately, they come from the same source, made of the very same 'stuff'. In creating the hierarchies, which can very easily be likened to rays of light, the One experiences itself.

> *It is through the world, and ultimately through you, that the unmanifested knows itself...*
>
> **Eckhart Tolle**

I initially raised questions with the Higher Realms about revealing the hierarchies so specifically and directly due to concerns that the knowing about individual hierarchies may cause additional separation within the human community. I was informed that this information may be used to assist the individual to bridge home to his/her own hierarchy, which will ultimately open the door home to the Oneness that created the Hierarchies. The Higher Realms understand that in opening us to new horizons by revealing their multidimensionality, we begin to reconnect to the Divine Presence or Being. This draws us away from the limitations of the mind engaged in the third dimensional constructs of the modern world. The Higher Realms anchor many types of teachings on Earth, knowing that some people will resonate to a particular teaching and other people to another sort of teaching. Their core intention is to craft teachings and paths to bring all of their children/human incarnates to awareness and awakening. The Higher Realms do not place one teaching as better than another. It is simply that one teaching will be more suitable in certain situations than another. This is always dependent upon the individual needs and inclinations of the human incarnates they are intending to reach.

The frequency and essence we call Jesus, as one of many manifestations of the Christ energy within the Central Sun hierarchy, anchored teachings as well as a vibrational frequency and a sound. This sound continues to this day, and the inner cores of humans hear this sound. The sound brings about awakening. Human incarnates of Christ energy anchored ancient keys on Earth and in the human vehicle so that once his body integrated the 'technology' all human bodies would find it easier to do the same. All hierarchies have sent highly evolved beings to perform similar functions and these are noted at the end of each hierarchy profile under ‘Publicly Recognised Human Incarnations’.

At the core of this universe is a Great Central Sun, the child of the Father and Mother of this Universe, and in many ways, this can be considered Jesus's 'home base'. You also have a 'home base', one that the Higher Realms are assisting you to reconnect to right now by triggering your awareness of it and by reminding you of your hierarchy.

The majority of human incarnates currently upon Earth’s floor belong to the Central Sun Hierarchy, which is the Divine Light of the Divine Mother and Divine Father of the All That Is. The sun that lights the Earth, is an aspect of the Central Sun. Incarnates from this hierarchy are here individually and collectively to hold the energy as Christ lights to assist in the evolution and ascension of humanity. This type of divine service is essential because there are also sections of other hierarchies who wandered far from their true nature in their attempt to answer the question 'Who Am I?' Such hierarchies have been returning home for some time and are restoring themselves to their highest offices and councils held within the Spiritual Hierarchy for Earth. The Central Sun is like a lighthouse that shines light through the dark night and helps ships to navigate their way; the torch bearer who guides all of creation home to the oneness.

The second largest group of human incarnates currently upon Earth's floor belongs to the Bethlehem Hierarchy, which among its many manifestations is also the fire womb of the Earth, the fiery core, the Earth's cauldron, the star grid of the Earth and the creatrix of the eternal realm known as Avalon. As the fiery womb, Mother Bethlehem has birthed entire species and hierarchies into existence on Earth as well as on countless other planets. With many human incarnates presently on the planet, Bethlehem members are here primarily to resolve aspects of themselves and return them to their rightful balance of masculine and feminine energies. They currently work to complete the karmic cycles and patterning introduced thousands of years ago in key times in Earth's history from Mu land, Lemuria, Atlantis, and Egypt. As with all hierarchies, this leg of their quest ends as they return to the Divine Source of All That Is of them. This returning can occur over many lifetimes, or it can occur within an instant, in any moment in time.

The third most prominent hierarchy on Earth (in terms of the number of incarnates) is the Tansafarie Hierarchy, also known as the Earth Hierarchy, because it holds the offices of Lord and Lady Terra – the physical earth, the soil, the dust, the ash. The Tansafarie Hierarchy, as the earth physical, has provided itself as the vicinity in which the final days of restoration will occur. The original Arcturians and the Venetians/Venusians are part of this hierarchy and have been holding the energy for Earth's ascension for thousands of years.

The fourth most prominent hierarchy currently on Earth is the Israel Hierarchy, which provides itself to be the 'mind' of the All That Is. Here, mind is defined as being different from consciousness. We may liken it to a mechanical structure where its anatomy consists of various parts such as the conscious and sub conscious mind with which consciousness is able to interact. Although in the highest dimensions, Israel is the expanded mind with limitless possibilities, closer to the Earth plane, this hierarchy holds the keys to the human intellect and mental body. Israel Hierarchy is home to the ancient creator gods and goddesses of the Order of Melchizedek, who, alongside many other tasks, hold the keys to the original genetic structure of human beings.

Israel's structure is complex and is thus categorised in terms of its four 'arms': the Israel arm, the Constantinople arm, the Chiron arm and the Albion arm. It desires peace to live within the hearts of its feminine and masculine aspects who, within several areas of the hierarchy, once feared and competed with one another. The Israel Hierarchy restored many of its aspects in ancient Egypt after many experienced the devastation of Atlantis. Among its many roles, it is the caretaker of numerous keys that allow creation to recognise beauty in other creations, and the keys to upholding the truth of beauty. It also holds keys to music and healing.

Many Israel Hierarchy members living on Earth at this time work in the medical, pharmaceutical and cosmetics industries. Some are involved in biochemistry and genetic research. Some work in advertising, marketing, film, television, fashion and beauty. These ones are challenged with ethical issues connected to youth/ageing, glamour, vanity, beauty and health, and are encouraged by their higher council to assist the hierarchy's cause to integrate compassion, empathy, and higher levels of understanding into these industries.

The Constantinople arm of the Israel Hierarchy is the next structure to hold the most members currently on Earth's floor. The arm is responsible for the forming of civilisations and has, due to the decisions made by incarnates from all hierarchies, struggled to maintain the balance of the masculine and feminine aspects of the civilisations it has anchored on Earth. Its challenge in the next phase of human history is to establish principles that ensure harmony between the masculine and feminine aspects of family, community, society and civilisations. The hierarchy's Chiron and Albion arms have less members incarnated at this time. However, those who are incarnated seek to strengthen the healing presence of the hierarchy on Earth and are often connected to herbs, healing through plants, the healing of animals, work in the equine related fields, and work with trees and forestry.

The Mu Hierarchy is another ancient and grand structure. It consists of many different planets, realms, kingdoms and species. The Mu Hierarchy is the keeper of the 'living library' of this universe and one of the keepers of the Akashic records, which houses the memory banks of all of the hierarchy's creations. Mu Hierarchy is both a cosmic womb that gives birth to creations and a Creator God who develops the vision for the creation. The ancient ones who created the vision for Earth to be a living library are part of the Mu Hierarchy. They include the Pleiadians, Lyrians, Sirians and the Orions (in this text, I am making a distinction between the Feline Lyrans and other related races and the Lyrians/Learians of Mu). Many Pleiadians and Sirians have incarnated in human bodies at this time to resolve karmic cycles that they instigated in ancient times either upon Earth or just prior to arriving on Earth. These ones are in the end stages of clearing old contracts with Earth and humanity so that they can complete their human incarnation cycle. This frees them to return home to their own planetary worlds, thus ending their need to return to Earth through human reincarnation.

Shiva Hierarchy is a highly advanced structure that has integrated all elements from other hierarchies and has introduced them to the physical plane. The Shiva Hierarchy, through Lord Shiva, delivered Yoga to the world. The hierarchy has balanced and integrated all chakras within the chakra system and continues to integrate, balance and evolve the chakras of the physical world. Shiva works with Mu to hold the keys to the Akashic records.

The Shiva Hierarchy represents mastery of all elements within the framework of a physical body living on Earth. It teaches the enjoyment of the physical plane as well as mastery over it. It enjoys the physical plane, but is not a slave to it. Contained in this hierarchy are keys to humankind's ascension into the fourth and fifth dimensional light bodies that are only available when a human incarnate makes peace with his/her individual challenges as part of being human and moves into the higher vibrational frequencies of acceptance of one's humanness, without judgment or fear. Shiva Hierarchy incarnates tend to return to Earth at pivotal junctures in Earth's history to aid in the movement of the consciousness to the next stage of its evolution. Many Shiva Hierarchy members have incarnated on Earth at this time.

The Pan Hierarchy is a frequency born out of the fiery core of Earth that carries the light of its father into the physical earth to seed races of beings who are the Forest Dwellers. The Pan Hierarchy fosters the earth-craft and is the parental lineage of the little people and many of the unseen ones who populate Earth's forests, marshes and caves. An awakened Pan Hierarchy incarnate stays very close to the Earth and to his/her own home space, usually choosing a life of homesteading, self-sufficiency and homeschooling. Some Pan aspects choose 'wild living' either alone or in small tribes or community clusters where the structures of the man made world do not inhibit their connection with the Earth and the realms of their hierarchy.

The Lemurian Hierarchy is the feminine twin of the Atlantis Hierarchy and is the child of Mu. The Lemurian Hierarchy holds the keys to the tribal frequencies of the Polynesian people, some African lineages and lineages within the Indonesian vicinity. The Lemurian High Council of Healing trained Initiates from many other hierarchies when the Lemurian civilisation was anchored upon Earth. It holds keys to healing through the vibrational frequency of sound, colour - light and crystal technology. This hierarchy represents the purity of childhood, the freedom of expression and the opportunity to grow, learn and live without burden. It is the highest ideal of childhood. The hierarchy holds the keys to the Inner Child and its healing, and the Awakened Child.

The Atlantis Hierarchy holds the key to the adolescence

of mankind, the opportunity to grow, experiment and explore through the freedom granted by the guiding hand of the Elders of Earth. It was born into the Earth's plane with a blueprint that allowed it to accommodate its own hierarchy aspects as well as become a 'home away from home' for many other hierarchies to experience Earth through living within a technologically advanced civilisation. Atlantis, the physical vicinity, housed beings from within the Spiritual Family who had traveled from realms, kingdoms and worlds beyond the Earth in order to experience life on Earth. These beings increased Atlantis Hierarchy's ability to accommodate many different frequencies, thus expanding its own frequency breadth. Technological advancement is of core interest to Atlantean members, who pursue studies in fields of interaction between humans, the digital world and machines. In ancient times, members of this hierarchy travelled to advanced planets to deepen their technological knowledge. Other Atlanteans who may not be interested in technology, often have great interest in the fields of human development science, sociology, and psychology where the focus is upon the evolution and spiritual awakening of the human species. The Atlantis Hierarchy is the Son of Mu.

The Gaia Hierarchy is the Angelic Spirit of the Earth and maintains a council of incarnated aspects upon the planet. Many of these aspects manifest as human beings, while others are the over-lighting devas of plants and trees. Some aspects live as Tree Beings within physical trees, while others live in the atmosphere as nature spirits and angelic beings who live in oxygen. The human incarnated aspects of the Gaia Hierarchy are committed entirely to Nature and her preservation. All awakened Gaia Hierarchy members currently incarnated on Earth immerse themselves in Nature either through their occupation, meditation, gardening, or outdoor interests. Gaia Hierarchy members are aligned to the highest requirements of Earth and are attuned to meeting their own needs through their relationship with Nature.

The Ishtar Hierarchy is the ancient dragon and serpent energy of the Earth. As a child of the fiery core, this hierarchy lives within the Earth's frequencies and many realms and dimensions that are part of Earth, but not completely known or understood by humankind. This hierarchy does have human incarnated aspects, but most of its aspects live in realms that co-exist alongside the physical, third dimensional realm that humans experience as Earth. Ishtar's origins are ancient, having entered many planets alongside Bethlehem to be the serpent energy that travels through Bethlehem's star grids. Ishtar has birthed itself into countless realms and worlds in an effort to experience itself in all frequencies.

The Jerusalem Hierarchy is the embryonic fluid of the Divine Mother of the All That Is. It holds minimal incarnated aspects on Earth with most of its aspects residing in Neptune or in the Earth's seas. The origins of this hierarchy are not on Earth, and yet the hierarchy has been present since the creation of the original blueprint for Earth. In the mid 1990s, a wave of Jerusalem Hierarchy children were prepared for incarnation and began incarnating in 2001. This new wave of children will become part of the building blocks for the awakened society that will integrate on Earth from approximately 2050. This awakened society is already in existence and is gathered above the Earth at present, interacting with earth-humans as they allow it. The awakened society forms part of a movement that will anchor in the physical plane soon as well as a task force that has been protecting Earth for many centuries. These two bodies are known as The New Jerusalem and Jerusalem Command respectively.

The following chapters explore each of the twelve hierarchies in more detail. At the end of each chapter, as mentioned earlier, there is a list of publicly recognised incarnations belonging to the hierarchy. By no means is this a complete list. However, this incomplete list is included to assist the reader to 'get a sense' of the signature frequency of each hierarchy and to be able to appreciate the extensive role each hierarchy has played in sending aspects of itself to Earth to facilitate human awakening. Human incarnates who are alive, serving their hierarchies in this current time, have very deliberately not been included in any lists in order to respect the privacy of their work and assignments.

A list of Divine beings belonging to each hierarchy is also included at the end of each hierarchy's chapter. When the terms 'Lord and Lady' are used, they are used to describe the masculine and feminine energies and aspects of a hierarchy as well as to differentiate between them. In these instances, the terms refer to vast energies, consciousnesses and frequencies, which could manifest as an office or council of beings rather than one 'being' or individual. However, there are instances where the terms may refer to an individual being.

Some hierarchies have chosen not to reveal all of their facets at this time and so the profiles below are not to be taken as the entire picture of each hierarchy. The details we have included at this time are here because the hierarchies have granted permission to reveal them.

CHAPTER THREE

Central Sun Hierarchy

You have made us for Yourself and our heart is restless until it rests in You.

Saint Augustine

Many aspects of Central Sun Hierarchy currently live on Earth, each with their own specific and individual assignments. As the levels and roles within the Central Sun are explained, those who belong to the hierarchy will resonate with the information at a deep cellular level. In time, this recognition will develop so that Earth representatives remember their place within the hierarchy. Some members will recognise their belongingness immediately and will not need a phase of integration where the information is processed at a deep cellular level before it can be accessed consciously. These members will awaken almost immediately to their place and role within the hierarchy for they programmed themselves to do so prior to incarnating upon Earth in this lifetime.

The information revealed about the Central Sun is accurate and appropriate for this current level of human evolution. As every member of the hierarchy awakens as they are destined to do, in their agreed time, more information about the hierarchy will become available to humanity. Human incarnates of the Central Sun will bring the information through into the physical plane for themselves. They will (and many have already) emerge as artists of a divinely inspired order - writers, teachers, poets, gardeners - creators in every sense. They will continue to heal as doctors, nurses, veterinary surgeons, dentists and other healing professionals, conscious of their multidimensional existence within their earthly life and the Central Sun simultaneously.

The Central Sun Hierarchy is a family of light within the greater family of this Universe. Within the structure of the Ancient Spiritual Family, the hierarchy has produced many races. One such race is the feline beings. Feline beings at the level of ascended master, travel to many planets and into many civilisations and races to work primarily as educators. They are an entirely benevolent race, with ancient genetic structures and family history. Their collective soul experience is extensive so much so that they are considered elders, teachers and guardians of various younger races.

The grand lion beings of Sirius are a good example of this. These huge beings have guarded the etheric structures of Sirius for millennia and have stood as guardians and facilitators of the ascension gates since the time of the 'fall through the frequencies'. The ascension gates are massive portals that release higher vibrational frequencies into the Milky Way as well as into specific planets to grant an opportunity for each conscious being to ascend quickly and easily to the next level available to them. The opening of these gates and portals can be considered a 'power up' for all those who choose to accept the opportunity provided to them. The lion beings preside over the opening of the gates at various important intervals in the ascension journey of the Ancient Spiritual Family and all planetary worlds and realms.

Aside from their role at the ascension gates, the feline race's only large scale interaction with humanity at present is through the physically incarnated cat family who act as transmitters and broadcasters for higher frequencies and important, telepathically communicated information. The feline beings do have some direct interaction with specifically chosen human beings on a much smaller scale. Such humans may receive visitations from feline representatives either directly or through the dream state.

Feline communities have lived so long on Sirius that some humans believe the felines are from Sirius. It is important to note that Sirius is not the original birthplace of the feline lineage although they share many assignments with the Sirians (whose spiritual lineage was birthed by Mu Hierarchy). When the Central Sun Hierarchy created the feline race, they were designed to be an evolving race that developed through their service to other planetary worlds and races as well as through the vicinities they incarnated into. For this reason, feline beings are found on many planets in large communities. They also travel, sending large delegations to countless destinations across the galaxies to aid in the evolution of the species with which they are sent to work. All of their work is done with the agreement of other hierarchies. These particular agreements are made in the Galactic Council levels of the hierarchies.

Feline beings are primarily fourth and fifth dimensional. They maintain fourth dimensional frequencies that allow them to interact with younger races and to have access to a broader set of grounding frequencies in the planetary worlds in which they work. They hold fifth dimensional heart frequencies and consciousness. They also have the ability to move upwardly through the frequencies from the fifth to the seventh dimension. Their multidimensional capacity is the result of the races' collective commitment through incarnation in multiple planetary worlds and realms.

Solar angels also belong to the Central Sun and work as a community of light to support life in many planetary worlds and systems. Otherwise known as the sun angels and the angelic community within the solar realms, the solar angels are the angelic frequency and angelic essence of the sun, sunlight, and sun rays. They travel to Earth and interact with human beings and all life on the planet as physical sun rays. These rays bring healing, rejuvenation and vitality. They are able to encourage rejuvenation within the human body and they assist to regulate the human body by supporting the natural cycles and systems of the body to find their harmonious rhythm. When so many unnatural external cycles disrupt the body's natural way and throw it into disarray, the solar angels remind the body of its true rhythm.

Sun rays as a physical manifestation of the solar angels, encourage the proper functioning of systems in the human body that lead to an increase in vitality. The right amount of time in the sun (and this time varies from person to person) will increase the person's life force levels. Individuals can fine tune their ability to detect when they have 'topped up' their life force levels and it is time to move out of the sun.

Solar flares are powerful offerings of energy from the solar family of light. The solar angels orchestrate as a community these outpourings of energy. Initiates who are attuned to these outpourings are able to use these instances to rejuvenate their energy fields and increase the vitality of their human bodies. The solar flares also contain technology and information that can be used to inform and upgrade programming within the body cell memory of the human vehicle. Once Initiates have understood how to work with this additional energy, they will not fear the solar flares, but engage with them safely and for the benefit of their ascension.

The solar angels when working as a single sun ray or as solar flares, have the ability to transmute debris lodged in the mental fields and emotional bodies of all species. The transmutational capacity of solar angels can easily be utilised by the Initiate. The ancient practice of meditating on a rising sun, and/or allowing the setting sun to penetrate the pineal gland is well documented. Integrating the solar angels through the form of sun rays into your daily practice enables you to elevate your vibrational frequency and bring more power to your ascension exercises. Your body will use this power to accelerate your ascension process.

When the Central Sun Hierarchy interacts with the Jerusalem Hierarchy in the physical plane, it results in sunlight shining into water. The interaction between the two hierarchies is an event that is older than all the planets and worlds, yet reoccurring. This triggers an awakening or remembering in your body cell memory of this original activation and beginning of life. It is for this reason as well as many others, that it is beneficial to drink purified water that has been reawakened by sun rays. Leaving your glass water jug filled with purified water in the sun for five to twenty minutes will activate this process. When you drink this 'activated' water, the water moves in through the systems of the body and reawakens ancient memory codes. This can be very useful for Initiates wanting to accelerate their ascension journey. The solar angels are available to all Initiates, regardless of their hierarchy of origin. It is very helpful to a physically incarnated Central Sun member to call upon the additional assistance of the solar angels and to incorporate the sun into their daily spiritual practice where possible.

Physically incarnated members of the Central Sun generally devote themselves to spiritual learning of some kind during their lives. They may pursue with great dedication a particular religious path or a more general spiritual education that encompasses a wide body of religious and spiritual thought. They are especially drawn to vicinities of spiritual contemplation such as monasteries, convents, temples, shrines and holy places. Members of this hierarchy, more so than other hierarchies, are likely to go on pilgrimages and retreats. They may even feel compelled to invest years of their lives to living in quiet communities or relative isolation in an effort to reach a higher state of mind, spiritual grace or enlightenment.

Central Sun members are very content with the 'simple life'; simple food, humble dwellings, and a close, loving relationship, friendship, family or community life. Even though they may show an interest in 'the world', such as the famous people of the world or current affairs, they are not particularly attached to it, and show interest more so to be polite rather than any deep investment in the news. They are, however, interested in the safety and happiness of others. Similarly, their interest in business and money is only out of necessity so that they are able to comfortably support themselves and their families. They have very little interest in making money outside of meeting these simple needs and even less interest in the corporate world. However, education is highly valued by Central Sun members, and may range from a basic ability to read the Scriptures, to holding multiple degrees in languages, philosophy, history, law etc. They often have an interest in human rights legislation and governing bodies created to protect the rights of minorities and citizens in general and have worked with members of the Jerusalem Hierarchy who are similarly inclined.

This legal interest may stem from the role the hierarchy plays as the guardian of the Spiritual Hierarchy for Earth. As part of its responsibilities as guardian, it holds the Spiritual Hierarchy's governing offices, such as the Office of Balance and Justice, within its jurisdiction. The Office of Balance and Justice stabilises the consciousness of the Spiritual Hierarchy for Earth, while hosting the Law of One Council. The Law of One Council ensures that hierarchies make choices that do not encroach on others' aligned will or restrict other hierarchies the freedom to choose their own expression or 'be within their own frequencies'. The Law of One is thus:

> *When all are allowed to be within their frequencies, all shall come into peace and harmony.*

Through its role as guardian, with impeccable integrity, the Central Sun Hierarchy steers the Ancient Spiritual Family through the waters of its evolution towards complete ascension and reunion with the Oneness.

While on Earth, Central Sun incarnates' most treasured 'possessions' are their time alone to contemplate and enjoy their own company, quietude, their loved ones, their spiritual texts or documents, literature, their ability to read and write, and their prayers, poetry, hymns, chants, and music. Their physical bodies can be easily affected by negative thought forms and ideas that do not align to their evolved and divinely aligned frequencies. For this reason, it is crucial for members of this hierarchy to surround themselves with people who are committed to refining their state of mind to reflect the higher consciousness of the fifth dimension and beyond. Such discernment will benefit the Central Sun incarnate immensely.

Central Sun Hierarchy Members

The Office of the Christ

- Christ Consciousness
- Jesus
- Mary Magdalene
- The Priestesses of the Magdalene Order, the Ladies of Magdalene
- Archangel Michael
- Overseer of the Holy Men of the Essene Order (Originating approximately 100 B.C., the Essenes were a Jewish mystical community. After the destruction of Jerusalem in 70 A.D., they disappeared from history. Many of their keys rose again with the Cathars, another spiritual community, which emerged in Europe in the eleventh century. Note that not all human incarnated Essenes and Cathars came from Central Sun Hierarchy)
- Overseer of the Sacred Nuns of the Essene Order
- Planetary Prince of Peace

King and Queen of the Elven Kingdom (the Elven King and the Elven Queen)

Keys to the Elven communities

Lord Hilarion

Lady Galadriel, spiritual warrior for the Central Sun and Elven kingdom representative

Lady Leto

Lady and Lord Assandra, Keeper of the Animal Kingdom - they are known by multiple names and titles across various traditions

Bast (Egyptian Feline Goddess)

Feline Beings, ancient Feline race

The Lion Beings who guard Sirius

Bees and the Council of Bees

Keeper of the Tree of Life

Keeper of the Keys to the Essenes and the Cathars

Lord and Lady Egypt

Atum-Ra (Egyptian)

Hathor

Falcon totem

Cow medicine totem

Horus

Keeper of the Eye of Horus

Keeper of the Keys to the Third Eye

Keeper of the Keys to the Pineal Gland (The Pineal Gland is an anchor point for the light of the Central Sun. This light can be drawn into the Pineal in meditation and is available for use by all human beings)

Lady Nada, Keeper of the Pink Ray (gentle, soft, rose gold pink)

Keeper of Rose Gold

Keeper of Rose Quartz (a crystal representative for Central Sun)

Lord Vishnu

Lakshmi

Enoch

Lord and Lady Sananda

Gautama Buddha

Lord of Compassion

He who is the Central Sun, She who is the Central Sun

Archangel Chamuel

Lord Metatron, volunteer overseeing Archangel of the Sirian High Council

Kwan Yin

Amaterasu Omikami (Japanese Goddess of the Sun)

Earth's Sun

The Central Sun

Photon Light

Light

Lord and Lady Gold

One of the Keepers of the Keys to Nursing (alongside Bethlehem)

Publicly Recognised Human Incarnations

Siddhartha Gautama - known as The Buddha

Zoroaster

Socrates

Plato

Saint Augustine

Empress Theodora (Byzantine Empress)

Saint Abigail (County Clare, Ireland)

Hildegard of Bingen

Rumi

Saint Joan of Arc

Saint Teresa of Ávila

Leo Tolstoy

J.R Tolkien (Elven Kingdom representative)

C.S Lewis

Aldous Huxley

Chico Xavier (Brazilian author of numerous titles including *Nosso Lar*)

CHAPTER FOUR

Jerusalem Hierarchy

The memory of life arrived on this earth carried by the soul of water. From this memory, life awoke, the human being emerged, and finally you and I were born.

Masaru Emoto

Although it has manifested itself into a multitude of creations, the Jerusalem Hierarchy in a nutshell is the embryonic fluid of the Source.

This hierarchy has two primary arms, which for ease of understanding, can be considered masculine and feminine arms, although both arms are naturally balanced in their masculine and feminine frequencies. The feminine arm is called the Neptunian lineage, line or hierarchy. Its function is to serve the All That Is through the provision of its signature frequency, which is the life force that manifests itself as the physical element of water on Earth. In this way, water can be considered 'liquid life force'. The master frequency, Lao Tzu, is part of this feminine arm and consists of multiple aspects working in a team to anchor the keys to the ancient mysteries of water.

The Lao Tzu team of incarnated aspects is a frequency belonging to Saint Germain.

The masculine line, known as Jerusalem, balances this as the life force, which has not manifested as physical water, but is still required in order for there to be life. When the two are balanced in harmony, creation and life is supported fully. This balance of the two arms then offers itself as a feminine balance to the Central Sun Hierarchy, who in this instance, becomes the masculine so that creation can manifest in solid form, colour, sound and light. The Central Sun is the light and provides the light. The Jerusalem Hierarchy is the womb from which intention emerges to manifest through the light and into light. The Central Sun and Jerusalem hierarchies have always balanced each other's masculine and feminine energies in a way that allows for the creations of the All That Is to be birthed into manifested form. Their relationship is an eternal one.

Jerusalem Hierarchy presently holds bases in France and Switzerland. Bases are like anchor points, which help hierarchies ground support infrastructure for their incarnated aspects.

The Neptunian Line

The Neptunians are energies of divinity who hold the essence of the cosmic sea in their physical forms. They exist on, in and around the planet Neptune. They sing in the planet's womb, which is her fertile, embryonic seas, and within this creative space they manifest into form. Beings classified as Neptunian angels are the wind and sound angels of Neptune and the sea angels of planet Earth.

When Gaia was born from Mother Neptune's womb, the Neptunian angels traveled the passage of light created by their father, Lord Neptune, also known as the God of Earth's seas. They followed this passage and manifested in physical form to support the beloved newborn, Lady Gaia. They still sit around her as the Council of the Angelic Realm of the Sea. This realm and council presides over the Angelic Light of Earth's waters. They ensure the balance of light within the sea and endeavour to maintain the purity of the physical water. Their mother, Mother Neptune, works through them, as their mother and also as part of them. They travel the passages between Earth and Neptune frequently and continue the flow of light and love between these two places and energetic bodies. These passages are pure and free of taint. In the tainting times upon Earth, these passages were never infiltrated. This has been a true support to Lady Gaia, and has allowed for great strength, wisdom and cleansing to reach humanity, from the Sea Mother, via the Angelic spirit of the Earth, who is Gaia.

The Merlin lineage within the Neptunian Line

The Merlin lineage within the Neptunian line allows for the masculine side of the hierarchy to express itself in various physical formats on Earth and in other planetary worlds. The Merlin lineage consists of members of the Neptunian line although participants from other hierarchies have, over the course of many thousands of incarnations, engaged in training and initiation through the Violet Flame system, office and council. This Violet Flame order is the creation and domain of the Merlin lineage within the Neptunian line of the Jerusalem Hierarchy, but has opened its doors to Initiates from other hierarchies for the purpose of offering the powerful transformational tool to the extended spiritual family for the benefit of the All That Is.

Thus, the key to transmutation through the vehicle of the violet light and flame is available to all hierarchies which choose for it to be so. In the past, hierarchies sent members to train in the use of the violet flame to bring expansion and where needed, cleansing, back into their own hierarchies. This process has been re-created many times on Earth, from the days of Lemuria onwards. Human incarnates have had the opportunity since Lemuria to receive this training while remaining in a physical body. The training is usually administered by the head of the Merlin lineage, Saint Germain.

Lady Germaine, St Germain's feminine balance, has manifested on Earth several times since Atlantis and holds the energy for humanity as creatrix and feminine aspect of the Violet Flame and Office of Transmutation. Her role, although not widely seen, is to remain available as a source of healing, restoration, transmutation, and to make available a particular path of ascension for humankind and other species also co-existing on Earth at this time. Her work and contribution is often administered through other members of her hierarchy, such as Lady Mary, Lady Neptune, the Lady of the Sacred Waters of Life, and Lady Jerusalem. Lady Germaine's work often goes unnoticed due to the subtle nature of her role within the transmutational process. Her subtle, gentle frequency allows for a grace to imbue the transmutational process. This allows the process to unfold gently, painlessly and at times, pleasurably within a human body.

Lord and Lady Amethyst belong within the Merlin lineage and hold the masculine and feminine balance for the transmutational capacity of the amethyst crystal. Their light and depth allows for the amethyst crystal to transmute debris without becoming contaminated by the very debris it is transmuting. The amethyst ray holds the energy for the long-term ascension of humankind by way of transmuting lower energies so that humankind has the opportunity to see its highest potential. The amethyst ray clears obstructions from the paths of human beings and is easily called upon by any individual or community who wants assistance in moving upwardly into a higher vibrational frequency.

Assistance from this ray always comes in a gentle, non-confrontational and graceful way, due to the frequency held by the feminine aspect of this lineage. The transmutational power of the masculine Merlin lineage balances perfectly with the grace of its own Divine feminine.

In the physical plane, one of the biggest areas for a male or female Jerusalem incarnate to master is learning when <u>not</u> to act or intervene. Much of the 'karma' accrued by Jerusalem members over the centuries has been in trying to assist when they would have been better to leave well alone. This is the basic, underlying tension in the life of a Jerusalem member: how to best be of service - when to withdraw and when to aid. When a Jerusalem member aids others, they can be of immense assistance because their skills, tools and abilities are relatively 'complete'. By 'complete', we mean that their lower incarnation levels (less time spent on Earth) have ensured that their abilities have been for the most part, preserved. (Please note: for some hierarchies, less time on Earth does not necessarily equate to stronger abilities. Often, Earth experience increases a hierarchy's 'toolbox of abilities' and gives incarnates a chance to master certain skills in the physical plane).

In the 'negative', this aiding, if it becomes excessive, can take the form of disempowering another in his efforts to 'stand on his own two feet'. It can also manifest as pushing for progress in another, which leads to disruption in the natural flow of energy. Jerusalem members must learn how, when in attending to others, to pull back at the first sign of tension. They need to also be mindful of not allowing this 'Achilles heel' of the hierarchy to be used against them by those wishing to exploit their calling to serve.

The Jerusalem incarnate may find it helpful here to examine the history of their hierarchy, particularly how this calling came to be. The calling to serve the recovery of the Spiritual Family evolved from an awareness that most of their abilities survived 'the Fall', where many other hierarchies sustained great losses. When we use the term 'the Fall' in this context we refer to the times when Earth's frequencies 'nose dived' like a stock market in free fall, such as occurred in the later stages of Atlantis. During those times, Jerusalem had only a small number of aspects incarnated in the Earth frequencies and even less aspects in human form (most aspects on or near Earth during these times were incarnated in the sea realms). Ninety nine percent of incarnated aspects left Earth for safe havens before the most significant drops in frequency occurred.

This exiting early has led some Jerusalem members to carry through their subsequent incarnations, a sense of guilt or feeling of unexplained responsibility for others as well as feelings of unworthiness, as though they do not deserve to be part of the human community, as soldiers do when they are the ones to return alive when so many of their comrades died. It is this very reason that compels many members of this hierarchy to try to convince others of a particular course of action when they perceive danger ahead.

They tend to be well organised and generally well prepared, walking carefully on the Earth, watching and listening, interpreting signs and the energetic waves emanating from the collective 'world mind'. When they sense danger they will not hesitate to move out of its way, and are not above 'hiding out' in a quiet and humble existence until the threat has passed.

The best example of Jerusalem preparedness can be seen in Noah's story, meticulously building his boat years ahead of the upheaval. Likewise, by the time of 'the Fall' of Earth's frequencies, Jerusalem incarnates had secured their keys and left Earth. The few members who stayed behind did so consciously and willingly as part of the higher plan of the hierarchy.

As well as foresight and preparedness, Jerusalem members also possess a type of technical training that has not yet reached Earth in the form of widespread education or formal learning available to human incarnates. It will be a long, long time before such training is available to the general population through the form of Earth based schooling, although it could be available if humanity chose to receive it. This technical training allows for Jerusalem members to navigate the corridors of each of the twelve hierarchies as well as the bridges that sit between and link the twelve. Jerusalem members are able to use this ability to become the 'mechanics' of the hierarchy system, just as car mechanics know the car they work on like the back of their own hand. Jerusalem incarnates tend to navigate the human condition and psyche in the same way, understanding it as a type of mechanical landscape that can be 'tuned' once the correct condition has been identified. We see the beginnings of this ability in the psychiatry work and writings of Dr Carl Jung, and the work of Dr Ainsley

Mears in developing meditation as a therapy for the West.

Members of this hierarchy have little tolerance for structures that attempt to govern the population through excessive laws and rules. Even social structures that consist of many unspoken rules can at times ruffle the Jerusalem incarnate's feathers. They become rebellious if they identify that they are being manipulated. Moving beyond being 'triggered' by such things will bring them peace.

They may, on occasion, come across to others as being non-conformists or rebels. This rebellion manifests only with human created structures. Regarding the spiritual structures, they do not only adhere to Divine Law, they have an active role in anchoring the Law of One on Earth and in many other realms and planetary worlds. They hold Divine Law in the highest regard, but eye the manufactured laws of man with suspicion.

Although Jerusalem incarnates avoid manipulative social interaction and structures, paradoxically they do move between various groups as diplomats and ambassadors for the Spiritual Hierarchy for Earth. They endeavour to remain distant from politics and yet some incarnates serve the divine plan of the Spiritual Hierarchy for Earth within political and legal frameworks. These ones regularly work alongside members of the Central Sun Hierarchy who are very often advocates for individuals and groups in vulnerable situations.

The Jerusalem incarnate has a strong constitution. However, they are extremely sensitive to emotional and psychic conditions. They do well eating edible flowers and foods from the plant kingdom such as leaves, roots and herbs. Teas made from tree barks, plant roots, leaves and edible flowers strengthen their energy fields and shield skin. (The shield skin being the outermost layer of physical skin encasing the body and the innermost layer of the energy field). If this invisible encasing weakens or tears, it allows external debris to infiltrate the physical system. (Please see 'Definition of Terms' section for a more detailed discussion of shield skins). If Jerusalem incarnates would protect and maintain their shield skins, many earthly challenges would be averted.

Jerusalem Hierarchy Members

Shekinah

Saint Germain

The Lao Tzu group frequency

Queen Mother of the West

Merlin (Magician, advisor to King Arthur)

The essence of the Divine Feminine Principle that for many is called Mother Mary/Lady Mary. Keeper of the Rose Ray (soft, dusty rose colour)

Mama Cocha (Incan, the Mother Sea)

God and Goddess of the Seas

Lord and Lady Neptune

Archangel Raphael

Lady and Lord of the Flowers

Lord and Lady of the Lake

Lady of the Sacred Waters of Life

Water Element

Keeper of the Keys to the healing power of salt

Planet Neptune

Lord and Lady Amphibian

Cosmic Sea

Well of Urd (Norse)

The Violet Ray and the Violet Ray Beings

Lord and Lady Amethyst (a crystal representative for Jerusalem)

Mother and Father of the Rosaceae plant family

Keeper of the Keys to Seaweed, Kelp and all sea plants and vegetables

Lord and Lady of the Pearl

Keeper of the Keys to Coral

One of the Keepers of the Keys to Geomancy and the Council of Geomancy (alongside Bethlehem, Tansafarie, Ishtar, Pan, Gaia, Lemuria and Shiva)

Lord and Lady Jerusalem

Sandalphon (Archangel)

Ascended Master Elijah

Publicly Recognised Human Incarnations

Taliesin (Great Merlin, Welsh Chief of Bards)

Zhuangzi

Francis Bacon

Comte de St Germain

Ellen G. White (author and founder of Seventh-Day Adventist church)

Beatrix Potter and husband William Heelis

Carl Jung (psychiatrist, founded analytical psychology)

Joseph Campbell (mythologist, writer)

Alan Watts

Dr Ainsley Mears (originator of Stillness Meditation Therapy)

Dr Masaru Emoto (scientist and water researcher)

Co-Creations Initiated by the Hierarchy

The grounding of the keys shared through the *Tao Te Ching*

Anchoring of the Keys for the American Constitution

CHAPTER FIVE

Mu Hierarchy

The Mu Hierarchy is the source of the air, the atmosphere, the mists and the ethereal realm that we call the etheric. The hierarchy is the keeper of the keys to the fourth dimension. In addition to this it holds the offices of the Great Sky Queen and Sky King. From these offices, the hierarchy oversaw the integration of the civilisations of Atlantis and Lemuria on Earth. The Mu Hierarchy is not the keeper of the Atlantean Frequencies, for this belongs to the Atlantis Hierarchy, but it holds the keys for all advanced civilisations entering Earth's vicinity. Mu created a station above the Earth and in this version of a mothership, trains all potential incarnates upon Earth.

All species, beings, frequencies and energies once gathered in the hierarchy's sacred halls of learning and wisdom before attempting to incarnate into Earth through the Holy Councils of Incarnation and through their own individual Offices of Incarnation. The hierarchy is the keeper of the Great Halls of Sirius - centres of advanced learning and higher wisdom. These halls include the Great Hall of Learning and the Great Hall of Wisdom. As part of its role as a caretaker of ancient keys and information, Mu Hierarchy sits with others on the Council of Elders that keeps the Akashic records and the Akashic Hall. Mu maintains high councils on Sirius, the Pleiadian realms, various

Sirian outposts and other planetary realms.

Although vast, the Mu Hierarchy is overseen by its Divine Mother and Divine Father, who sit in the twelfth dimensional levels of the hierarchy - Ancient Mother and Ancient Father Mu. The size and scope of this level is not easy for the human mind to comprehend. To help put this level into perspective, Ancient Mother Mu birthed the Milky Way. As we move down through the dimensions, particularly at the fourth and fifth dimensions, these ancient beings manifest as Lord Mu and Lady Mu.

Sirian Line

If you consider Mu as a tree, Lord and Lady Mu and all of their direct offices are the tree trunk. The Sirian arm is a major 'limb' and in its own right has many councils, offices, and creations housed within its arm. The Sirians are part of the community of this universe and have members living in the fourth dimension and beyond. The Sirian High Council is a powerful body that has overseen the colonisation of many realms, including bringing many Sirian delegates to Earth in Earth's history, namely Atlantis and Ancient Egypt. This council once permitted its members to have aspects of themselves in the fourth and fifth dimensions. This policy was changed after Ancient Egypt. Since that time, due to infiltration, Sirians wishing to serve on the Sirian High Council can only do so if they have attained fifth dimensional consciousness or above.

The original genetics and frequencies of Sirius belong to the Mu Hierarchy. However, the Sirians have welcomed Initiates from other hierarchies to incarnate into their genetics (see Chapter Nineteen "The Sirian Family" for a more in-depth exploration of this). The home base of Sirius consists of outposts, and each of these houses other species belonging to the core Sirian Family. Although this family is self-governing, in reality, it is an 'arm' of the Mu Hierarchy and not a separately existing hierarchy. The other species that belong to the core Sirian Family include the Sirian elves, the Sirian canine community, and various other communities.

Within the canine community, the Canine Shapeshifters of Sirius maintain an important function. Although they have been distorted and exaggerated in literature as malicious werewolves for the purpose of scaring small children, the true canine shapeshifters are gentle beings who have the capacity to shift in and out of canine form. They are a guardian and protector race, which champions and protects emerging species. When they are not in their canine form, they enjoy a domesticated life, creating and living in their gardens that they tend with great care. They are able to shift back and forth effortlessly and remain entirely in control of the process.

Pleiadian Line

Although functioning differently from the Sirian arm, the Pleiadian line is another one of the major arms of the Mu family tree and although four arms are recorded in this book, Mu has many more arms than this. The Pleiadian line not only encompasses the region in space that we know as the Pleiades, but is home to the Pleiadian races. The term 'Pleiadian' is a broad term used to categorise beings of a unique set of genetic codes birthed by Mu. The Pleiadian line within Mu consists of a governing council, which oversees the genetic experimentation and development of the lineage. This governing council is labeled 'Lord and Lady Pleiadies', a term used to encompass the masculine and feminine aspects and representatives of the Pleiadian genetic codes and frequencies.

The Pleiadians are highly advanced in terms of their technological advancements. As Keepers of the Living Library for the Mu Family, they hold the keys to the vast resource that is the memory banks and genetic codes of thousands of species throughout the galaxy.

Orion Line

The third arm of the Mu Hierarchy, the Orions are a technologically advanced species that shares its technology with humankind. Members of this species are in direct communication with many people on Earth and are involved in training Initiates to awaken their higher abilities. The Orions have developed the technology to easily penetrate the channelling systems of human beings to bring messages and guidance. They work to strengthen the channelling systems of individuals on Earth. They carry the plans to develop the telepathic abilities of humans and will activate these plans in the future.

Over thousands of galactic years, the Orions have had the opportunity to evolve their communities into centres of advanced learning that allow for emotional and spiritual development. Some phases of their evolution were born out of harsh learning experiences whereby the Orions were required to re-evaluate the principles that underpinned their societies. From this, the Orions recognised the necessity to restructure these societies and reconsider the values that they held. Because of this history, many Orions have developed deep empathy for evolving races and are currently working as guardians and mentors for the human race.

Lyrian Line

The Lyrians have many gifts and strengths to contribute to their hierarchy. As a species they possess exceptional organisational abilities and the ability to structure resources and beings in such a way as to provide security for everyone in times of scarcity. The Lyrians are very much an 'explorer race'. They have travelled to uninhabitable planets and due to their resourcefulness and military-like organisation, have been able to establish colonies where others could not.

Their combination of determination and ambition is of exceptional value when it is kept in balance by other attributes. However, over the course of their history, the Lyrians have needed to contend with small factions within their society that have lost this balance. This has resulted in the ambition becoming excessive, leaving some Lyrians to value power above harmony. This aggressive and overly ambitious streak within the line has caused challenges for the Mu family and has led the Lyrians into war with the other lines of their hierarchy.

The Lyrians have been studied by many beings in other hierarchies for their ability to identify weaknesses and correct them. Through observing and learning from their struggles, other hierarchies have gained enormous knowledge from the Lyrians. To this day, the Lyrians continue to colonise worlds and establish infrastructure to support the evolution and expansion of their species.

•••

Beyond the arms or 'limbs' of the hierarchy, the higher realms consider the ancient levels of Mu to be likened to a great and ancient Grandmother Spider who weaves an intricate web of ideas, dreams, and creative possibilities. This web is like her blueprint and at any time fragments of this web may be harnessed and manifested in the planetary world that has anchored it. As a master weaver, she is the visionary and creatrix of ancient species, worlds and entire dimensions of consciousness. One of the Elder Goddesses, Mu sits upon one of the oldest overseeing councils of this universe and will always hold her office and title as the Ancient Mother of the Milky Way. She and Ancient Father Mu have many sub-aspects and children. They are manifested and incarnated across numerous planets including Earth.

Many Mu members have come to Earth at this time of great ascension. They bring keys and ancient advanced technologies designed to aid in the ascension of the human being into the fifth dimension and to aid in the establishment of new systems and new ways of living in co-operation with Earth and the nature realms. Innovations in architecture that allow for human beings to live connected to nature will be anchored by Mu members over this coming phase. Mu has developed civilisations on other planetary worlds and has contributed to the development of new sustainable ways of living on Earth, and will continue to do so.

Mu sent many of its members to Earth and along with the Atlantis, Central Sun and Israel hierarchies, built the Egyptian civilisation. They established structures that would serve as tools to educate, inspire and remind generations of humans to come. The Egyptian era was extremely important to Mu and became an opportunity and a vehicle for the hierarchy to reduce karma acquired by its many aspects who had served in Sirius, Orion, Pleiades, Lemuria and Atlantis.

Thousands of Mu aspects ascended from third and fourth dimensional levels to fifth dimensional levels through multiple incarnations into the Egyptian era. Some aspects reincarnated many times through consecutive lives - leaving a life and almost immediately after briefing with their councils, returning to a new body. Mu members still completing their final karmic contracts are incarnated on Earth at this time. They have incarnated across the globe into all religious, socio-economic and physical conditions to release the final levels of their karmic contracts, awaken, and begin their ascensions. This is a time of healing, expansion and growth for Mu.

With many incarnates on Earth at this time, the hierarchy has an opportunity to transcend the last of its limitations and expand into its full potential on this planet. The hierarchy has always enjoyed the diversity of experiences that incarnation on Earth provides. Where all hierarchies appreciate good craftsmanship and objects of art and beauty, some Mu members pursue paths where luxury, fame, wealth and the acquisition of beautiful man-made goods are of central importance. We have said 'some' because this is not the case for the entire hierarchy.

For those who pursue this luxury and/or fame, they can easily tip into an ostentatious lifestyle where they live far beyond their means. For these ones, they can be swept up in an ideology, a vision, a peer group, celebrity worship, or even a 'cult', and lose sight of the ground beneath their feet. However, paradoxically, in directing their thoughts towards such lifestyles, they often draw to themselves opulent experiences and opportunities and share the gifts of such lifestyles with their wide circle of loved ones. Reconciling their desires and generosity with the financial cost of such things, can be a difficult balancing act and one that is refined over the years as the incarnate reaches spiritual maturity later in life. Regardless of the tools at their disposal, they excel at creating the sense of a special occasion encapsulated in that beautiful Italian phrase 'L'arte di arrangiarsi'.

Many Mu members have pursued fame over the course of their incarnations. It is very important to Mu members to feel loved and valued, and to create either for themselves or others that exquisite feeling of 'specialness'. This may not take the form of fame on a world stage, but may be as simple as manifesting an ideal table at a restaurant or receiving special attention or service in some way. Equally, Mu members have an innate ability to make others feel treasured and important, often creating elaborate birthday or other special occasion celebrations so that others feel loved and cared for. They are exceptionally good at bringing people together, especially for a party, cultural event or theatrical presentation, and creating a festive atmosphere.

One can find more Mu members at the world's most prestigious fashion shows than any other hierarchy. They love physical beauty and beautiful clothing and will either be the fashion designers, the people who purchase this haute couture, the press who promote it, or the models on the catwalk. Their collective energy creates the 'buzz' or feeling that fuels these shows. Where other hierarchies' members may feel exhausted at or after such an event, the Mu member feels enlivened and ready for the next gathering. For those with the sight, they may notice that Mu members possess a shiny, sparkling or misty-like magic that sits in their energy field. They often like to colour their hair and/or wear colourful or highly fashionable clothing that others may not have the confidence to wear. For those interested in astrology, think 'Leo' and you will understand the characteristics of this aspect of Mu members.

They are generally very good at creating beautiful or amazing physical vicinities using their innate knowledge of architecture and design. From table settings to interior design, they love to use colour and they use it with great skill and flair. When they create sacred spaces, these spaces combine their ancient intuitive knowledge of sacred geometry, colour healing and sometimes sound or acoustic therapy elements and are generally uplifting and inspiring vicinities.

Although innately spiritual, Mu members tend to be more connected to 'alternative' spiritual paths rather than traditional religious structures. Some enjoy tarot, palm reading and other tools that look into the future. They are not against formal religion, but find it difficult to confine themselves to a strict doctrine or set of beliefs over a long period of time, preferring to explore many different ideas, tools and paths. In general, they are very accepting of the ideas and choices of others and are considered by other hierarchies to be 'open-minded'. In the physical body, Mu holds the keys to the lungs and the function of breathing. Mu is the angelic essence of air itself, through the hierarchy's aspect, the Angel of Air. If the hierarchies were contained inside a human, Mu would be the lungs of the body.

Mu Hierarchy Members

Ancient Mother and Father Mu

Lord and Lady Mu

Prince and Princess of Air

Sky King and Queen

Archangel Uriel

Ptah

Lords of Time

Lords of Karma

The Star-walkers

Sirius

Lord and Lady Sirius (Masters of the Grand Lodge on Sirius)

The Pleiades – the Pleiadians

Lord and Lady Pleiades

Orion Star System - the Orions

The Lyrians (Learians)

Zeus

Ether

Air

Keys to the Lungs of the Human Body

The canine family (and the dogs of Sirius who guard the Hall of Learning)

The Canine Shapeshifters of Sirius

Anubis

Keeper of the Keys to the Diamond

Lord and Lady Diamond (crystal representatives for Mu Hierarchy)

Pink Diamonds (a direct manifestation of Lady Mu)

Keeper of the Pink Diamond Ray (this is different in frequency to the Pink Ray of Central Sun's Lady Nada and the Rose Ray of Jerusalem's Lady Mary. The Pink Diamond Ray is robust, bright and strong - an electric pink)

Keeper of the Keys to Uranium

One of the Keepers of the Akashic Records (alongside Shiva)

Keeper of the Fourth Dimension

Publicly Recognised Human Incarnations

Cleopatra

King Louis XIV

King Louis XV

Christian Dior

Princess Grace of Monaco (Grace Kelly)

Liberace (singer, performer)

Princess Diana (Diana Spencer)

CHAPTER SIX

Israel Hierarchy

The Israel Hierarchy birthed its first stage of creation in the Vega star system. The Vega race came entirely from this hierarchy. The Vega family has since created many planetary worlds and seeded different species within its planetary worlds.

Israel existed before Vega, but not in its hierarchy form. It was originally brought into form as 'mind'. Birthed by the Mind of God, Melchizedek was brought forth to be the structure for Self Love for the All That Is and from there the Israel Hierarchy developed. Then, as the Melchizedeks (the Creator Priests and Priestesses of the Melchizedek frequency of Israel who are Master Geneticists) created species that began evolving to inhabit worlds, the hierarchy also provided the mechanics of the intellect and within this, the ability to perceive oneself and love oneself. If all twelve hierarchies were encased in a single human body, Israel would be the human's mind and mental body, as well as the human mind's highest potential.

As an extension of its role in the creation and evolution of species, Israel's collaboration with other hierarchies led it to provide the first human prototype for integration into the Earth's environment. In order to integrate the first human prototype on Earth, this hierarchy received input in the form of genetic material and DNA coding from other hierarchies. This input was essential given that the Earth's environment was/is made up of the genetic materials and coding from other hierarchies. For example, the Neptunian family, which provides the oceanic realms and waters of the Earth, supplied the coding and materials for the waters of the human body, including the embryonic fluids that support and nourish the unborn child in the body of the mother.

As another example, Pleiadian genetics from Mu provide keys to the galactic travel and telepathic abilities that are beginning to awaken in human beings who have the desire for this to occur. These genetics allow human beings to communicate and interact directly with the communities and species beyond Earth. This telepathic communication function lying dormant in the human body will be a tremendous asset to human beings in the future. By collaborating with other members of the spiritual family, Israel Hierarchy, through its Israel and Chiron 'arms' (see below), has been able to create a human prototype that thrives in the Earth's environment, but also possesses the potential to adapt to conditions beyond Earth.

There are four 'arms' to this vast structure we call the Israel Hierarchy. For ease of understanding, we are placing the four arms under the umbrella term, the Israel Hierarchy, although the hierarchy could easily be labeled according to any of its arms. These arms serve Earth directly while being simultaneously involved in many projects on multiple planetary worlds.

Israel Line

The Israel line of the hierarchy anchored itself on Earth through the seeding of tribes that carry genetic codes from multiple planetary worlds, including the Vega star system. This arm anchored itself in the Middle East thousands of years ago and created the seeding of a breed of humans whose origins are not of Earth due to the breed's ancestry being of Vega star system. This race is encoded to awaken at this time in Earth's history. The race is not understood in the way humans understand bloodline. It is a spiritual race, which awakens over many generations regardless of human ancestry. The race can be born into different cultures and human genetics time and time again through reincarnation, but its spiritual origins, or spiritual race, remain the same. This ancient line was the creation of Lord and Lady Israel, which is the name or title for the masculine and feminine balance of this arm of the hierarchy.

For centuries, the Israel line has been instrumental in anchoring support systems on Earth. In recent times, the Israel line established the Red Cross through anchoring the keys for this to occur. In other instances, they have collaborated with the Chiron line of their hierarchy, sharing their keys to manifest modern allopathic medical infrastructure on Earth and create charities focused on delivering emergency medicine.

Constantinople Line

The Constantinople line allows for the hierarchy to interact with Earth and humanity through the creation of civilisations. This arm created the Byzantine, Constantinople and Roman empires. In order to truly understand the Constantinople arm, one needs to identify its masculine and its feminine aspects that at certain times in Earth's history opposed each other. The Constantinople line was created with distinct and powerful feminine and masculine aspects, that when in harmony with each other create the synergy that allows for the practical aspects of life to be blissful. When this arm balances its masculine and feminine frequencies, people the world over will enjoy the benefits of harmony between the masculine and the feminine within their daily lives. Men will appreciate at the very basic level, the differences between them and women, honouring and cherishing these differences. Women will accept this genuine appreciation and the forgiveness they extend will enable a deep healing to unfold throughout the human race.

Many Constantinople arm members are currently incarnated as members of the human race and have experienced lifetimes in Atlantis, Sumer, Ancient Egypt, Ancient Greece, and Ancient

Rome. Two central Constantinople members, Lord and Lady Constantinople, gained much experience as a Lord and Lady of Civilisation prior to the human incarnation of hierarchy members. They worked within many planetary worlds and worked on the council that star-seeded races of Homo sapiens within the Vega star system. As Lord Vega and King of Vega, Lord Constantinople stood beside his feminine balance Lady Constantinople, the Queen of Vega. They worked with other hierarchies to bring the first human being to Earth and created a unique set of frequencies within the first humans on Earth so that they could ascend to accept higher frequencies very quickly. The multidimensional capacity of these humans, although latent, was extremely powerful. This was a landmark race and had the ability to accept genetic material from other star worlds, including Sirius and the Pleiades.

Alongside other Spiritual Hierarchy for Earth members, Lord and Lady Constantinople incarnated in the physical plane in Ancient Egypt with a desire to build the foundation of a new civilisation that could hold the memories of the star-world people. This information was designed to be decoded at a later time, when humanity most needed it and was also able to assimilate the keys contained within the information.

The Constantinople line of Israel Hierarchy anchored the fifth root race when the energy shifted from the fourth root race (whose foundation of power was held in Ancient Greece by the Atlantis Hierarchy) to Emperor Constantine. It was here that Lord and Lady Constantinople reincarnated with many other Constantinople line members to create the Roman Empire and the Roman Catholic Church. Emperor Constantine was an incarnated member of the Constantinople line and an aspect of Lord and Lady Constantinople.

While the masculine aspect of the Constantinople arm anchored the keys and frequencies mentioned above, the feminine aspect of the hierarchy established an ancient lineage on Earth, drawing from its ancestral roots, its parent hierarchies the Central Sun and its own Israel arm. The feminine aspect of the Constantinople arm is anchored in the ancient lands of Great Britain and manifests itself through the Albion arm of the hierarchy.

Chiron Line

Lord and Lady Chiron are the masculine and feminine balance of the third arm of the hierarchy, the Chiron line. While on Earth, this arm is charged with the task of anchoring the work of the Israel line into Earth so that the hierarchy's aspects can become human in the physical boundaries of the planet itself. This third arm was the overseer of the human race, the guardian of it, as well as the orchestrator of the race's development and eventual formations of the race's civilisations. Where Lord and Lady Israel created the race and gave birth to it in the Vega star system, the Chiron arm implemented the creations of Lord and Lady Israel in a very practical, physical way, which is compatible with the Earth's frequencies.

In ancient times, prior to the settlement of humans on Earth, Chiron worked with many of its creations to build sacred realms on the planetary worlds it created, such as Pluto. As the Keeper of the Keys to the Horse Medicine, Chiron gave birth to many horse tribes on Pluto and also within other planetary worlds. These sacred horse tribe orders have developed over many, many generations to hold higher healing keys and energetic medicine for various races, including humans. Through their highly developed specific techniques, they are able gently to restore damaged humans by healing frequencies related to trust, telepathic damage and issues connected to power – abuse of power and/or powerlessness. Because of their ability to communicate with human beings, they have been sent to Earth over thousands of years to strengthen weakened areas within the human psychological framework. Their role in the healing of humans is extremely important to them and they remain committed to this assignment until they are no longer required in this capacity.

Albion Line

The fourth arm of Israel is called Albion. The Albion energy is the guardian spirit of Great Britain. It oversaw the establishment of Stonehenge, but later in its history it supported the establishment of Christianity in its lands by the hierarchy's Constantinople line. The Albion line is the Keeper of the Round Table and facilitates the coming together of this Brotherhood to serve the assignment of the reconnection of each individual on Earth to his/her higher self and hierarchy. This council is also the Champion of the Divine Feminine. In this role, it supports the return of the Divine Feminine in the hearts and minds of all human beings.

As an anchor for the hierarchy's four lineages, the Star of David is a unique star grid that allows for the infusion of frequencies and technologies from advanced civilisations developed through the Israel Hierarchy to embed in the physical bodies and consciousness of humans. The Star of David is an advanced technological device in its own right, capable of activating ancient codes to advanced technologies and codes embedded in the human structure and consciousness. The Star of David is both an activating device to 'turn on' these codes, and an instrument to make them 'bio-compatible' with the Earth/humans. The Star of David is the creation of Lord and Lady Israel (again 'Lord and Lady Israel' is the name for the masculine and feminine lines within this arm) and is the structure through which many of the hierarchy's creations are birthed.

The Star of David, the Star of Jerusalem and the Star of Bethlehem come together to hold the energy for the thriving of the human species and the coming of the ancient ones through the incarnation process: for it was always meant to be that the Creators of Earth and Earth's Divine and Holy Guardians, incarnate through the human vehicle to experience the magnificence of their creations.

Just as the Star of David unites all four arms of the hierarchy, so does the hierarchy's office of healing. Israel's office of healing is overseen by Lord and Lady Chiron as the high priest and high priestess of the office. The office is fed by the Divine Mother of the hierarchy whose waterfalls of energy and love fill the lake that is the office of healing. Through the waterfalls that flow from this lake, four rivers are fed. These rivers are the four arms of the hierarchy.

All four arms recognise the necessity for all of creation to have a core resonance that is pleasing to all and is, in truth, beautiful. What creates the beauty in all of creation is not its appearance or form, but the core resonance within creation that allows it to sing with the core resonance of the rest of creation thereby creating a symphony. What allows creation to appreciate the rest of creation is the recognition of other core resonances as part of the oneness of the All That Is. Creation recognises the core resonance in the rest of creation and experiences pleasure – peace and joy. The Israel Hierarchy holds the keys to this core resonance symphony and is its master conductor. Appreciation is the music of the symphony. As master conductor of the symphony of the hierarchies, it is the caretaker of the keys to appreciation. It orchestrates the harmonising of the core resonances, which occurs in the space between the twelve hierarchies, but does not have jurisdiction inside other hierarchies.

Israel has long held the keys to this harmonising of the hierarchy symphony through the frequency that allows one hierarchy to recognise the core resonance in another hierarchy and have that recognition bring peace and joy. Other hierarchies contribute also to the harmonising of this symphony, each holding keys to other frequencies that build bridges between the hierarchies. The Israel Hierarchy holds the keys that support creation to be pleased by the presence of other creations. This pleasing experience occurs through creation recognising the core resonances of other creations. On Earth, the recognition of core resonances is interpreted as finding someone or something beautiful. Human beings attribute this recognition of beauty to certain physical characteristics, but in actuality, the human being observes creation and recognises the core resonance within creation.

Music is perhaps the one area where a human being is not distracted by physical characteristics that can be seen or felt by one's hands, and is instead drawn to find the beauty in each note and in the way the notes harmonise. One is drawn into the music, recognising the core resonance of each note, so that within each note and the piece as a whole, one finds beauty in the music. Israel Hierarchy members have long understood the transformational power of music; that music can heal, inspire and transport individuals from one vibrational frequency to another. Often Israel members have incarnated on Earth to bring this power to humankind, manifesting as conductors of music, musicians and composers. Israel members hold deep appreciation for the Arts either by creating artworks, designing, or enjoying the creations of others.

The Israel Hierarchy has created physical and etheric bases for itself on Earth many times over the thousands of years since Atlantis. Currently, Israel has five physical/etheric bases on Earth. The Israel arm has a base in the Scandinavian region, which moves depending upon the assignment and fluctuations in energies. The Constantinople line has small bases located in Jerusalem city and Rome. The Albion line still holds bases over Great Britain and France. These bases move depending upon the requirements of the hierarchy's human incarnates. The Chiron arm has a large base on Pluto, and the entire hierarchy anchors within a planetary world in the Vega star system. Israel has maintained these bases to support its ongoing commitment to human beings and the Children of the Earth Hierarchies, which are Gaia, Shiva, Pan, Atlantis and Lemuria.

Israel holds the seed of the Adamic man and the keys to the 'Adam and Eve' frequencies. As previously mentioned, the hierarchy holds the prototype and the blueprint within its structure for the first human beings, indeed the first human man and woman. Israel experimented with many prototypes, understood within the context of pre-historic man. Some of these prototypes walked in other planetary worlds, but the first man was developed through collaboration between the Tansafarie,

Central Sun, the Children of the Earth and Israel hierarchies, with Bethlehem supplying the keys to the blood and Jerusalem the keys to the internal waters. This collaboration saw the seeding of the first Homo sapiens on Earth and much later on, the seeding of the root races on Earth. Israel holds the keys to the root races alongside and in conjunction with the corresponding hierarchies.

Israel Hierarchy Members

Lord and Lady Melchizedek

Order of Melchizedek - Melchizedek Priests and Priestesses of Israel Hierarchy

Lord and Lady Israel

Archangel Gabriel

Ascended Master Abraham

John the Beloved

Merkabah

The Adamic Seed

The Adamic Man

Keys to the 'Adam and Eve' frequency - Homo sapiens incarnation through the Earth's frequencies and offices

Lilith

Keeper of the Keys to the Twelve Tribes of Israel

Keeper of the Keys to Judaism

Keeper of the Keys to Tektites such as Moldavite

Lord and Lady Moldavite (crystal representatives for the Israel Hierarchy)

Ascended Master El Moyra

Lord and Lady Mercury (Planetary Prince and Princess of Mercury)

Publicly Recognised Human Incarnations

Queen Elizabeth I

Wolfgang Amadeus Mozart

Ludwig van Beethoven

Albert Einstein

Sigmund Freud

Coco Chanel

Constantinople Arm

Lord and Lady Vega

Lord and Lady Constantinople

Lord and Lady Byzantium

Lord Kuthumi

Keeper of the Keys to the creation of the Abrahamic religious structures

Keeper of the Keys to Copper

One of the Keepers of the Platinum group metals (alongside Pan and Tansafarie)

Publicly Recognised Human Incarnations

Pythagoras

Isabella I Queen of Castile

Christopher Columbus

Constantine the Great, Roman Emperor

Julius Caesar

Augustus (first Roman Emperor)

Leonardo da Vinci

Many (but not all) Popes in service to the Vatican

Co-Creations Initiated by the Hierarchy

The creation of the Roman Empire

The creation of Catholicism

Albion Arm

Lord and Lady Albion

Ancient King and Queen of Britannia (also hold the office Lord and Lady Britain/Britannia)

King Arthur frequency

Goddess Gwenhwyfar and Queen Guinevere frequency

Sir Gawain frequency, Knight of the Round Table and Defender of The Land / the Earth goddess

Guardian of the Round Table

Publicly Recognised Human Incarnations

King James I

Winston Churchill

Chiron Arm Members

Lord and Lady Chiron

Lord and Lady Pluto

Pluto

The Centaurs

The Unicorn Herds

The Horse Herds

Pegasus

Keeper of the Keys to Mercury

Keeper of the Keys to Lead

Publicly Recognised Human Incarnations

Hippocrates (considered a founder of medicine)

St Francis of Assisi

Louis Pasteur (medical pioneer)

Samuel Hahneman (anchored many keys to Homeopathy)

CHAPTER SEVEN

Tansafarie Hierarchy

The Tansafarie Hierarchy and its Venetian/Venusian race hold the keys for the Indigo children frequency upon Earth. In addition to this, the hierarchy holds the energy for the crystal children who come as part of a collaboration between the Tansafarie and Mu hierarchies. Tansafarie holds the energy for many crystal children to pass through the passageway from Mu Motherland to Earth. These children pass through the vibrational frequency of Venus and enter Earth through the Tansafarie corridor. Many species who consider Mu their motherland contributed vibrational frequencies into the energetic structure of these children. Some of the crystal children hold primarily Sirian frequencies, others hold frequencies of star worlds not yet understood by the human mind.

True Indigo Children belong to Tansafarie and their origins are on Venus and planetary worlds seeded by Venus. They have a certain criterion in common, and this criterion is the ability to hold as an embodiment in human form, the violet ray, borrowed from the Jerusalem Hierarchy for the purpose of transmuting fear frequencies in the human mind, and a specific higher frequency of the blue ray pertaining directly to the Will of God and overseen by Archangel Michael, borrowed from the Central Sun Hierarchy, which establishes the new foundation of Divine Will upon Earth.

When these two rays are combined, the Indigo Child holds great power, aligned to the Light. The true indigo frequency and ray belongs as a unique frequency, to Tansafarie, and all Indigo Children are Initiates of this most powerful ray and frequency.

Indigo Children hold the ancient memories of their mother Venus, who is both their mother and an aspect of them. The Indigo Children come as a gift from Ancient Mother and Father Venus, to star-seed the consciousness of Earth with a higher vibrational frequency. While they are often misunderstood within the current social and emotional climate upon Earth, Mother Venus and their father, Sanat Kumara, who is Father Venus, encourage them to remember their ancient roots. This is done through returning home to Venus in meditation. A great being known to some simply as Paul the Venetian, shall welcome these children of Venus and begin the complete awakening of their memory banks. This process occurs over several months, as the Indigo Child returns to Venus nightly or daily in meditation. Initially, the Indigo may not see Paul the Venetian, or even feel him, but slowly, as each meditation unfolds, the Indigo's true ability of sight and hearing will awaken, and the Indigo will see and hear home.

Some individuals on Earth believe they are an Indigo because of the year or decade they were born. Technically, this is not accurate. Remember that an Indigo holds the unique frequency of the Venetians/Venusians upon Earth, and they originate from the Tansafarie Hierarchy. One is technically an Indigo if one belongs to the Tansafarie Hierarchy.

Indigo Children have been on Earth since the seeding of Lemuria and a large influx of Indigo incarnations occurred in the late 1800s. Now, more than ever, Indigo Children are entering Earth. These children will continue to incarnate upon Earth for as long as Earth calls for it, and requires it.

Odin's Realm – A Gift from the Tansafarie Hierarchy

Odin is a multidimensional being who has had the capacity throughout Earth and humanity's history to travel through fourth and fifth dimensional realities. In ancient times, prior to Lemuria, he and others co-created many realms within the Earth's structures. His light and keys allowed many beings from various kingdoms to collaborate within the realms he created. In these realms, he was a caretaker, a guardian, and in some instances, a father to the beings and species in residence there. His light allowed for collaboration without judgment and thus were fourth and fifth dimensional beings cohabitants within his realms. His realms allowed for the free will of others to be exercised always. As a Creator God, he created and allowed, but did not govern with authoritarian control.

Odin recognised how the evolution of beings and communities through the allowing of free will created chaos at times, but also created growth and ultimately ascension. Although he slumbers now below the Scandinavian lands, his 'golden era' of creating was before Lemuria, around the time of Hyperborea. He was benevolent and aligned to the governing principle of creating on Earth and through the Earth's frequency. This governing or primary principle for creating was simple: respect for the right and opportunity of others to learn and grow through the unencumbered execution of their own free will.

Valhalla was a fifth dimensional construct created by Odin to assist in the ascension of fourth dimensional beings and members of his own hierarchy. It was misunderstood to some degree by humans, but the essence of it being a sanctuary was understood well.

Odin came to Earth at a time when many souls were seeking elevation through the difficulties resulting from various galactic wars in Sirius and the Pleiades, which engaged many races in a karmic cycle. Odin's family members were seeking to ascend their frequencies in a vicinity where free will remained intact for the most part and the fourth dimension was still accessible. Planetary worlds that maintained their genuine free will status had, generally, ascended beyond their fourth dimensional residency, or had never been fourth dimensional and therefore lacked the capacity to provide it. Odin's hierarchy had lost some warriors in the Sirian wars. After this, he decided to retreat to Earth. These warriors had fallen into lower fourth dimensional frequencies and needed a platform to work their way back up through the levels. Upon moving an arm of his hierarchy to Earth, he was able to restore many frequencies to his warriors and bring about their ascension through the systematic recovery of their aspects (parts of themselves). Some infiltrations occurred into his hierarchy's aspects through bringing this arm to Earth, but much of this infiltration has been resolved. Odin's reason for choosing Earth was also linked to the co-creational ties his hierarchy has had with Earth since her embryonic stage and birth.

Aspects from other hierarchies utilised the vicinities provided by Odin as a platform to experience themselves within a fourth dimensional structure on and/or close to Earth and her energy fields. They also contributed keys and aspects of themselves to support Odin's project. Loki, for example, is an aspect of the Ishtar Hierarchy, the Well of Urd is of Jerusalem/Neptune and Yggdrasil of the Central Sun. Such hierarchies benefited from these Tansafarie realms while contributing to the realm's diversity by way of manifesting their unique frequencies through their respective creations.

In the physical plane while in human bodies, Tansafarie incarnates are generally robust and strong. The hierarchy's members are the most physically powerful warriors to have ever incarnated in human form. The men are usually larger framed - taller and/or with wider chests than the incarnates of other hierarchies. They can also be quite 'stocky'. For incarnates in the current emotional climate of the modern world, special attention must be given to stress reduction. They can easily store decades of tension in the body, resulting in heaviness of the emotions, trouble sleeping in a desired routine (staying up later and later), complaints with the shoulders, legs and feet, and in the long term, issues with the heart, heartburn and indigestion. If a Tansafarie incarnate would only give themselves some quiet time and take themselves for a walk, they would find that in many situations, difficulties can be prevented long before they manifest through the simple act of a daily contemplative walk in nature. In general, Tansafarie incarnates do especially well eating foraged and traditional foods, particularly those that are naturally and properly fermented according to old, time-tested methods.

Although they can survive decades in the wilderness in relative isolation, Tansafarie members shine most brightly when they live with their clan or tribe. It is interesting to note that many Tansafarie members incarnated into and established the old Scottish clan system. The will of the clan pulses in the blood of Tansafarie members. Loyalty to the clan is strongest with this hierarchy. Although they may argue from time to time with members within their clan, they will never break ranks to betray one of their own. The Tansafarie woman is deeply nurturing of people and animals. She will 'adopt' people without clans and animals who are injured.

As only a fool would get between a wild animal and her offspring, it is sensible not to interfere with or try to control Tansafarie members' plans. Once they have decided on something, they need the space to discover for themselves the outcome of their choices. In all matters, it is wise to enrol a Tansafarie member gently into a new perspective, never directly challenging them once their passion or anger has been roused.

Some (not all) members of this hierarchy can be quick to anger. Once set on the war path, few can persuade them to abandon it. This is partly due to their protector instinct. They have a strong sense of justice, right and wrong and will defend what they understand to be the honourable position or the position of their clan, tribe or family. They have deeply loving hearts and when they love, they love fully, with passionate loyalty. When Tansafarie incarnates manifest their higher aspects, they can be extraordinarily effective as administrators and directors of large organisations, armies, and entire countries and populations. Their ability to take charge and lead the tribe, regiment or nation is well known throughout this universe and they are highly regarded in many councils because of these skills.

When aligned and operating from their higher aspects while incarnated, Tansafarie members have the ability to manifest their Master Healer level on Earth. This is a title given to Initiates by offices within the Spiritual Hierarchy for Earth and is rarely attained in one lifetime. Generally, an Initiate works towards attaining this title over multiple incarnations. Often, the Initiate who attains this level has had experience working with the populations and/or environment of other planetary worlds and systems. Such an individual is usually dedicated to the healing sciences in their lifetime and is deeply committed to the role that he/she renders as selfless service. This is not 'self-sacrificing' service, but a willingness to perceive when the higher councils have placed the Master Healer in a situation for the purpose of assisting someone. Here, the Master Healer does not pretend not to notice the need in the other, but steps in and offers the appropriate support at the appropriate time, never over-servicing and never under-servicing. There are a few older Master Healer aspects of Tansafarie incarnated on Earth at the moment as well as many Tansafarie Initiates in training to attain this level of themselves while in human bodies.

As the spiritual warriors of the Ancient Spiritual Family, Tansafarie Master Healers will 'go where angels fear to tread' in pursuit of opportunistic or malevolent beings. These healers see the innate weakness of malevolent beings and thus carry no hidden fear of them. Due to their fearless nature, traditionally Tansafarie Master Healers have been the most competent at removing indwellers, entities and lower spirits from the physical bodies and energy fields of those afflicted. Over the centuries, Tansafarie Master Healers have incarnated as priests, priestesses, holy men and women and shamans in order to perform this service.

Tansafarie Hierarchy Members

Lord and Lady Tansafarie

God and Goddess Terra

Lord Olympus, Guardian of Mount Olympus

Soil

Earth Element

Odin

Frigg

Thor

The Valkyries (part of the angelic guard of Tansafarie)

One of the Keepers of the Platinum group metals (alongside Israel and Pan)

Lord and Lady of the Turquoise (a crystal representative for Tansafarie)

Grandmother Willow (tree being)

The tree beings of the various Willow varieties and the Aspen tree

One of the Keepers of the Keys to Geomancy and the Council of Geomancy (alongside Jerusalem, Bethlehem, Shiva, Pan, Gaia, Lemuria and Ishtar)

Sanat Kumara, Lord of the World, ancient elder of the Earth, Keeper of the Council of Shambhalla. Trainer of Spiritual Warriors

Lord and Lady Venus

Paul the Venetian

Ascended Master Serapis Bey

The Venetian/Venusian People

Planet Venus

The Indigo Children

Keeper of the Keys to the Rainbow Bridge

Home star planet Arcturus

Lord and Lady Arcturus

The Keepers of the Arcturian genetic codes and keys

Publicly Recognised Human Incarnations

Ngawang Lobsang Gyatso, Fifth Dalai Lama

Boudica (Queen of the Celtic Iceni tribe)

Chief Seattle (Si'ahl)

William Wallace

Robert Roy

Co-Creations Initiated by the Hierarchy

Valhalla

Anchoring of the Native American healing system on Earth

CHAPTER EIGHT

Bethlehem Hierarchy

A hierarchy of great light and power, Bethlehem committed many aspects to work with Tansafarie to establish the foundation blocks for the creation of planet Earth. As the Great Fire Goddess at the core of planet Earth, she allowed herself to be the spark that ignited the creation of the planetary forces to work as one body in the natural systems of Earth. Her fire warms the homes of Earth incarnates, cooks the people's food and burns away debris in the ritual of fire ceremony. It is a life-giving and a destructive force. The Fire Queen is revered and feared, and humanity is now, in this next phase of evolution, integrating the light and the feared aspects of this force and this hierarchy.

Prior to the creation of Earth, Bethlehem manifested itself as the fiery core of planets too numerous to mention. Since the creation of Earth, Bethlehem has co-created many more planets by offering itself to be the fiery core and the fire womb. As their fiery core, she is a mother to countless planetary worlds and provides life giving sustenance to billions of species across multiple galaxies through her fire and her ability to decompose matter. Through these roles and many more, she meets the criteria of an Ancient Mother Goddess and sits upon the Council of Ancient Mothers and the Council of Elders - the wise ones who are the founders of the Spiritual Family and the guardian elders of the Spiritual Hierarchy for Earth.

Although all hierarchies have their own version of this element, Bethlehem also represents the side of the goddess that we prefer to avoid: death, destruction - the mother that takes away. She fulfils the essential role of the crone, and can become the hag when need be. She is the crow that feeds on the remains sprayed across the battlefield. However, some may not realise that as she searches the battlefield, she searches for the spirits of people who need assistance in transitioning to a safer realm; those who would otherwise be at the mercy of the lower spirits in the astral plane. Bethlehem saves humans and spirits from the torments of the astral realms. In that vicinity and other such places, she is a force to be reckoned with. The darkest creatures tremble when she comes. Journeying into pockets where many fear to tread, she retrieves the souls who earnestly request to be rescued. Thousands and thousands of years of experience has allowed her to serve in this way. To fulfil this assignment she works closely with Christ and Archangel Michael.

Her light is in her fire, in her ability to burn and consume. Her force is also contained in her ability to decompose. This force is essential in order for life to be sustained on Earth and on all planets where the natural environment has within itself this form of a life cycle. When a fruit or a leaf falls from the tree and onto the ground, it decomposes and provides sustenance for the microorganisms that depend on this process for survival. All members of the Spiritual Hierarchy for Earth must make peace with their version of this energetic in their lives, indeed, how the symbol of Bethlehem manifests practically for them, if they are to ascend and leave their fear behind.

As Bethlehem represents the side of the Goddess that many wish to avoid, so too does the hierarchy represent masculine energies that can be confronting and often misunderstood. One such example is the Great Fire God. As the Fire God, his force ignites matter, creating movement and change. However, this change is often instigated through destruction. Destruction in any form can be very distressing to people, although it plays a necessary role in creation and evolution.

Bethlehem's Goddess aspect sits upon the High Council of Goddesses, a council that consists of a Goddess from all twelve hierarchies. This council is aligned to the Divine Will and remains in the highest level of service to humanity. The aspect of Bethlehem that sits upon this council is Lady Avalon, balanced in her masculine and feminine frequencies as Lord and Lady Avalon.

Avalon is a vibrational frequency, a collection of principles, an advanced training course for high Initiates, and a pathway home to the Divine Mother of the All That Is. Avalon is also a vicinity that is entirely transportable, likened to a grand mothership that is organic in its structure and contents. It maintains itself as a transportable, 'living realm' and is home to its own creations as well as a home away from home for other species. Within this portable realm, many tree beings gather and experience themselves as they journey with the realm wherever the realm is stationed.

Avalon existed in the physical and the etheric levels of Earth when Lemuria, Atlantis and Ancient Egypt also existed on Earth. Avalon never truly disappeared when Lemuria and Atlantis did, and remained as a realm of safety and sanctuary for Initiates of the High Council of Goddesses, in service for the benefit of humanity. Its existence coincided with Ancient Egypt, and some Initiates left their training in Egypt and reincarnated immediately into Ancient Britannia and its surrounding vicinity in order to join the Sacred Order of Avalon as either a priestess, a druid, or as a support to those holding these roles.

Lady Avalon worked tirelessly over thousands of years to give the High Council of Goddesses a voice in times of darkness upon Earth. She initiated many men and women through her Sacred Order of Avalon, in an effort to teach them how to hold the energy for the return of the true balance of masculine and feminine frequencies upon Earth. The Lord and Lady Avalon office continues to restore harmony and balance between the masculine and feminine frequencies on Earth, particularly where the twin flames (the masculine and feminine balance of a hierarchy, office or council) sit.

Lord Avalon worked also, often as a druid priest, and frequently as a healer, occasionally as a bard, and later as a physician and teacher, in an effort to restore the masculine light of Bethlehem to Earth.

The Holy Isle of Avalon still exists in a realm above the physical vicinity of Glastonbury, in England. Initiates who vibrate at a higher vibrational frequency and hold the intention to balance the masculine and feminine frequencies of God/Goddess within them are granted entry into the sacred realm. These ones may experience physically being inside this realm, or may enter it in dream and meditation. Lady Avalon remains available to train and guide Initiates who enter the realm, and works alongside her spiritual sister, the Lady of the Lake, who belongs to Jerusalem and the High Council of Goddesses.

The realm of Avalon is a fifth dimensional realm and only those vibrating at the fifth dimensional level and above and abiding by the Law of One are allowed to be present in the realm. On occasion, Initiates who have not yet attained the fifth dimension will be 'lifted up' in the dream state or in meditation, to experience Avalon. They are granted this gift because of their service to Avalon over many thousands of years, and/or their intention to serve the Avalon assignment in the physical plane. They are then returned to Earth after their short experience in Avalon, with their memories intact and with a stronger awareness of their link to this sacred realm.

Avalon left the physical plane and disappeared into the mists of the etheric and the fifth dimension after infiltration entered its holy vicinity towards the end days of its physical co-existence with Britannia. Some Initiates entered the physical order on Earth with the intent of upsetting the natural and equal balance of power within the masculine and feminine frequencies and attempted to corrupt the choices about how power was used and who could use it, within the Sacred Order of Avalon. Lady Avalon and the High Council of Goddesses recognised that this infiltration could not be permitted and so caused the realm to ascend into the fifth dimension, accessible only to those abiding by the Law of One.

Since that time, Bethlehem has continued its work through sending key Initiates into human form to hold the energy for the restoration of the Office of Avalon in the physical plane. This work continues to this day with the original priestesses of the Sacred Order of Avalon incarnated, here, now, in female form at this pivotal time in Earth's history. These women are incarnated across the globe, to ensure that a network or web of light and information is established for the benefit of the entire hierarchy, not just the members of the Avalon arm. Although these women may not consciously know each other through meeting each other's human form in this lifetime, they have worked together in this way for thousands of years.

The High Priestess of Avalon is incarnated in human form on Earth at this time, working tirelessly to restore the ancient realm of Avalon to the Earth's frequencies. This restoration can occur once Earth ascends its vibratory rate to meet the higher vibratory rate of Avalon. When this meeting occurs, many beneficial gateways will open into Earth and the ancient magic and wonder will return. Through these beneficial gateways, many of the 'old ones' will return. The Elders and keepers of the land, who have long retired from the Earth will feel inspired to return. This will aid in the ascension of individual aspirants who have long wanted to ascend, but who have struggled to hold the focus, discipline and stamina to do so. These 'old ones' will ease the burden dramatically by returning many specialised frequencies to the Earth that were used by Initiates in past eras.

In addition to this work conducted by the Avalon arm of the hierarchy, Bethlehem holds keys to the blood within the human body. Blood is not the domain of just one hierarchy as it is made up of elements from other hierarchies. However, Bethlehem has been the keeper of these keys to the sacred mysteries of blood for thousands of years. The hierarchy understands the power that lives within the blood and the ability of blood to link the person/creature/animal, to the sacred feminine and Divine Mother. Bethlehem also holds the keys to the temperature regulation of the human body. Hierarchies work together through the human body and planet Earth and this collaboration provides the experience that we understand as life on Earth. The profound diversity found on Earth is the result of the harmony and work-ship between the twelve hierarchies that make up the Spiritual Hierarchy for Earth and Spiritual Family.

The silver ray is a manifestation of the Bethlehem signature frequency and the silver ray beings are an extension of this. These silver ray beings have, over the course of many centuries, organised themselves in councils and teams for the purpose of supporting human incarnates while in human bodies and also at the point of transition from the Earth's plane.

One such council is the silver nurses who journey the astral planes and lower levels of the fourth dimension to rescue people who have died, often tragically, and have not felt sufficient support from spiritual family members to know how or where to transition after physical death. These people are often in states of such immense fear, anger, pain, grief, regret and shock that their emotional bodies prevent their becoming aware of the level of assistance being presented by their spiritual family and the higher realms upon their departure from the physical body.

The silver ray beings identified this very issue around the First World War and formulated rescue teams to provide the support needed, especially at times of 'mass exits' where many people exit the physical body at the same time in the same place under very chaotic conditions. Many human incarnated aspects of Bethlehem leave their bodies while their bodies are sleeping and travel in their spirit body to battlefields, hospitals and accident sites to assist people to transition from Earth as easily as possible. Other hierarchies have also offered their assistance to the silver nurses and have sent aspects of themselves to train with these teams. Archangel Michael also champions this council and provides much tactical support by way of his own teams.

The silver ray beings are the keepers of the keys to the silver cords and use their knowledge of silver cords to support safe astral travel in those incarnates who choose to journey through the astral planes while the physical body sleeps. The silver ray beings assist the guardians of a human being to protect their human incarnate while astrally traveling. The silver ray beings work at clearing pockets of debris in the astral plane in order to provide safe passage for travellers and people exiting the Earth plane permanently.

In the physical plane of the human incarnation, Bethlehem incarnates often integrate the wisdom and strength of the hierarchy into family or business, or both. The Bethlehem woman in her strength is an astute business woman. If she hasn't chosen to manifest these attributes in her incarnation through business, you will find her the matriarch of a family, which she steers strongly and towards success. If she is not the matriarch, she will still be a major decision maker of the family, from whom most members draw strength. Generally, she is excellent at managing money and wealth accumulation and may be considered by others as shrewd in certain circumstances. The Bethlehem male is also very good at turning his profession into a business that allows him to accumulate wealth. For example, other hierarchies may be content to be, say, a grocer in a small village, whereas the Bethlehem male will turn that profession into a thriving business, he may have a chain of grocery stores with many people working for him and then he will continue to invest those profits into other, unrelated businesses or properties.

The Bethlehem woman's generosity towards her own family usually knows no bounds. She sees the protection and prosperity of her family (either blood related or those she considers family) as part of her incarnation's higher purpose. In the 'negative' she can become overprotective of the family to the extent that she views 'outsiders' with unwarranted suspicion. This can be a tricky area for Bethlehem incarnates, because both male and female members are extremely psychic, their intuitive selves read people and their intentions very well. The challenge for them is to keep in check what information is coming to them from their intuition and what is manufactured by their fear.

Even though Bethlehem incarnates are excellent socially, they have lived many lives on Earth and have experienced 'the sharp end of the stick' many times, which leads them to examine others carefully. Some Bethlehem incarnates, but not all, deep down do not trust the rest of the world. Many times this lack of trust has been warranted. The important thing here is self awareness, where the incarnate recognises his/her tendency to be suspicious and with this in mind, objectively evaluates the person/situation to ascertain whether the suspicion is limiting their ability to draw the best from the situation and, at a spiritual level, to ascend into a higher experience during their incarnation. Both male and female incarnates have the ability to be exceptional healers, regardless of the form that this healing work takes. Part of their strength as healers lies in their familiarity with and deep understanding of the human condition. They have the capacity for deep compassion while at the same time maintaining a practical approach, nourished by a dry humour that many people find enormously comforting.

Bethlehem members when their energy fields are depleted, struggle living in the world and managing the requirements for functioning as a part of a family, community or society. Here they can withdraw from relationships with others and find it difficult to maintain intimate or genuinely close relationships. A representative from the animal kingdom may be sent to assist in bridging them back to deeper interaction with others. This representative may manifest as a dog, cat or horse etc which comes to live with them. If the emotional isolation continues, they may begin to manifest health issues, although these can be slow developing and quickly corrected through lifestyle changes, as their constitutions are generally very strong.

Bethlehem Hierarchy Members

Mama Quilla (Incan, Mother Moon)

Chang O (Chinese Goddess of the Moon)

Lord and Lady Lunar

The moons of many planetary worlds

The Moon Goddess and the Moon God (in relation to the Lunar frequencies of many planets far beyond Earth)

The Sea Moon (the oceanic aspect of Bethlehem in service to Earth)

Lord and Lady Avalon

Office of Morgana

Keeper of the World Cauldron

Egyptian Goddess Nephthys

Cerridwen (Goddess)

Goddess Diana/Artemis

Aradia (daughter of Diana)

The keeper of the keys of the Crone

Keeper of the Keys to the Old Religion, and the anchoring of the more recent 'Pagan' keys, to provide a path home via the Ancient Goddess Mysteries with the Pan Hierarchy

Keeper of the Keys to the anchoring of the Ancient Goddess Council on Earth.

One of the Keepers of the Keys to Nursing (alongside Central Sun)

The Silver Ray and the Silver Ray Beings

The Silver Nurses

Keeper of the Keys to the Silver Cords

Lord and Lady of the Silver Ray

Mother Goddess Silver (one of the Ancient Mothers and co-creatrix of many building blocks within this Universe)

Father God Silver (one of the Ancient Fathers and co-creator of many building blocks within this Universe)

The Sapphire Ray

Lord and Lady Sapphire (a crystal representative of Bethlehem)

Keeper of the Keys to Moonstone

The Star of Bethlehem

The Keeper of the Flame of the World

Goddess Vesta

Oromasis, Prince of the Fiery Element

The Guardians of Fire

Fire spirits, fire devas

Salamanders

Fire glyphs

Lord and Lady Bethlehem

Mother Bethlehem

Methuselah frequency

Pele

Fire Element

The fiery core of the Earth

Agni, Lord of Fire

The Great Star Grid of the Earth

Co-keeper of the keys to the dragon, ley lines

One of the Keepers of the Keys to Geomancy and the Council of Geomancy (alongside Jerusalem, Tansafarie, Ishtar, Pan, Gaia, Lemuria and Shiva)

Publicly Recognised Human Incarnations

Michaelangelo (painter)

Caravaggio (painter)

Francisco Goya (painter)

Helena Blavatsky (founder of the Theosophical Society)

Florence Nightingale

Mother Teresa

Margaret Thatcher

Co-Creations Initiated by the Hierarchy

Anchoring Avalon into Earth's energy fields for the benefit of all of Earth's inhabitants

The Founding of the Theosophical Society

CHAPTER NINE

Ishtar Hierarchy

Child of Bethlehem (mother), Ishtar Hierarchy possesses the power of the Great Serpent energy. This energy has inspired and terrified humankind for thousands of years. Although born of Bethlehem, Ishtar was not born of her earthly fire womb and was born away from Earth. Ishtar is not considered one of the Children of Earth hierarchies and does not sit on their councils. Some of Ishtar's work appears not to be relevant to the world today. The hierarchy's keys are often buried in folklore and legends, and yet the hierarchy's work is very much alive. Ishtar's dragon energy courses through the old paths that cover the Earth - the old tracks both above and deep in the Earth that many have forgotten. Many tribes, whose roots travel back into ancient times, remember these old tracks and pathways, and they remember the dragon spirits and the rainbow serpent whose energies they can still feel and with which they can communicate.

There are three levels to the dragon energy: the universal dragon, the planetary dragon and the elemental dragons. The universal dragon is part of the inner workings of the cosmos, being both a creative and destructive force. The universal dragon is usually only approached by the most advanced sages and shamans who have attained the knowledge and wisdom that allows them to do so safely. Such a person would need to be thoroughly cleansed of all arrogance, lust for power and greed before attempting to do so.

The planetary dragon is part of the inner workings of a planet. Many planets have a planetary dragon. Earth's planetary dragon was well known to the ancient people of the Earth. Merlin worked with this great being during Arthurian times and only the most experienced shamans still train today to be able to do the same.

The elemental dragons are individualised incarnations of the dragon energy - incarnated aspects of Ishtar Hierarchy in physical form. These dragon beings live primarily in the etheric, although they have the ability to live on Earth in physical bodies. They are powerful guardians and protectors of the Earth and her many realms. They serve as guardians not only of realms, but of knowledge and mysteries also. Their love of learning, wisdom and beauty makes them great protectors of physical and spiritual treasures.

The dragon energy is in many ways the manifested flame. Where Bethlehem is the fire, the dragon which carries the fire within itself is one manifestation of the spirit of fire. Bethlehem is the mother flame that all Ishtar dragon members carry within themselves as the daughter/son of Bethlehem. The ley lines, the dragon lines that run through the Earth are created by and kept through a collaboration between both Ishtar and Bethlehem which share these offices and their responsibilities equally.

Where Bethlehem is the keeper of the flame of the world, Ishtar carries the will of the flame through the dragon lines to the cauldrons. The cauldrons are the high energy places where the energy accumulates and can be used to facilitate awakening. Various religions understood this and so these cauldrons are often easily found by tracing the places where certain cathedrals, temples and ancient stone monuments were erected, often one superimposed over the other. The lines that join the cauldrons are the dragon lines and often the cauldrons manifest where these lines intersect. Whether they are consciously aware of it or not, modern people have built churches and temples over these sites in order to harness the energy generated by the cauldrons.

In the cases of ancient stone monuments, the ancient people utilised the power generated by the cauldrons to facilitate a stronger interaction between the Earth plane and other planetary worlds and higher dimensions. Some of these vicinities also had the capacity to open portals to allow for direct interaction, communication and travel between Earth's inhabitants and 'star born' communities. The portals allowed for Earth to receive energies from the celestial bodies at certain times in Earth's cycles. These energies facilitated dramatic enhancements of the human vehicle, a 'power up' of sorts, where the human vehicle received 'downloads' of information, spiritual technology, the activation of memory banks and the transfer of frequencies that resulted in the raising of the vibrational frequency of the physical body and human energy fields.

The Jade Lady is the manifestation of the harmonisation of the Divine Feminine principle within Ishtar. A member of the Council of the Keepers of Jade Mountain where ancient dragons slumber, she maintains balance within and between the primordial forces at play on and within Earth. She acknowledges the interplay between these forces, recognising that one cannot dominate or be suppressed for too long. These forces must have equal opportunity to express, release, submit and dominate. She balances the potent primordial forces present within her hierarchy and within the fabric of Earth.

The masculine dragon energy of the hierarchy manifests itself in and through various forms, one of which is the physical stone of jade. This potent force interacts with the Keeper of the Jade Stone (another office held by the Jade Lady) and creates a masculine and feminine balancing of this ancient primordial energy within the wearer of the jade stone. The Jade Lady holds the feminine principle, whereas the male dragon lineage holds the masculine principle. For this reason, and many others, the stone of jade is a powerful balancer of the human energy field when it is interacting with unpredictable elements within the Earth plane.

Just as a human being has a shield skin (the innermost level of the energy field and the outermost layer of the physical body), so too does the Earth. Ishtar holds the keys to this important terrain. Many species born of Ishtar call this terrain their home.

The human incarnated Ishtar member isn't commonly found living in modern western society, preferring the subtleties of thought embedded in the ancient cultures of China, Japan, India and South East Asia. In the past, many Ishtar members incarnated in Africa, Babylonia and various settlements in the Middle East and many members are still incarnated in those lands. Ishtar had the highest number of incarnates on the planet during the time of the Persian Empire. They, like all hierarchies, also had their share of incarnates sent into ancient Egypt to anchor the keys and mysteries for the coming times of rapid human ascension.

Ishtar still has bases in Iran, within the old Persian frequencies. It holds bases in Lebanon and in Syria, for there remain many ancient keys hidden in those lands. The recent war in the region is a battle that is not only fought on the physical plane, but is unfolding at a fourth dimensional level also, with various parties wanting to possess these most ancient keys. These keys, buried deep in the land, will rise over these next few decades and create a rediscovery or rebirthing of sorts, of many ancient etheric 'books' of knowledge and wisdom. The true treasures of the ancient world will be revealed as the doors to enlightenment that they were designed to be. Simultaneously, a deep awakening will occur in the incarnated aspects of Ishtar so that members can claim their true heritage.

Connoisseurs of ancient artistic expressions, architecture and poetry, Ishtar members will begin to reawaken their love of these most refined expressions of earthly life. Their own divine sensuality and appreciation of the 'romance of life' although already strong, will deepen and expand to include the higher, fifth and sixth dimensional frequencies of their hierarchy. These frequencies are now beginning to anchor in earnest into the incarnated members of this hierarchy. This is most certainly the age of ascension for the Ishtar family.

In their human manifestation, Ishtar human incarnates have a subtle, 'snake like' energy that slithers quietly but intently through life's events. They recognise and are innately connected to, the primal energy that underpins everything that unfolds on Earth. This primal energy of the Earth Mother intimidates some incarnates, but not Ishtar members, who feel it course through their veins and consciousness.

Ishtar has given birth to a multitude of species over billions of years. Many of these are benevolent, have loyally served the Spiritual Hierarchy for Earth in its work with humanity and some live in the shield skin of the Earth. However, when attempting to make contact with them it should be recognised that there are numerous creatures that dwell in the Earth's shield skin and some are unpredictable. Some of these creatures should only be approached with caution (if at all) and great vigilance should be exercised before allowing them to enter your channelling system. If in doubt as to the integrity of a species, call forth the High Council of the Law of One and ask for the council's intervention and/or protection.

A number (not all) of Ishtar members possess the internal characteristics that allow them to act without allowing their emotional bodies to become overwhelmed and burdened by their decisions. For this reason, they have often been used as assassins and mercenaries. Historically, they have been known to carry out orders masterminded by other hierarchies and have made highly competent spies. Generally, these particular members do not tend to join groups or organisations and do not develop emotional ties to ideologies, preferring to remain neutral and free to be or serve whomever they please as the occasion arises. However, over the course of history, where necessity has required it, they have banded together with others for short periods of time in order to successfully carry out the task at hand. Many times, they have been found at the helm of underground resistance groups. They have an ability to disband and disappear, never to be seen again, to protect themselves and their work.

No stranger to the complexities of the human condition, the

Ishtar member sees all the shades of grey between the positions of black and white. Among the least judgemental of the hierarchies, Ishtar members are well acquainted with their own shadow, having navigated that inner landscape themselves over many incarnations. They accept human frailty as a natural part of life, as certain and necessary as the sun rising and setting each day. Within this acceptance, they generally have no intention or hidden motive to 'redeem' other people, but can make outstanding transpersonal psychologists, shamanic healers, counsellors and psychotherapists.

Like the snake, quiet, efficient and purposeful as it slithers over the earth on its belly, Ishtar members do best in their incarnations when they stay close to the land, keep their heads down, listen to everything and stay attentive. They benefit from not allowing themselves to become attached to the workings of the world, to be "in the world, but not of it", as the great Master advised. They thrive when they remain in regular, if not continual, communication with the Primal Mother. Again, this is achieved through staying alert to the present moment and remaining close to the natural world.

Ishtar Hierarchy Members

The Star of Ishtar

God/Goddess Ishtar

Inanna

Lord and Lady Persia

Lord and Lady Babylon

Tezcatlipoca (God of the Aztecs and brother of Quetzalcoatl)

The Snake Goddess (known by multiple names throughout many cultures)

Jormungandr (Norse sea serpent)

The Jade Lady, Lan Tsai-ho

Keeper of the Keys to the Jade Stone (a crystal representative for Ishtar)

Dragon species

Keys to the Dragon Energy

The fire knights of the Dragon Guard

The Dragon Guard (Earth's protector Battle Dragons)

The Angelic Dragons

The Water Dragons and the Sea Dragons (the oceanic representative for the hierarchy)

Keys to the Serpent Energy

The Kundalini energy of the Earth

Keeper of the Keys to the Kundalini energy

The Great Rainbow Serpent

Serpent-being Muchalinda

Serpent and reptile species on Earth

The Goanna people

The Lizard King and Queen

Co-keeper of the keys to the dragon, ley lines

One of the Keepers of the Keys to Geomancy and the Council of Geomancy (alongside Jerusalem, Bethlehem, Tansafarie, Ishtar, Pan, Lemuria and Gaia)

Loki (Norse)

The Phoenix, keys to the Phoenix medicine

The Carian species (ancient/off planetary)

Keys to the Snake medicine

Earth's shield skin

Publicly Recognised Human Incarnations

King Gilgamesh

Queen of Sheba

Persian king, Cyrus the Great

CHAPTER TEN

Gaia Hierarchy

I am made to love the pond and the meadow,
as the wind is made to ripple the water...
Henry David Thoreau

The Gaia Hierarchy is a structure of light, essence and frequency that allows itself to be the Angelic Spirit and Light of the planet Earth. Gaia constantly showers the Children of Earth with unconditional love and healing. Gaia is the star of the galaxy, indeed an adored angel, a young mother, youthful and vibrant, mother to the Children of Earth, and indeed all Earth Angels. Lord Gaia is the masculine aspect of Gaia. As a young father he is conscientious and pure. He is here to guide his children as they return to the full knowledge of who they are. He holds the energy of early fatherhood as Lady Gaia holds the energy of the first-time mother and early motherhood.

Gaia Hierarchy brought forth ancient seeds from the realm of Arcadia and the realms of Neptune to anchor its ancient purpose into the core of the Earth. Gaia wished to bridge the keys of its ancient parentage to the creation of Earth and the people who would come to be the indigenous ones of Earth. The indigenous Earthlings are divided into distinct groupings and have a deep affinity with the Earth and the nature realms.

Gaia has a base in India and Russia. It also has a base in Tibet, in a land that is more etheric in its frequency than it is physical. This land is the working and waiting place of Lord and Lady Himalaya. The Tibetan lineage of Buddhism has its base in this holy vicinity also and has existed, in one form or another, in this vicinity to hold the energy for humanity since ancient times. The hierarchy uses this base to transport many of its aspects into and out of the human incarnation state.

All hierarchies love nature, but a Gaia member is entirely lost without it. Gaia members rely upon nature for their emotional and spiritual sustenance and although one could argue that this is fundamentally true for all humankind whether they realise it or not, Gaia members wither without an intimate relationship with the natural world. These ones generally have their own gardens, organic vegetable gardens, orchards, farms or may even work in professions as landscape or garden artists and caretakers, in forestry, or in environmental protection and sustainability. The more business minded members of this hierarchy will look to incorporate environmentally sustainable practices into their businesses or will invest in environmental initiatives, land, sustainable forestry, organic agriculture, herbal products etc. Looking after their home, which is the Earth, is extremely important to every member of this hierarchy.

A Gaia member who was not born or raised in a lifestyle that is closely connected to nature, will seek out a change in lifestyle at some stage in their adulthood. They will relocate in order to live a more natural life as soon as they have the practical/financial ability to do so. Generally these ones also have a deep affinity with animals, birds and sea creatures, easily relating to other species and the needs of other life forms on Earth.

Gaia Hierarchy members have a deep affinity with herbal and plant medicine and may pursue this as a vocation. They allow the spirit of the plant to speak to them, advise them as to the most appropriate use of the plant for the condition/person they are treating, and also open their minds to other ways the plant may be used for healing and spiritual awakening. Gaia members respond well to healing strategies that incorporate plant wisdom. Their bodies are especially attuned to the signature frequencies of plants. As well as many general herbal medicine keys, the keys to traditional Tibetan medicine belong to this hierarchy.

An awakened Gaia member will hear the Earth speak to them, often hearing the voice of Lady/Lord Gaia, which for Gaia members, is their own inner voice. They use this connection to guide them and so it becomes part of their 'lifeline' throughout their human incarnation. They need to stay close to the land and nature in order for this voice to remain strongly with them. The voice fades if they remove themselves from nature for an extended period of time, but is easily restored when they put their bare feet and hands on the ground or lie upon the Earth and consciously reconnect home to their Divine Mother and themselves.

The Maitreya line of the hierarchy is held by Lord and Lady Maitreya who act as Guardians of the Earth. The members of the hierarchy who are a manifestation of the Maitreya line generally hear the voice of Lord or Lady Maitreya more strongly than that of Lord and Lady Gaia. Because Gaia members are generally very grounded and tend to be immensely practical and level-headed people, they are also generally very good with money and managing resources in a balanced, calm and fair way. The Maitreya line members in particular have an interest in money management, whether this belongs to their own household or part of their profession, and they do well in business and finance. They are able to apply their mental clarity and clear vision to finance and can navigate this territory without the greed that often clouds the thinking of others. These attributes combined with their inbuilt ethics means that Gaia members are naturally trusted by other hierarchies in business and with money and thus they develop loyal clientele and business networks over their lifetimes.

All members of the hierarchy have an interest in meditation, exploring ideas through open-minded discussions, education, philosophy, and self-development in one form or another.

Gaia Hierarchy Members

Lord and Lady Gaia

God and Goddess Gaia

Archangel Gaia

Archangel Ariel

The Spirit of the Earth, for whom Earth is her physical body

The Gaia Field

The Angelic Realm of the Earth

The Angelic Light of the Sea on Earth

The Angelic Light of the Rivers, Lakes and Streams on Earth

Ganga, Goddess

Anastasia of Arkaim (see Vladimir Megre's work, The Ringing Cedars Series for a more in-depth exploration)

Lord and Lady Himalaya

Ascended Master Djwhal Khul

Lord and Lady Meru

Lord and Lady Maitreya

Lord and Lady Emerald

Keeper of the Keys to Tibetan Buddhism religious structure

The Light Green Ray of Earth and the Light Green Ray of Earth's Beings

The Emerald Ray of Earth and the Emerald Ray Beings of Earth

Mother and Father of the Cedar trees

One of the Keepers of the Keys to Geomancy and the Council of Geomancy (alongside Jerusalem, Bethlehem, Tansafarie, Ishtar, Pan, Lemuria and Shiva)

Publicly Recognised Human Incarnations

Dr Edward Bach (Bach Flower Remedies/vibrational medicine)

Alice Bailey (Author, Member of the Theosophical Society)

Ralph Waldo Emerson

Henry David Thoreau

William Ricketts (Australian sculptor)

CHAPTER ELEVEN

Shiva Hierarchy

To love oneself is the beginning of a lifelong romance...

Oscar Wilde

The Shiva Hierarchy is named after the Hindu god Shiva. In Hinduism, Shiva is one of the three great energies, the others being Brahma and Vishnu. The three are all emanations of Brahman – the infinite limitless All That Is. Shiva is the divine parent of the Shiva Hierarchy and all members of the hierarchy are manifestations of this essence.

Shiva created the chakra system (a system of interacting 'wheels' that perform as portals, energy storehouses and engines in the body), when Israel Hierarchy first developed the human prototype. Shiva also provided Yoga to humanity. These two systems can be used as paths and provide protocols to be applied by Initiates wanting to ascend and attain reunion with the Divine. A dynamic and vibrant hierarchy, Shiva creates and destroys: the destroyer of negativity and a transformer of energy.

The Shiva Hierarchy encompasses the full gamut of human experience, offering its members the experience of all aspects of the human condition. The hierarchy supports its members through its bases on Mount Kailash, as well as through its 'mothership' stationed above India. It also has a race of non-humans called the Blue Hue, or the 'blue people' who live in Inner Earth. The race provides a great deal of unseen support to its human incarnated hierarchy members. It is a hierarchy that although born on Earth and to the Earth, will in time come to populate other planetary worlds and kingdoms. It will come to inhabit planets that have already an indigenous population. Such populations will invite beings from other worlds and frequencies to their lands, and Shiva is poised to accept these invitations. The hierarchy looks forward to experimenting, learning and growing on other planetary worlds once this assignment on Earth is complete and the human experience fully mastered.

The Shiva Hierarchy, balanced in its masculine and feminine frequencies holds keys to the ability of a soul to experience the human body, to live through its challenges and celebrate its blessings, and to then raise the human body's vibrational frequency to become ascended and fully enlightened. These keys are of utmost importance to the ascension of all human beings, regardless of their hierarchy of origin. The Shiva Council of Elders has been the caretaker of these keys since the first human colonies appeared on Earth.

The Shiva hierarchy will, in time, incarnate into other bodies that are not human and live in these non human bodies on planetary worlds other than Earth. This ability to integrate into its environment effortlessly, individually and also in communities, is a key component to the Shiva Hierarchy. Its members are extremely tolerant of other people and deeply accepting of the human body and its difficulties and limitations. Its members are tolerant of heat, multifunctional spaces, changes in temperature, crowds and crowding. They harmonise their own frequencies well and apply this to their interactions with others.

Members of the hierarchy excel in setting social structures and also in challenging them and dismantling them when people outgrow these structures. They work well in groups and communities, their individual agendas harmonising to fulfil the agenda or the needs of the whole and the greater collective good. Shiva members possess an ability to tend to their own needs and serve the needs of others in gentle, loving acceptance, without fear or anger. Their selflessness is evident in the characteristic that defines most Shiva members; their loyalty and commitment to Divine service, attuned always to sensing the course of action that will best serve the collective good.

Having experienced all the human world has to offer, the Shiva Hierarchy records the history of the human condition in its memory banks. It is the keeper of the history of the Children of Earth and of human beings on Earth and is the keeper of the future human – the human that understands his role on Earth as a citizen and a caretaker. Through this role, the Shiva Hierarchy is also a mirror, reflecting the choices, the actions, the thoughts and the words of humans back to themselves. Through the Shiva Hierarchy's mirror, a human being can see itself and reflect on its choices, thoughts, words and deeds. The hierarchy offers the key of reflection to human incarnates on Earth – the ability to have one's reality reflected back to oneself by the outer world, and the ability to go within oneself while incarnated on Earth to reflect on one's life path and choices.

While Shiva, alongside other hierarchies such as Mu, holds keys to the entire incarnation cycle on Earth, the hierarchy is also the caretaker of a stage of incarnation that exists beyond the veils of forgetfulness. A baby encounters these veils of forgetfulness upon entering the Earth's plane. The veils force the baby to have but a vague recollection or forget entirely the realms in which he/she existed just prior to incarnation. The baby forgets the higher realms and often his own spiritual connection to his higher self. Shiva is the caretaker of the stage of incarnation that is available to souls who have attained a level of spiritual advancement in previous incarnations and who are thus not required to wear these veils (some souls volunteer to wear the veils again even if they attained full awakening in previous lives because to do so may help clear the veils for others).

This higher stage of incarnation provided by Shiva is not specific to a region of Earth or a race of people, but encompasses all parts of the world and all human beings. This stage supports the higher potential of human experience on Earth, and is offered to all Homo sapiens once they have attained a certain level of awareness. This level of awareness is the evolution of all human experiences, where the human being has come to peace with oneself, other human beings, and life on Earth. It is the transitional stage whereby human incarnates experience themselves in conscious transition from the endeavour of acquisition and competition with other races and species, to the higher manifestation of oneself as an awakened being living in an awakened family, community and society.

Some individuals are within the frequency bands of this stage, having a personal vibrational frequency that allows them to live beyond the veils that are acquired at the beginning of their incarnation. Such individuals also hold the energy for this stage from within their own societies across the globe. Many children currently incarnating bypass wearing the veils of forgetfulness altogether and incarnate directly into this incarnation level.

Shiva Hierarchy members have over many centuries explored the many layers of the human condition. They have acquired great knowledge of every facet of what it means to be human. While some hierarchies have stuck to very definite paths, Shiva has explored them all. Like explorers who set off across the seas to bring their findings back to their country, Shiva has provided profound insight to the rest of the Spiritual Family through its willingness to explore, learn, understand and then share. The hierarchy's members have lived all sorts of lives: many decadent and others pious; many wealthy and others poor; some lives have been spent in palaces, castles, ashrams and universities while others have been in overwhelming poverty. Shiva members designed these lives so that the hierarchy could truly understand the full gamut of human experience. Thus Shiva's knowledge supports individual incarnates within all hierarchies to transcend the limitations of human incarnation and become a fully ascended human being.

Shiva Hierarchy Members

Lord Shiva

Durga

Shakti, Divine Consort of Lord Shiva and embodiment of the Divine Feminine principle for the Earth's plane

Parvati (Hindu Goddess of Love), she is also the wife of Shiva and their children are the gods Ganesha and Kartikeya

Kali

Kartikeya (Hindu God of War)

Ganesha (Elephant-headed Hindu god of wisdom, success, remover of obstacles, patron of the arts and the god of beginnings).

Jyoti (Hindu Goddess of Light)

Lord and Lady India

Keeper of the Keys to the Hindu religious structure

Keeper of the Keys to the Ayurvedic healing system

The Weaver of the Tapestry of the World

Shiva Lingam (Shiva Lingam is a crystal representative of Shiva Hierarchy)

Mother and Father Tulsi (holy basil)

Mother Ayahuasca

One of the Keepers of the Keys to Geomancy and the Council of Geomancy (alongside Jerusalem, Bethlehem, Tansafarie, Pan, Gaia, Lemuria and Ishtar)

Lancelot frequency (Round table knight)

The Blue Hue race, sometimes known as the 'blue people' who inhabit Inner Earth

One of the Keepers of the Akashic Records (alongside Mu)

Publicly Recognised Human Incarnations

Lord Rama

Babaji (Ascended Master who, after his ascension, chose to maintain his presence on Earth to serve humankind)

Queen Marie Antoinette

Lord Byron

Oscar Wilde

Mahatma Gandhi (A spiritual father to India, advocate of non-violence)

Paramahansa Yogananda

Jiddu Krishnamurti (spiritual philosopher)

Co-Creations Initiated by the Hierarchy

The settlement and creation of India on Earth

The creation of the powerful healing substance Turmeric

CHAPTER TWELVE

Pan Hierarchy

There slumber in every human being
faculties by means of which he can acquire
for himself knowledge of higher worlds...

Rudolf Steiner

I am Lord Pan and I come forward this day to aid the children of my hierarchy to return home. They are the warriors of the Earth, the most ancient clansmen who walked far into the desert and into the forests to protect loved ones from invaders. They are the warriors, the tribesmen, the fighters, but not the invaders. This is an important key. My hierarchy has sought to defend itself over these last 35,000 years approximately, but it has never sought to invade the sovereign land of another race or tribe.

My people are spread across the globe and they will soon remember who they are. The men will awaken; they will hear my horn blow across the plains, through the desert, within the caverns, caves and ravines. The women will awaken; they will hear the gentle whisperings of the fairy folk, indeed, when they collect their fruits in the forest, the mushrooms in the pasture and the kindling for their fires, the fairy folk will hear their footsteps upon the path and they will place a sign along the way. This sign will be the first communication and it will be followed with unexpected gifts, good fortune, dreams and the hearing of music, and indeed miracles. The fairy people of Earth want to call their human counterparts home now and they will seek out their human selves and awaken them soon.

This is very important to understand. Approximately 35,000 years ago and then again approximately 25,000, 17,000 and 6,000 years ago, Earth fairy folk incarnated into human form. This was done intentionally by the Pan Hierarchy. We recognised a damaged frequency in the ability for Homo sapiens to access true connection with the unseen realms of Earth and we foresaw great turmoil on Earth because of this. We incarnated in many places across the Earth, and entered the human karmic cycle voluntarily. We have maintained educational opportunities for Homo sapiens by frequently reminding them of the presence of the fairy folk, and we have done this through stories and creating visual images.

Many of our human incarnates are artists, woodcarvers, potters, painters, wool spinners, players of folk music instruments, and singers. We use materials and mediums that connect us directly into the Earth. We allow the natural fibres to blend with our skin to link us with the Earth. We sleep upon natural fibres, we prefer to eat foods we have foraged or hunted ourselves. We share our hunt with our clan. We are loyal to the Earth, our home, our Mother Goddess.

We of the Pan Hierarchy awaken our human incarnates and encourage you to return home now. Your return home occurs the moment you remember who you are. Are you Homo sapiens, or are you fairy folk, masquerading as human for the purpose of fulfilling your voluntary assignment? Many of you are fairy, incarnating for the moment in human bodies so that you can complete tasks that all members of our hierarchy agreed upon some centuries ago. Ask for assistance to remember who you are. Assistance will come and you will forget no more.

I Lord Pan am the Lord of Light, Creator God and Father Light of the Pan Hierarchy. I stand beside my feminine balance, my

Lady of the Light, the Creator Goddess and Mother Light of the Pan Hierarchy. Together we call our children home to us and into the womb, the great cave-home of our hierarchy.

Pan Hierarchy members draw their emotional and spiritual power from music. All hierarchies love music and have created their own forms of it. Pan Hierarchy members connect to themselves and to the guardians and spirit of the land through the medium and bridge that is music. They also sculpt, paint, perform needle craft and woodwork as a way of remaining deeply connected to themselves and each other. Their music and artisan crafts act like the glue that connects them.

Pan members recognise that the Earth provides all of the nourishment, abundance and gifts that they require. To one who has pursued the treasures of the modern material world, the lives of Pan members may seem humble, quaint, even primitive in some cases, and yet Pan incarnates recognise that by remaining very close to the Earth, Her caverns and caves, Her mountains and forests, Her rivers and streams, their soul is nourished and they truly have all that they need. Pan members hold the keys to the way of the artisan, to home crafts, homesteading and home 'self-sufficiency', homeschooling and learning through allowing Earth and nature to be one's teacher.

These ones carry the totem of the bear as well as many other totems. Through studying the bear, one is able to understand the wisdom of following the seasons, withdrawing into one's cave to reconnect with oneself and also to rejuvenate one's life force or qi (chi). The bear understands how to maintain this essential balance within the energetic cycles of the body and all Pan members have this instinctive knowing.

In the early period of the hierarchy, when the decision was taken to enter the human incarnation cycle, many safeguards were programmed into the Pan members who volunteered for this task. These safeguards ensured that Pan members would receive clear messages or indicators from their human vehicles if they strayed onto paths that were destined to lead them too far away from their assignments and true essence. The safeguards were designed to activate feelings in the emotional body as well as symptoms in the physical body. Such feelings include a feeling of loss, as though something is missing or has been lost to the incarnate. Other feelings may also arise depending upon the individual member and what he/she programmed into the emotional body prior to incarnation. The feeling of loss or loneliness is the most prominent encoding.

The encoded physical symptoms are such that they create a discomfort in the body that can be remedied through daily walks, soaking in water with sea salt, daily sunshine 'baths' where sun rays warm the skin, and drinking water from mountain and running streams as pure and fresh as possible. If the food comes from natural sources only and is home baked, this will contribute greatly to the easing of the physical safeguard indicators. These simple practices will assist to realign the incarnate to his/her correct path, which is also the fulfilment of his/her assignment on Earth. The Pan incarnate must remain vigilant so as not to become caught in the 'net of the world', to remain the free creature that he/she was destined to be; free to walk in the true rhythm of the natural world and according to Earth's timing and seasons - not for he (or she) the clocks and calendars of men.

Fairies have their own structure within the Pan Hierarchy. This structure includes 'elemental versions' of their essence that reside in the second dimension with the physical plants. This is where the 'unformed' prenatal essence builds its energy body through communion with the plants, minerals, rocks, crystals, trees and the physical earth. When it is then born through its fairy parents into the fourth dimension on Earth, it carries into its physical form, the energetic fibres formed through its time as a prenatal elemental energy, that forever link it to the many facets of nature. One could say that its very being is an intricate tapestry woven of the fibres that are its interaction with the natural landscape.

In addition to this, the fairy carries also the signature frequency of the Pan Hierarchy, the same signature essence it shares with the dwarf, leprechaun and gnome communities. They draw strength and experience from their shared hierarchy memory. The ancient records kept by the dwarves in particular contain an ancient magic and inform the fairies just as texts written by civilisations older than ours inform the modern human. The dwarves are much older than the fairy, although the fairy themselves are not young, being much older than the first Earth human prototype. They have their own 'arm' within the Pan Hierarchy, having created a self-governing structure for themselves within the greater hierarchy.

Depending upon the evolution and assignment of the individual fairy aspect, an incarnating fifth dimensional fairy may enter Earth's fourth dimensional nature realms. A fairy who has ascended comes to rest in the seventh dimension. Fairies live in communities on Earth. These communities are considered their 'home base'. However, over the course of billions of years, fairies have expanded and evolved as a race and have thus established various 'outposts' in other realms away from Earth, including other planets. Fairies have developed a solid community framework within Sirius. They have enriched the Pleiades with their presence. In older times, they experimented with outposts in Venus, Earth's moon and various other local vicinities.

At present, most of their family members are here, in their home base of Earth, assisting with the shift in consciousness occurring in human beings. The fairies have invested many resources into co-facilitating this shift with many other races and species so that human beings awaken to the awareness of the many other species co-existing in the fourth and fifth dimensions. The fairies have been committed to this removing of the veil, as it were, so that humans can reclaim their true history and take up their mantels as responsible, devoted caretakers and guardians of the fairies' home base and true home, planet Earth. The education of human beings so that fair and just co-habitation of the races can occur, has been a long-standing project that the fairies assigned themselves around the times of Atlantis and Lemuria, where the veils became fixed upon the eyes of human beings. These veils have been of various thicknesses over the centuries. However, they began to thin permanently in the latter half of 1800s.

Many light-workers volunteered to incarnate and participate in a highly organised assignment that combined the efforts of many hierarchies. This assignment activated in the 1850s. However, some light-workers began incarnating in the early part of 1800s to prepare the ground for the coming seeds. Pan Hierarchy sent thousands of incarnates to Earth to assist in the assignment. Many Pan Initiates incarnated into England, Ireland, Scotland, Wales and France during this period. Others incarnated into or traveled to Australia, New Zealand, South Africa and India to begin this important seeding of the consciousness. Many fairy beings living in the etheric began reincarnating into physical fairy form during this time to assist the project. The Pan Hierarchy has remained committed to the project since this time.

The hierarchy has a large base, a sacred meeting place, in the vicinity of Uluru in Australia as well as a base in central Ireland.

Pan Hierarchy Members

God Pan

Goddess Brigid

Ereshkigal (Mesopotamian Queen of the Underworld)

God and Goddess of the Underworld

Keeper of the Mystical creatures on Earth

Guardian of the Stones

Lord and Lady Oberon

Keeper of the Keys to the Kingdom of the Fae

King and Queen of the Earth-born fairies

All fairies

Dwarves, the Elders of Earth's nature kingdoms, and realms within the Earth

The Green Man

Leprechauns

Gnomes

Pixies

Brownies

Nisses

Celtic Lord of the Forests

Celtic Lady of the Forests

Lady Erin, Queen Erin (Guardian of Ireland)

Bear medicine totem

Goat medicine totem

Reindeer medicine totem

Deer medicine totem

One of the Keepers of the Platinum group metals (alongside Israel and Tansafarie)

Keeper of the Keys to Iron

Lord and Lady Amber (Amber is a crystal representative of Pan Hierarchy)

Mother and Father of the Pine trees

Keeper of the Keys to Native Australian Flora

Part of the Guardian Council of Uluru

One of the Keepers of the Keys to Geomancy and the Council of Geomancy (alongside Jerusalem, Bethlehem, Tansafarie, Ishtar, Gaia, Lemuria and Shiva)

Keeper of the Keys to the Royal Stag lineage (although it has been carried by other hierarchies, this mantle is bestowed upon the kings of the lands as is determined by the Pan Hierarchy)

The Keeper of the Keys to the Faun

Keeper of the Keys to Homesteading and Homeschooling

Keeper of the Keys to the Way of the Artisan

Pan Hierarchy hosts:

The Council of Poets

The Council of Bards

Publicly Recognised Human Incarnates

Empress Joséphine (first wife of Napoleon I)

Rudolf Steiner (founder of Anthroposophy, basis of Steiner/ Waldorf education)

Ita Wegman (Anthroposophical medical pioneer)

Joni Mitchell (American folk singer)

Jimmy Little (Australian singer/performer)

Co-Creations Initiated by the Hierarchy

The creation of Ireland on Earth

CHAPTER THIRTEEN

Lemuria Hierarchy

The Lemurian Hierarchy holds the energy for healing and restoration between families, tribes and nations. Many hierarchies hold keys to this, but the Lemurian Hierarchy has a deep desire to see healing and restoration on this level, and has thus sent many incarnates over the course of its incarnation history to bring awareness and healing to large groups of people.

Anchoring the keys to the foundation of family in the physical plane, this hierarchy provides solid learning structures to those individuals and communities who choose to create harmony within the family unit as well as in society. The Lemurian Hierarchy holds the keys to tribal law and the restoration of harmony within the tribe and between different tribes.

Lemuria holds key frequencies to the development of peoples in close relationship to the sea. Those who are seafaring, those who live by the waterside or in houses on stilts in the sea, and those whose survival is directly dependent on the ocean and her bounty are held and protected by the Lemurian Hierarchy. The Lemurian Hierarchy is also deeply connected to the islands that support the ancient energies, indeed the Elders of humankind. Those who are of the Fijians, the Samoans, the Polynesian peoples, are connected to the ancient lineage of the Lemurian Hierarchy. The Lemurian Hierarchy is the daughter of Mu and receives from the Mu

Hierarchy, the ancient seeds of consciousness and genetic material to birth its human lineage. The people of the Lemurian Hierarchy have inherited ancient genetic materials from their ancestors of the Mu Hierarchy and carry within them a love for their home, the Earth and for the ancestors of the stars. The Lemurian Hierarchy's grandmother lineage is that of the Neptunian line of Jerusalem - the keeper of the oceanic frequencies. In the honouring of their grandmother line, this hierarchy treasures the sea and all creatures that come from her realms.

The Lemurians understand the movements of the Earth, watch her tides and interpret her signs. They recognise the key to life on Earth and, just as they surrender gracefully to the ebb and flow of the oceans and seas, they accept Earth and her rhythms, finding their peace within her cycles. They currently hold bases across the South Pacific, Hawaii, New Zealand, Japan, Canada, Australia and Africa.

The Lemurian Hierarchy is the keeper of the realm called Telos, which houses an advanced civilisation of ascended Lemurian members. The Lemurian community in Telos holds the energy for Lemurian family members working on Earth assignments. The Telos realm was established as a physical and etheric base for Lemuria and saw the influx of many Lemurians after the fall of Atlantis on Earth. It continues to provide a safe place and community environment for Lemurian family members to return to when their Earth assignments are complete.

Before the fall of Atlantis, the Lemurian High School of Initiation worked closely with its brother council, the Council of Atlantis. The two Hierarchies parted ways when members on the Council of Atlantis deemed the strict initiation codes of the Lemurian High School of Initiation unnecessary. Eventually, over the space of many years, the Lemurian Hierarchy disappeared into the ethereal realm of the fourth and fifth dimension, and beyond, and established its civilisation in the frequency band known to some as Telos. Telos is indeed a bridging band, with the core Lemurian civilisation living within a realm beyond the Telos portal. This realm is sacred within every aspect. It is beyond the experience of taint and impurity.

Many members of the Lemurian Hierarchy remain upon Earth to complete their personal aspect's karma and hold the light for the restoration of the human family of light to the upper levels of the fourth dimension, and ascension into the fifth dimensional consciousness. Polynesian descendants are generally Lemurian Hierarchy incarnates. There are many Lemurian Hierarchy aspects incarnated in America at this time who are not of Polynesian descent. They consider themselves Americans for the purpose of healing unresolved feelings towards the Atlantean Hierarchy. Some Lemurian Hierarchy members view the Atlantean Hierarchy members as destroyers of their peace and the purity of fourth dimensional Lemurian frequencies. They have incarnated in America as Americans in an effort to restore the Atlantean/American frequencies to their masculine and feminine balance.

This work by the Lemurian Hierarchy holds a very important place in the Great Ascension. Many Lemurian Hierarchy members belong to oceanic conservation movements and are also involved in the restoration of Mother Earth to her highest office. This is done through education and raising awareness, through organisations and educational institutions. Many Lemurian Hierarchy members prefer to live in the natural environment, preferring country, wilderness or seaside lifestyles.

During physical incarnation in human form, Lemurian incarnates require as natural a diet as possible, consisting of foods that are alive with the life force. Lemurian incarnates have the sensitivity and awareness to feel the freshness and life force levels within food and choose according to this energetic indicator for suitability. For this reason, freshly foraged foods are particularly beneficial.

(For additional information on the Lemurians, see the Atlantis Hierarchy below).

Lemurian Hierarchy Members

Daughter of Mu (mother) and Central Sun (father)

Lord and Lady Lemuria

Keeper of the Keys to the Polynesian People Family

Keeper of the Keys to the Maori People Family

Hawaii settlement

Guardian Spirit of Fiji

The Crystalline beings of the Earth

The Keeper of the Keys to the Crystal Resonators in the Earth (the Lemurian Crystalline beings hold the office of the Crystal Resonators with the Tansafarie, Pan, Bethlehem, Atlantis, Ishtar, Shiva, and Gaia hierarchies)

Keys to the Inner Child

Keys to Inner Child Healing

Keeper of the Keys to Childhood on Earth

Keeper of the Tribal Keys, harmony within and between tribes and clans.

Keeper of the Clan Frequency on Earth (jointly held with Tansafarie)

Keeper of the Tribal Frequency on Earth

The Dolphin Species (the oceanic representative for the hierarchy)

The Keys to the Dolphin Family

Coconut tree being

One of the Keepers of the Keys to Geomancy and the Council

of Geomancy (alongside Jerusalem, Bethlehem, Tansafarie, Ishtar, Pan, Gaia, and Shiva)

Publicly Recognised Human Incarnations

Abraham Lincoln

Martin Luther King

Steve Biko

Nelson Mandela

Co-Creations Initiated by the Hierarchy

The creation of the Lemurian settlement on Earth

The creation of Telos, a Lemurian Hierarchy settlement

CHAPTER FOURTEEN

Atlantis Hierarchy

If you want to find the secrets of the universe, think in terms of energy, frequency and vibration...

Nikola Tesla

Lord Atlantis was the high king in the time known as the Atlantean civilisation. His queen, Lady Atlantis was a keeper of the circle of stones and was able to call forth many great beings to Earth to participate in the Atlantean experience. Greater Atlantis was a thriving settlement with many outposts, seeded by smaller Atlantean tribes. Atlantis was a powerful civilisation because it was the cradle of Homo sapiens multidimensional development. Damage occurred within the Atlantean civilisation when experiments were conducted to raise the multidimensional capacity of Homo sapiens without honouring the necessary balance of masculine and feminine frequencies within all things. One cannot have extraordinary growth of particular attributes without the balancing function of one's heart awakened within authentic compassion. People who had not yet raised their heart frequency were given access to power without the wisdom and knowledge gained through slow ascension or initiation into the truth of such power.

Often described as 'The Fall of Atlantis', this phase was not only dislocating for groups of people and for beings from other planets who had congregated on the continent, but also marked the breakdown of core units within the Atlantis Hierarchy itself. It was at this time that the Council of Atlantis parted ways with the Lemurian High School of Initiation.

The Atlantis Hierarchy has established itself in America. This was a very deliberate act. The Atlantis Hierarchy made a decision to explore ideas such as material advancement, scientific exploration, and karma relating to civilisation itself. Atlantis Hierarchy members are not restricted to incarnating in America, nor is a person's race always an indicator of their hierarchy origins. Many Atlantis Hierarchy members chose to incarnate in Atlantis as human beings and have since incarnated in many different racial experiences as a path to fulfilling their soul's higher blueprint. Most Atlantis human incarnates are incarnated in America (although not all Americans are from the Atlantis Hierarchy), working to resolve the karmic cycle that they began in Atlantis many centuries ago. There are currently ten physical/etheric bases for the Atlantis Hierarchy, which move depending upon the requirements of the hierarchy's human incarnates. The bases are currently located in Beijing, Seoul, Tokyo, North America, Zimbabwe, Berlin, Brussels, Luxembourg, Washington, New York region.

The core Atlantean frequency is: soul evolution through community and inter-civilisation cooperation. Very soon this will evolve out of necessity to become inter-planetary cooperation. When the Atlantis Hierarchy learns to work together for the benefit of the All That Is, this hierarchy will have the opportunity to reincarnate in other planetary worlds, star systems and kingdoms for the purpose of creating colonies and civilisations to ascend within and with their habitat. Without this level of cooperation, the hierarchy creates pain and suffering for itself and others. The hierarchy can work as one. It is programmed with this highest potential. It has done so before, and it will in the future, create circumstances for its members that promote the ability to strengthen latent attributes and lift them to the surface of experience, making this potential an everyday reality.

This hierarchy will thrive as it understands its core relationship with nature and its direct habitat. Until it recognises that it is reliant upon the harmonious experience of its habitat, it cannot ascend. It must learn to respect its habitat and treat its habitat as equal to itself. This is the key learning requirement of all Atlantean human incarnates. Evolution and advancement can only occur when incarnates remain in balance with their environment.

In the physical plane, human incarnated Atlantis Hierarchy members have a highly advanced understanding of computer systems, digital and wireless technology and artificial intelligence (AI). They embrace technological advancement where other hierarchies may be reticent in certain situations. They believe that the technology that they have either invented or received from other planets and races will eventually liberate humankind from suffering, but they are also learning that technological progress must be balanced with regard for the environment. Generally, they believe that technology *is* liberation in that it has the capacity to one day end physical body suffering, loneliness, environmental problems, poverty etc. During the Atlantean period on Earth, they collaborated with other hierarchies, namely Israel and Mu in areas of genetic research. Atlantis Hierarchy members still pursue some of this research today.

Since the time of the Atlantean civilisation, Atlantis Hierarchy members have needed to work towards recovering aspects of themselves that remain lost to that time. For Atlantis Hierarchy members, reconnecting to and 'grounding into' the natural world may prevent or remedy any feelings of being lost in their lives and may also assist them to heal lost aspects. As a source of tremendous healing, nature has the ability to 'recalibrate' the mind and the senses.

Atlantis Hierarchy Members

Son of Mu (mother) and Central Sun (father)

Lord and Lady Atlantis

King and Queen of Atlantis

Lord and Lady of Athens

Pallas Athena

Poseidon (the lineage of Poseidons and the Atlantean Kings. King Neptune and Poseidon are different beings from different lineages)

Goddess Minerva

Keeper of the keys to the ancient Greek civilisation

Keeper of the Keys to Confucianism

American civilisation (but not Hawaiian islands, which are Lemuria Hierarchy lands)

Publicly Recognised Human Incarnations

Confucius

Genghis Khan

Marco Polo

Alexander the Great

Madame de Pompadour

Nikola Tesla

Richard Buckminster Fuller

Co-Creations Initiated by the Hierarchy

The creation of Atlantis and Atlantean society on Earth

The creation of Greece and the Grecian culture

The creation of the Mongolian Empire

The establishment of North America

CHAPTER FIFTEEN

How to Discover Your Hierarchy of Origin

Generally, a hierarchy reveals itself to its human Initiate in a dream, meditation, or through some other kind of direct contact such as communicating through the Initiate's artwork or sacred journeying through music etc. It is rare for a hierarchy to use a third party to reveal the incarnate's spiritual origins.

Even if a third party has revealed to you your hierarchy of origin, it is wise to check this yourself through your own meditation work. A hierarchy may use a third party if that party is a trusted source who has received permission from the High Council of the Law of One and the Spiritual Hierarchy for Earth High Council to release such important information. This scenario may occur if the person's low self worth will not allow them to receive for themselves through meditation etc, the truth of who they are and their true spiritual family origins, or there may be other blocks beyond their ability to reach that prevent them from remembering. In this way, the third party functions as a type of 'divine intervention', giving the Initiate a 'boost up' to help them move forward and out of the cycle in which they are caught.

If a third party wishes for the role of revealing hierarchy

origins to Earth incarnates, they are required to be initiated into that task by the Spiritual Hierarchy for Earth's High Council. This initiation takes place in the higher realms with permission from the person's own higher councils. Such a role is a tremendous responsibility and is to be taken very seriously. When functioning in the role, the third party is not permitted to 'guess' when declaring a person's hierarchy, potentially casting that person into confusion and diverting their energy and focus away from their true hierarchy.

The process of an Initiate discovering their hierarchy for themselves is an empowering one and functions as part of their higher training. Some Initiates know immediately their hierarchies. As soon as they read about their hierarchies, there isn't a single doubt in their minds that they belong to that structure. Others receive the name of their hierarchy in meditation, dream etc and do not resonate with it initially, the revelation doesn't mean anything to them or they may feel some misgiving. For them, the relationship grows over time or may require some work to heal. There are several reasons for this: the Initiate may feel estranged from their hierarchy, such as feeling abandoned by them on Earth or let down in some way; the Initiate may find it difficult to accept their divinity or greatness; the Initiate may feel unworthy of their hierarchy; the Initiate may fear the responsibility that knowledge and awareness brings; the Initiate may still have unresolved energies or issues with their hierarchy that have carried over from past incarnations; the Initiate may not appreciate the significance of the information revealed to them (the significance will dawn upon them over time).

Only through working regularly with your hierarchy can these areas of difficulty be overcome. Communication heals many things. Meditation and contemplation provide good opportunities to communicate with your higher council. For those who have the ability, journal writing that develops into 'automatic' writing, whereby a two-way conversation emerges through the writing process, can be an excellent way to build the foundation for communication between you and your higher council.

If you are unable to work through unresolved areas yourself, a third party may be called upon to assist. This is where another person who has the ability to bridge between human incarnates and their higher councils acts as a communicator and intermediary. Only seek advice from a person whom you trust beyond any doubt, and whom you understand to have the genuine skills to aid you. You do not want someone who is emotionally or energetically unclear interfering in that sacred space between you and your higher council. This terrain must be kept clear of debris in order for you to develop a clear, trusting space where communication can occur easily and consistently.

Below is a suggested meditation that may assist you in discovering your hierarchy of origin. Try not to push for the name of your hierarchy or for any other answers to come. Pushing can cause you to receive incorrect information. Instead, when you are in meditation or any form of communication with your hierarchy, allow information to flow naturally toward you. Even though this strategy may feel slower, ultimately it is a more effective path.

Meditation for Connecting to Your Hierarchy

Gently close your eyes and move around a little until your body is in a comfortable position.

Listen to the sounds outside your room.

These sounds will now fade away and your mind will slowly drift through the different thoughts of the day.

Your mind will now visit a most magnificent blue shimmering lake surrounded by ancient green mountains.

You find yourself standing on the soft sandy bank of the lake surrounded by mountains.

The fresh cool air calms your body as you breathe deeply.

You turn away from the lake and discover a cave entrance in the mountain behind you.

Follow the rocky wall of the mountain around until you come to a cave like entrance.

Move slowly into the depth of the cave leaving the outside world behind you.

The cave becomes very dark yet comforting as you move deeper and deeper into it.

Up ahead you see the faint glow of a warm lantern light.

As you move closer you realise that two lanterns light an entrance of a heavy door. The door looks ancient and in some ways familiar with certain patterns and symbols etched into it.

The door opens inwards slowly to reveal a marble floor, again with symbols on it.

As you step onto the marble floor, the large door closes behind you.

Look across the floor, you see that you are on what appears to be the ground floor of a multi-story building. You look towards the ceiling and realise it is a glass dome structure allowing the sunlight to enter into every aspect of the building.

There are levels leading up to the dome, and a glass elevator to take you to each level.

You look towards the centre of the ground floor and see a large round table – a council table. You can sense that there are some Beings of Light spread around the table chatting informally.

You walk towards the table and sit down gently.

A Being of Light across the table smiles at you. You know that this being has a special connection with you and in some way feels very familiar.

The Being of Light stands up from the chair and moves to a seat closer to you. As it does you begin to sense what the Being of Light may look like.

As it sits next to you, spend some time feeling into the love and the light that it is beaming at you.

The Being of Light reaches out and takes your hand. As it does this you feel warmth and love. The being welcomes you home to your hierarchy.

Take some time now with the Being of Light to feel into your hierarchy and have a look around if you wish. The being may show you into certain areas of the hierarchy and explain the certain areas to you as you go. You may wish to use this opportunity to ask some questions about your hierarchy and your role/mission. You may ask for a symbol or name to help you to understand your hierarchy.

When you are ready, the Being of Light, your spiritual friend, leads you back to the entrance door you came in through. You embrace and thank your friend of light and know that you can return whenever you wish to.

As you step through the door, it closes behind you and you are back in the cave.

You make your way back through the cave and into the sunlight.

The sunlight warms and welcomes you as you walk back to the shimmering lake.

When you are ready to return from the lake, bring your awareness back to your body and to the room or area you are lying in.

Breathe in deeply to ground your spirit back to earth and

gently open your eyes.

Return to explore the many levels of your hierarchy as often as you feel the need. Allow yourself to develop strong connections with the Beings of Light who come to greet you as you visit your hierarchy.

Working Consciously with the Spiritual Hierarchy for Earth

When you learn your hierarchy of origin, as a natural extension of this knowledge you begin to develop an interest in working consciously with the Spiritual Hierarchy for Earth. Here, a deeper understanding of the Hierarchy becomes useful. The core principle essential in understanding the Spiritual Hierarchy for Earth is that it is entirely a function and process of collaboration, and that everything within the All That Is is interconnected and interacts to some degree with something else. Everything that lives, is, by way of its 'aliveness', a collaboration between the hierarchies. A human being breathes and is therefore collaborating with air (a function overseen by the Mu Hierarchy). Blood flows through the human body and thus the body collaborates with the Bethlehem Hierarchy, which in turn collaborates with other hierarchies. Like a solar battery, the human body is 'charged up' by the sun, allowing it optimal function. This gift comes from the Central Sun Hierarchy. Isolation, abandonment and even independence are illusions; ideas birthed only because humankind temporarily forgot the Spiritual Hierarchy for Earth and the essential role each human fulfils within it and in their own hierarchy families.

To be alive is to be automatically connected and continually interacting with the Spiritual Hierarchy for Earth. As you remember your automatic connectedness, in time your important and unique role will also reveal itself. You may arrive at this understanding through attaining a level of full awakening, which will automatically deliver to you all of the knowledge you need as well as direct experience of the knowledge – the knowledge becomes experiential. You may also arrive at this understanding through the systematic learning of each level as you reach it, training level by level, or through a combination of training, meditation and study.

Understanding the hierarchy you have come from, may or may not lead you to a full awakening. Full awakening is always dependent upon your hierarchy's plan for you – in essence, your plan for yourself. Your divine plan may see your complete awakening stretched out over several lifetimes for various reasons. You may be gathering souls, as it were, bringing many people up and along with you and this may take some time to achieve. Many believe that they are in charge of their full awakening, but even in this they must yield to the divine plan that they have co-created with their higher councils even if they do not recall it fully while on Earth. Refusing to yield blocks the natural flow of energy, which in turn blocks awakening and brings the person the very opposite of what they wanted in the first place. Trusting the divine way brings your energy field into a calm state and opens you up to the greater knowledge of your hierarchy, which may lead you to full awakening as part of a natural unfolding.

Higher knowledge does play a useful role in your ascension and in attaining levels of awakening. It can anchor a strong foundation of understanding within you, leading you towards wisdom. It may help you harness your personal and hierarchy power, so that you are able to gain access to a higher, broader perspective when making choices. It will expand your consciousness and assist you to think beyond this earthly paradigm. It is always beneficial to allow the expansion of your mind through assimilating ideas of a higher vibrational frequency and consciousness than your own. This can facilitate and significantly expedite your ascension.

When you begin to consciously work with the Spiritual Hierarchy for Earth, you will find that knowledge of the significance of your incarnation will bring you a greater appreciation for who you are. In understanding your contribution, you become more confident. Your seemingly insignificant life reveals to you its significance. You begin to understand with greater clarity, the sequence of events in your life, why you are here on Earth and why you decided to arrive here in the first place, well before this current incarnation.

You may ask yourself: 'How do I know that I truly contribute to the All That Is in this way? What if I am sugar-coating my life with an illusionary story?'

Humankind has forgotten the importance of story, of the Dreamtime, of the old myths that acted as a connective frequency bridging the third and lower fourth dimensions of humanity to the upper fourth and fifth dimensions of the higher worlds. The higher realms use these 'stories' as mediums through which they travel to reach you. Humanity has replaced this most necessary medium with the most disturbing illusions; illusions that many higher beings consider to be corrosive in their nature. Humanity has transposed false meaning and significance over the true meaning of things so that you are unable to see meaning beyond fourth dimensional constructs.

However, these challenges you face here are the same challenges many of you have faced in other planetary worlds and systems, and so you are well placed to overcome them. The Spiritual Hierarchy for Earth stands ready to assist in your conscious collaboration. For you are already collaborating with the Hierarchy, it is only that now you will be aware of it. This awareness will be soothing and comforting to you and will assist in your rising above the challenges of the earthly plane. These challenges of the earthly plane do not need to be *your* challenges. When you attain conscious awareness of your *real* purpose here, your understanding assists your movement beyond the vibrational frequency bands where these challenges have manifested into form.

For when you raise your consciousness beyond this lower fourth dimensional band, you will find connection to the higher realms becomes significantly easier to maintain. You will feel the

Spiritual Hierarchy for Earth with you, in some form. A desire to return to genuine collaboration will activate within you – you will want to feel truly part of something greater once more, as you did prior to incarnation when you were in your ancient form.

When resuming to work consciously with the Spiritual Hierarchy for Earth, you may find it useful to remember your hierarchy of origin. This knowledge isn't essential to your work, but it may help. As we discussed earlier, rarely is a person's hierarchy revealed to them through another medium such as a spiritual teacher, channel etc. It is mostly given to the Initiate through his/her own channels, meditations or dreams. Some hierarchies inform their human incarnates while they are coming out of a deep sleep. Often the hierarchy that they belong to may come as a surprise and they may not warm to the knowledge straight away, even though something inside them knows that it is the truth.

You are able to enter into meditation and request information from your hierarchy on any topic you would like. Such a facility is very helpful when the Initiate is ready to work consciously with the Spiritual Hierarchy for Earth and understand his/her assignment. For assistance in seeking the answer, follow the above meditation: Meditation for Connecting to Your Hierarchy. In this meditation, you travel to a council within your hierarchy. When you locate this council, spend some time connecting with the beings of light there and ask them to show you somehow, or even tell you directly the answers to your questions. As with any form of channelling, you are more likely to succeed in allowing yourself to hear the correct answer if you do not restrict your questions to 'yes' or 'no' answers. Ask for a broader discussion on the answers you seek. They may tell you or they may lead you into other councils or areas within your hierarchy that will act as clues.

Sometimes you may encounter beings from other hierarchies in your councils. This can occur when other hierarchies are acting as guardians, overseers and general support for your incarnation. For example, just because St Germain is your guide, does not necessarily mean he is a member of your hierarchy. Certain beings like St Germain, Mother Mary and Sanat Kumara act as guardians and instructors of new Initiates.

A great deal of comfort can be derived through consciously interacting with the Spiritual Hierarchy for Earth and although we have used that term extensively here, it is important to remember that access to the Spiritual Hierarchy for Earth is nearly always through your own hierarchy; that your own hierarchy is invariably the portal to that greater structure beyond. Through opening up your life to higher communication you come to understand the purpose and higher significance of events in your own life and on a global scale. Your interactions with other people will also be understood from an entirely new perspective.

CHAPTER SIXTEEN

Your Hierarchy's Service at the Earth/Physical & Etheric Level

As we discussed in the previous chapter, in understanding the function and structure of your own hierarchy, an interest in the Spiritual Hierarchy for Earth and Ancient Spiritual Family, which contains all hierarchies, naturally emerges. The following chapters outline the function of the Spiritual Hierarchy for Earth in detail and how your hierarchy contributes to this grand structure. If you now know the hierarchy to which you belong, you can use the information contained in these chapters below to further understand your own assignments on Earth, part of your higher purpose for incarnating on Earth in the way that you did and the life path you have chosen. Through understanding the manifestations of your hierarchy and how it contributes to the Spiritual Hierarchy for Earth, you may identify these unconscious 'drivers' that have propelled you down certain career or interest paths.

As you observed when learning about your own hierarchy, you have solid infrastructure that connects you with the planet and allows for you to function and ascend on Earth. We call this the earth/physical level of your hierarchy. The Spiritual Hierarchy for Earth also exists at the earth/physical level, and has a highly developed infrastructure at this level to support the functioning and ascension of all species on Earth.

At the earth/physical levels, the Spiritual Hierarchy for Earth can be seen as a cradle in which Earth is held. Like a baby who learns to walk with just enough room to fall, but not enough to do any permanent harm, Earth is supported by the Ancient Ones who observe your progress well. Every person on Earth at this time is part of this greater assignment initiated by the Spiritual Hierarchy for Earth and every person is known to the Ancient Ones. Earth is held in the arms of the Spiritual Hierarchy for Earth, which in turn is held by the Ancient Ones. The Earth is both supported by the Spiritual Hierarchy for Earth and part of this structure. In order to understand this fully, it is necessary to examine the Earth's structure, which earthlings call Mother Earth.

The term given to the planet, 'Mother Earth' implies one being who gives birth to and supports all life on Earth. However, Mother Earth from our perspective, refers not to one being, but an office or council where many beings sit. For example:

The lord and lady of the air (the lungs of Earth – Mu Hierarchy)

The lord and lady of the water (the waters and womb of Earth – Neptunian lineage within the Jerusalem Hierarchy)

The lord and lady of the earth (Overseer of the harmonisation between the rocks, minerals and bones of Earth – Lord and Lady Terra of Tansafarie Hierarchy)

The lord and lady of fire (the molten core – Bethlehem Hierarchy)

Lord and Lady Gaia – the angelic spirit of the Earth (Earth's spirit – Gaia Hierarchy.)

There are five sub-offices within the overseeing office of Mother Earth. However, when these sub-offices come together and harmonise, they form the higher consciousness of planet Earth. When you pray to Mother Earth, you may be praying to one specific function or office within the overseeing office, or you may be praying to the overall consciousness of Earth – the combined offices that form Mother Earth. Many people pray directly to one sub office, the Angelic Spirit of Earth, Earth's spirit, who is otherwise known as Gaia.

The office of Mother Earth is supported by a group of beings and frequencies called the Council of the Children of Earth. This council is made up of five out of the twelve hierarchies within the Spiritual Hierarchy for Earth, and these five also function as sub-offices within the overseeing office of Mother Earth. They are: Gaia, Shiva, Pan, Atlantis and Lemuria.

The Council of the Children of Earth Diagram

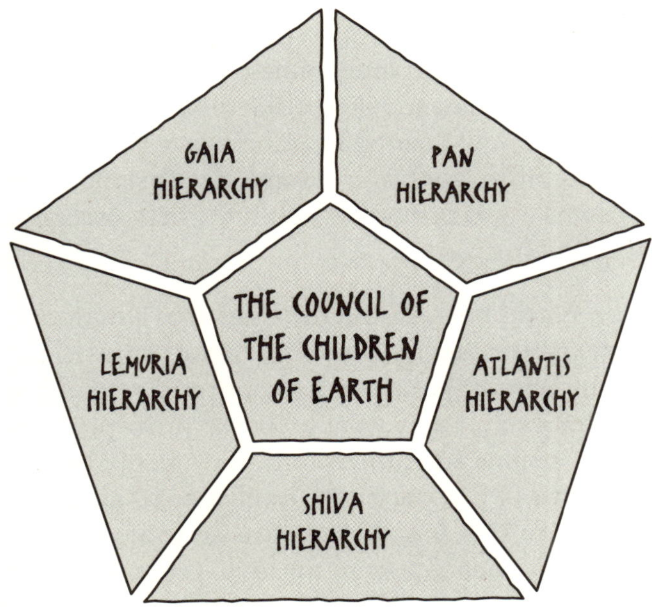

Those who are considered Children of Earth are technically members of one of the above hierarchies and have a place within the Children of Earth council. Many species and 'peoples' throughout the galaxy consider this group the indigenous people of Earth.

Like the earth/physical and etheric levels of one's own hierarchy with their various offices and councils that facilitate life on Earth, the Spiritual Hierarchy for Earth has its own version of these offices, albeit on a much larger scale. Most prominent in the earth/physical and etheric levels are the Nature Realms and Elemental Kingdoms. Without these realms, councils, offices, and the beings who furnish them, the Spiritual Hierarchy for Earth would not be able to anchor and operate within this section of the galaxy or planet Earth.

Understanding the Nature Realms and Elemental Kingdoms

The elemental kingdom holds great power on Earth. The many realms within this kingdom interconnect with many of the nature realms and yet their rules and laws often differ from those of the nature kingdom. The elemental kingdom concerns beings who are primarily fourth, fifth, sixth and seventh dimensional, whereas the nature kingdoms exists primarily within the first, second, third, fourth, and fifth dimensions.

While on Earth, beings from the elemental kingdom live within the nature kingdom and her many realms. They understand the laws of the nature kingdom and work within their perimeters. However, if they were to live on other planets and in other planetary realms and dimensions, they would live according to the natural laws of that vicinity. The elemental kingdom requires the nature kingdom to provide a sense of place. In return, the nature kingdom benefits from the loving care of the elemental beings as they tend to and support the plants, trees, waterways and the land itself. The nature kingdom of Earth consists of human beings, all creatures, plants and trees, which are the Divine's creation. Minerals, water, air, soil, sand are all part of the nature kingdom.

While on Earth, human beings belong to the nature kingdom and the Human Hierarchy as well as their own hierarchies. They are requested to be responsible members of all three structures. They are requested to love and support the nature kingdom, be caring, compassionate members of the Human Hierarchy, and make choices and complete actions that serve the highest good of their own hierarchies. By complete actions, we mean to finish assignments that were begun in earlier or ancient times, to fulfil one's higher plan and leave no previous action unresolved or unfinished. When all previous actions are resolved, healed or complete in the way that they need to be, a human's karmic assignment with the Earth is finished and they are free to move beyond the Earth plane permanently if they choose to do so.

Humans are required not to prey upon the nature kingdom and instead tend to it lovingly and respectfully. This may be done by following the elemental beings' example of how they interact with the nature kingdom. The elemental kingdom consists of many groups of beings. Every group has its own realm, which comes together with the realms of the other groups of beings to form the elemental kingdom. These groups together are called the elemental kingdom because they are all beings who depend upon a living connection with nature realms in order to survive, unlike certain angels for example who are not dependent on an external environment for their survival.

The elemental beings may not eat as humans do, but they do require nourishment from the life force that nourishes all creation and is amplified by the plants, trees and water belonging to the nature kingdom. An energetic exchange of life force nutrients and properties occurs between the elemental beings and the nature kingdom - an exchange that ensures the survival of both parties.

Below is an outline of some of the beings of light who are part of the elemental kingdom. Through understanding these beings, you grow in confidence to make contact with them. Making contact may occur through gardening, walking or sitting, drawing or painting in nature, and through meditation. Every small interaction develops a bridge between you and the elemental kingdom that grows and fortifies over time.

Lady Gaia (Gaia Hierarchy)

Like all plants, the planet itself has an overlighting guardian. One may invoke her to carry out a higher purpose such as the creation of a garden. Although she has received many names throughout human history, here we refer to her as Lady Gaia. As the overlighting guardian and the angelic essence of Earth, Lady Gaia's angelic presence gives Earth its beautiful aura and magical quality.

Gaia is the light and the essence of Earth's spirit and in her arms she holds Mother Earth and all of her children that are known as the Children of Earth. Gaia is the spirit that runs through Earth's heavenly body, and supplies the light and the essence within earth. Her role is specifically to fulfil the need for Earth to have a spirit. Every living entity must have a spirit, an energy that creates a conscious, communicative connection between the solid, physical form and All That Is, and provides a home for the signature frequency; the unique original essence of the living entity. Gaia is an individual aspect of the All That Is, as is the spirit within you. In truth at one level we are all the one energy, but on other levels we have individuality within our life force and thus Gaia's section of the All That Is has been named Lord and Lady Gaia.

Gaia contributes to the overall creation of Earth by casting an angelic, celestial light on the planet that provides its magical and heavenly feel. There are certain areas on Earth that feel otherworldly and it is likely that you have experienced some of these. These places evoke the feeling that you have walked into a completely different realm, and you have interrupted a party that was teaming with mystical life of fairies and spirits you can't quite see. Gaia's angelic and celestial spirit helps to create this feel on Earth. Her energy opens the corridors for other beings from kingdoms far away to visit Earth and to stay awhile.

Fire Knights of the Dragon Guard (Ishtar Hierarchy)

The fire knights are protector dragons that have protected and championed Lady Gaia since before Atlantis. This guardian band was formed when many incompatible species began frequenting Earth. These species were originally considered incompatible by the Children of the Earth Hierarchies, which are Gaia, Shiva, Pan, Lemuria and Atlantis, because they held a different understanding of how to utilise and distribute the Earth's resources and how Earth should be 'governed'. These species came from other planetary realms and did not respect the ancient Council System that had already been functioning for millions of years. These various species groups began depositing their own eggs and seeds (genetic materials) and began experimenting with the genetics of Earth-based species. The fire knights which pledged to protect Earth from these species are a particular order contributing to the Dragon Guard. It is not the role of this book to examine these 'incompatible' species in depth, they are mentioned here only to explain the core assignment of the fire knights.

Sea Dragons of the Dragon Guard (Ishtar Hierarchy)

Another order within the Dragon Guard, the Sea Dragons are part of the Oceanic representatives of the Ishtar Hierarchy. This band of warriors pledged to support the Neptunian visitors as they journeyed between Earth and Neptune as well as the entire oceanic family within the Earth's seas, lakes, rivers and streams. The sea dragons guard the Sea Gates that are the etheric barrier between the Earth's seas and oceans and the travellers from other planetary worlds and realms. This is particularly in relation to landing craft in the seas. There are what humans may call 'alien races' living in the seas. Some of these races are protected by the sea dragons of the Dragon Guard as these races are in the seas as part of their service to Earth and humanity. The sea dragons do not support the work of opportunistic or malevolent off-planetary visitors and serve as guards for the purpose of protecting Earth from such groups in areas of their jurisdiction.

The Faerie (Pan Hierarchy)

The elemental kingdom also contains the Faerie kingdom, which consists of many realms and many orders and groupings within these realms. The Faerie have homes away from Earth also, and have a kingdom realm in Arcadia. At times they have had a large outpost on Venus and a small outpost on Earth's moon. The Faerie belong to an ancient family that helps Earth to evolve and ascend. Their assistance harmonises the energy that flows from and between humans, animals and the elemental kingdom. In some cases, they have played a diplomatic role, communicating with the Human Hierarchy on behalf of the elemental kingdom. In the physical plane they work to raise awareness in the human being of the importance of the nature and elemental kingdoms.

Many human beings have forgotten that their own health and life-giving energy depends on the health and life-giving energy of the nature and elemental kingdoms. The Faerie work to remind humankind of this link that is part of universal law. It is part of universal law that humankind's destiny is linked with that of the nature and elemental kingdoms. Humankind will not be able to avoid this law and reality. The elemental kingdom and the Faerie in particular, have pledged to remind humankind of this shared destiny whenever it is possible.

The Faerie generally favour reminding humankind of its belonging to the nature kingdom through positive, motivational methods. Through fostering humankind's innate love for the natural world, the Faerie stimulate the memory banks hidden and often lying dormant in human beings. Scent, particularly the scent of a flower is a most potent tool for awakening these memory banks. The Faerie work in conjunction with the flower realm and flower spirits to bring pure scent to humankind to bridge human beings to the ancient memory banks contained inside their bodies.

Council of Bees (Central Sun Hierarchy)

Bees operate in multiple dimensions, having developed themselves over thousands of years of evolution in a multitude of settings on other planets. They work in tandem with the flower spirits and the two councils incarnate together - where the flower spirits go, the bees go, and vice versa. In many ways, this reflects the ancient connection and closeness between the two councils, who could almost be considered to share a 'sibling-like' bond.

Bees are fully telepathic and have advanced abilities yet to be mapped by earth-based science. They communicate through an intricate 'web-like' network that allows them both telepathic individual conversation with one other bee and the ability to broadcast messages across their entire community. They have the ability to mentally 'photograph' terrain or a site with their minds and send this data home telepathically.

Bees communicate effortlessly with the channelling systems of other species, particularly humans whose telepathic capabilities vary wildly from person to person depending upon their commitment to their spiritual development. For humans who have opened their channelling systems and who take the time to listen to a bee, the information they receive is highly insightful, often providing perspectives that the human may not have encountered before. The bees' unique perspective comes from 'surfing' the unseen energy waves that exist between all living things. They can detect the subtlest intrusion or 'disturbance in the force' in humans' energy fields and their advice can be invaluable in, among other things, healing work and the work of repairing energy fields.

Like all advanced beings, bees have organised themselves to form a Council of Bees that functions as an overseeing body of support for their species.

Flower Spirits

The flower spirits belong to the elemental kingdom and live within the natural worlds of countless planets. The home base of the Rosaceae family flower spirits within this universe is in Neptune. Neptune is much more than the physical planet that humans call 'Neptune'; it is a consciousness that includes a variety of beings belonging to the Neptunian family who populate realms and dimensions created by these beings. As well as their home base, these flower spirits have a large home base in Arcadia and an outpost in the realm known as Avalon, which is currently residing above Earth in the fifth and sixth dimensions waiting for the time to return to Earth and Earth's physical vicinity of Avalon.

The flower spirits are a unique race within the elemental kingdom. They are part of the essence of flowers. A flower has more than one manifestation – the physical flower, its scent, and its spirit, which lives within it and also beyond its physical manifestation. A flower's scent can be harnessed and taken in the form of essential oils (which are of exceptional benefit in maintaining the energetic integrity of the shield skin and energy fields), but its spirit is never harnessed. The spirit returns to the realm from whence it came when the physical flower dies – it is never lost.

The Lady of the Rose (Jerusalem Hierarchy)

Lady Mary is the Lady of the Rose as well as the caretaker of the signature frequency of all flowers. It is this specific caretaker role that allows her to hold the office and the title, the Lady of the Flowers.

The original rose (which lives in the flower realm of Arcadia) is a direct manifestation of the Lady Mary aspect of Mother Mary. Lady Mary is the aspect of Mother Mary who is the caretaker of the flower realm and the creatrix of many sacred flower realms within this galaxy. Her role as Lady of the Flowers sees her as a caretaker within the realm of flowers and flower communities on Earth. Through this service, she works alongside the guardians of sacred places, overlighters and archangels of the nature realms.

Water Spirits (Jerusalem Hierarchy)

Like the flower spirits of the Rosaceae family, the water spirits live in their home consciousness of Neptune, and come to Earth as part of their divine service. They are the manifestation of the spirit of water and are direct extensions of the Lady of the Sacred Waters of Life. They attend to the physical manifestation of water, maintaining its life force and purity. They also carry messages from the water itself to other beings such as the elemental kingdom members and human beings.

Mer People (Jerusalem Hierarchy)

The elemental kingdom expands beyond land and encompasses the underground waterways and the above ground waterways such as the marshes, seas, rivers, lakes and oceans of Earth. Here, we find the Mer people who are originally from the watery realm within the planet Neptune. Their primary task at this time is to carry information between Earth and Neptune and serve as caretakers of the seas and waterways.

As a multidimensional humanoid sea creature, the Mer people are upper fourth dimensional beings. They experience Earth through their physical bodies and yet carry the technology to pass from the Earth's physical dimension into realms and dimensional planes that overlap with Earth. In this, they are able to appear and disappear at will. When a human sees a Mer person, it is because the being has chosen for that human to see him/her.

Being of ancient Neptunian descent, the Mer people race was born of the womb of Mother Neptune, which also manifests as the Earth's seas. Exceptionally intelligent by human standards, they are able to interact in the physical and etheric realms simultaneously. Both in the physical and etheric, they form a body of light known as the Mer People Council. This council monitors changes and developments within different sea councils established to manage and oversee the sea family. Such councils service sea creatures, beings, frequencies and the various realms that make up the sea realms, regardless of the planet these sea realms happen to be located. The Mer people's role is to record all data and take this information home to Neptune. Nothing escapes them - they see all, hear all, and know all according to their Divine assignment. In this role they are protective of the realms they oversee and will not hesitate to take forceful action to defend their realm when necessary, such as when a boundary is crossed or their resources are plundered. As a manifestation of the essence of water, the Mer people carry not only water, but the very signature frequency of water within themselves. In this, they are frighteningly powerful; their power transcends the physical world and draws from the mysterious origins of the spirit of water itself. They have thus gained a reputation in multiple realms for being fierce, strategic and unrelenting.

Their reputation extends to Earth and causes them also to be feared among humans. This fear is compounded by the fact that water is essential to life; humans need water to live and they must cross perilous tracts of water if they are to find new land where their numbers can flourish. But only water itself could determine whether they have the right conditions to survive at home or across the hazards of the sea - and water is an unpredictable force. And so, just as there are gods or higher powers who can be petitioned to intercede in the affairs of daily life, similar appeasement was sought by humans to ensure steady supplies of water and safe sea voyages. However, given the capricious nature of water, the beings that came to be associated with it were often seen to display the same dual or contradictory characteristics. Of all the sea creatures, mermaids (and mermen) exhibit or are perceived to exhibit this duality more than others. And in this sphere of activity, it is the mermaids – as partly familiar beings - to whom humans have largely appealed to safeguard their interests. Inevitably, on the shadow side mermaids are also the ones regarded as the most contrary - beautiful and beguiling, tempting and treacherous.

For all that, they have retained their allure, as strong today as in the past. On one hand, their imagined features offer a perfect blend of the human and oceanic realms. On the other hand, they also reflect an underlying or assumed fickleness, with the capacity to flip from one identity to the other in ways that unsettle most humans and cause them to mistrust. They also remind us of the elemental power of water and the need to respect it; not to trespass or violate their domain. Yet perhaps they and our attachment to the imagery surrounding them indicate something more fundamental: that is, the visceral awareness that our bodies, being themselves mostly made of water, are linked to the spirit of water in ways we are still fathoming, from both a scientific and metaphysical perspective. Along the way, we are challenged to confront duality as to the very nature of our being, belonging and identity. They exhort us to remain open-minded and fluid; to withhold our prejudices and not to pre-judge, offering themselves as a mirror whereby we may glimpse another reality: that things are not always what they seem.

In line with the above, there is a very compassionate, gentle, family-orientated side to the Mer people, a quality to which many humans would relate. They organise themselves primarily in family and small community clusters. Their families are of central importance to them. Their undying loyalty to all sea kingdoms has always been recognised in the higher realms.

There are different 'categories' of Mer people within the species group, all protected by the guardianship of the Office of Lord and Lady Neptune. Depending upon the physical oceanic vicinity they patrol, they have variations in their frequency and appearance. Those who live in the underground waterways appear differently from those who live in the oceans above the surface. Those who live in lakes and rivers are able to 'blend in' with the human population more so than the oceanic Mer people, although both categories do carry this capability. Some Mer people enjoy crossing the threshold of the waters to fully interact with land-based communities. As water covers so much of the Blue Planet, they feel very much 'at home' in either environment and cherish their role as co-custodians of Earth.

Angel of Water (Jerusalem Hierarchy)

The Sacred Waters of Life has within its guardianship an angel who is neither masculine nor feminine, but androgynous in its structure. This angel of divinity is known as the Angel of the Sacred Waters of Life and the angel of water. The angel of water is the angelic essence of the water itself. This being is seventh dimensional and yet has the ability to live in all dimensions. The angel's home frequency is in the seventh dimension.

The angel of water serves the nature and elemental kingdoms and is also available to individual humans who ask for assistance. This angel provides healing through the water's frequency and energy and serves as a conduit for higher vibrational frequencies to reach the human being. A human may pray over or in front of a pond or waterfall for example, and receive higher vibrational frequencies sent by the higher realms to Earth. Water can accept these frequencies, intensify or modify them, and make them available to the human being. This method is useful when the individual's vibrational frequency is not at a vibratory rate high enough to accept direct interaction with the higher realms beyond the physical plane.

When humans swim in the rivers or ocean, they bathe in these higher vibrational frequencies and energies so that they are cleansed and purified where possible and their vibrational frequency is raised. If that human was to call upon the angel of water while entering the water, more assistance is available to them because the angels will grant permission for changes to be made to their vibrational frequency. Such intervention in a human's energy field never takes place without their agreement.

Only those who consciously request help either from the angel of water or from the water goddess, receive additional and often intense assistance. This assistance may extend into their dreams where they recall traveling into the sea realms to meet with the beings of the sea.

Honour the angel of water first by recognising that all water is sacred, even the tap water that may come to your house from the city reservoir. Make sure that the water that leaves your home is as pure as possible. Refrain from using toxic chemicals in your clothes washing and shower that lowers the water's vibratory rate. When preparing your drinking water, avoid storing it in plastic containers. Glass, porcelain or sealed clay is more appropriate. When you first receive your water vessel, place it in your house and put your hands over it. Close your eyes and feel the angel of water near or within you. Ask the angel to move through you and your water to charge it, purify it, and raise its vibratory frequency so that it can serve the highest needs of your body and the bodies of others who will drink it. Use the water regularly or change it regularly if you haven't been able to drink it all to avoid consuming water that has been stagnant for too long.

Office of Neptune (Jerusalem Hierarchy)

The Office of Neptune is the practical arm of the Neptunian line (see Jerusalem Hierarchy) in the physical plane. Its core bases are presently on Earth and on planet Neptune. This office, as well as other Neptunian offices, also has bases in other planetary worlds. The Office of Neptune connects directly to the Neptunian Council of Twelve, the Council of the Oceanic Family, the Office of the Seas and the Office of the Lord and Lady of the Sacred Waters of Life (which includes its other aspects the Lord and Lady of the Lake and an aspect of Lord and Lady Neptune) and the Office of the Lakes, Rivers and all Waterways (which includes aspects of Lord and Lady Amphibian).

Sea Moon (Bethlehem Hierarchy)

The sea moon is a celestial body of light which lives many kilometres beneath the surface in the depths of the Earth's sea. She radiates high vibrations through the sea kingdoms to assist humans to move upwardly to attain upper fourth dimensional consciousness. In addition to this, the Earth's star grids pulsate with her frequencies, which are in turn maintained by her hierarchy. She communicates with and is continuously connected to the Earth's moon, of which she is also an aspect. As she interacts with Earth's moon, the two moons provide a balancing function for the planet.

The sea moon, although feminine, is balanced perfectly in her masculine and feminine frequencies. She is the oceanic aspect of Bethlehem (see Bethlehem Hierarchy).

Angel of Air (Mu Hierarchy)

The angel of air is of utmost importance in the survival of all living creatures upon the planet. This angel is the very angelic presence of the air you breathe and carries the angelic aspect of oxygen into your lungs and cells. This essence brings feelings of joy and exhilaration when you inhale deeply, followed by deeper relaxation and peace. The angel of air heals through the life-giving properties of the angelic frequency, which it provides to the element of air.

The angel of air is best able to interact with you when you breathe in air that is flowing. As one would not drink water from a pool that has been stagnant for some time, one should be likewise vigilant in allowing air to flow as water does. The flowing of air is alive and joyful. Air that is stagnant becomes heavy and burdened. The angel of air is most active when air moves. This can be most easily facilitated by opening the doors and windows during the day to allow for circulation in your home, as well as sleeping with the window open a little at night where possible.

The angel of air interacts with your physical lungs, the keys to which belong to the Mu Hierarchy. The angel of air is a representative of the Mu Hierarchy.

Office of Venus (Tansafarie Hierarchy)

The office of Venus anchors the strength of the Tansafarie Hierarchy into the physical plane both on Earth and on planet Venus. This office is part of a network of offices belonging to the Tansafarie Hierarchy, which support the hierarchy's role on Earth. As part of this network, the Council and Office of the Rainbow Bridge provides a form of access to Earth through the Venetian/

Venusian incarnation process. The original 'People of the Stars/ Sky People' came to Earth through this bridge. Also included is the office of Lord and Lady Terra - the office of the physical substance that is earth/soil, mud, clay, rocks and minerals, and the Council of the Directorship of the Rays for the Spiritual Hierarchy for Earth as overseen by Sanat Kumara. This council has twelve members - one member from each hierarchy. The council directs rays of light and healing technology into Earth's consciousness to assist humanity's healing and ascension.

Angel of the Earth Physical (Tansafarie Hierarchy)

The Angel of the Earth Physical is the angelic essence of the physical substance of Earth. This angel incarnates in the soils, the clay, and the volcanic rock. As you walk barefoot on the dirt, rocks and natural surface of the Earth, your feet reconnect with the Angel of the Earth Physical, allowing this angel to help heal you through anchoring and grounding your energy. Grounding functions as a 'discharge facility', where the body can release built up energies and excess 'electricity' into the Earth so that it can bring its 'electrical circuitry' back into balance naturally. This is becoming increasingly important in today's modern world with the additional exposure to electromagnetic radiation, which builds up in our energy fields until it is discharged. Many people experience reduced physical body inflammation and other associated conditions through using grounding as part of a healing program. The healing path of grounding is provided by the Angel of the Earth Physical who comes from Tansafarie Hierarchy.

Office of the Sun (Central Sun Hierarchy)

The Office of the Sun is part of the Central Sun Hierarchy, which houses the Council of the Central Sun, the Law of One Council, the Council of Balance and Justice for the Spiritual Hierarchy for Earth and the physical sun of our solar system. This council provides the frequencies that allow for the vitalisation of sun rays, from which life on Earth feeds.

Angel of Sunlight (Central Sun Hierarchy)

The angel of sunlight provides the angelic essence of the sun itself and the rays of sunshine that come to the Earth. The sun is a physical manifestation of Christ consciousness. This angel heals by being the angelic essence of this unique and powerful light that provides healing and life-giving properties to the Earth, the nature and elemental kingdoms and humanity. Those who understand the full power of sunshine will utilise it in their self-healing and healing work without fear or doubt. To develop this understanding of sunshine's healing properties, enter meditation and create a bridge of communication with the angel of sunlight. This angel will educate you and explain how you may use sunlight in your healing journey or work.

Sunlight can be used to 'charge up' materials and items with life force and energy that in turn can assist to rejuvenate or feed your energy field and physical body. Your glass of drinking water will benefit from a moment in the sun. Watch the rays penetrate the water and make it shine from the inside. When you see this occurring, drink the water, charged with the sun's vibrant force, and allow it to strengthen your body and energy field.

Dry your clothing, towels, and bed sheets in the sunshine. Allow sun energy to filter through the fibres of your washing (natural fibres such as cotton and wool are recommended). The energy of the fibres will interact with your skin and assist in the energetic rejuvenation of your shield skin. Your shield skin is the outermost layer of your physical skin layer and the innermost layer of your energy field. The strength and vitality of the shield skin is key to physical wellness and maintaining your life force or 'qi'. A corroded shield skin can lead to weakness of physical stamina as well as weakness in your emotional and energetic resilience. This is why refraining from using toxic chemicals on your skin is critical to maintaining the integrity of your shield skin. The ancient practice of anointing Initiates with plant and flower oils and embalming to assist in preparations for the afterlife, build this essential layer for the next level of their spiritual ascension journey.

The foods you consume that are of nature, such as fruits, vegetables, nuts, seeds and grains, have grown with the assistance of the sun's energy. When you eat these foods, you take this life giving energy into your body. The cells will take what they need and anything left over will travel from the physical casing of the body and out into the body's energy field. The energy field will use this additional life force to repair any weaknesses in the layers of energy and the overall energy field. It will use this additional energy to restore its reserves and reinforce the boundary of the energy field.

This boundary acts as a barrier of defence against electromagnetic interference. Without a strong barrier of defence, electromagnetic interference may penetrate the physical body and affect human cells. Nutritious, sun-filled, life-giving food helps to strengthen the human energy field.

Lady of the Sacred Waters of Life (Jerusalem Hierarchy)

If the Divine Father breathes life and light into a body in the form of spirit, then the Divine Mother helps nourish the body in its very first stage through her embryonic fluid, her liquid life. At all levels, masculine and feminine elements are required for the generation of life and in order to sustain it.

On Earth and in the human body, water is also connected to the emotional body, and is the essence that governs emotions. Indeed, as tears of built-up emotion are shed, 'flood gates' are opened to cleanse the emotional body, creating a sense of relief and release.

By immersion or contact with holy waters, one hopes to clear the past and restore purity to mind, body and soul. For centuries, people have made pilgrimages to sacred sites because of a belief that the power and presence of the Divine reside therein. At the Chalice Well of Glastonbury, England, the force of feminine love bestowed by the Goddess upon those who seek connection is palpable. As she dispenses unconditional acceptance and wisdom, the place seems to hum such that it emanates an ethereal quality, and there in her presence, one feels remembered, held, restored and then released. The Goddess does not seem to encourage pilgrims to linger for as soon as they have collected the keys she has left just for them, paid their respects and walked her garden of healing to hear her messages, with her blessing, support and protection it is time to go.

Every year, millions of pilgrims seek the healing water at Lourdes in France, which became sacred in 1858 after twelve-year old Bernadette Soubirous (later Saint Bernadette, whom we met earlier) revealed the visions and communication she received there from the Blessed Virgin Mary. That encounter - between Mother Mary and a young girl - and the subsequent discovery of a spring that performs miracles have in a number of ways reminded humankind of the healing power and constant presence of the feminine principle. Mother Mary as an aspect of the Neptunian line (see Chapter Four on the Jerusalem Hierarchy) also illustrates the link between Mary and water; that she is/was a manifested aspect of the water element.

Deep within the psyche of humankind is an ancient spiritual memory of the higher purpose of water. The water goddess has lived at the periphery of humankind's psyche for a very long time indeed. As the Lady of the Lake (also the Neptunian line) she presented the magical sword Excalibur to Arthur and retrieved it again at his death. From her enchanted waters she set in motion a great cycle of spiritual initiation and, along with the Grail Quest, its ripple effects still surge through humanity today.

As Lady Neptune, she is the feminine aspect of the old sea god. Where God Neptune is the father and masculine aspect of the sea, she is the great womb that is the sea, giving birth to the consciousness of earth and humanity. She flows through all rivers, streams and seas, her essence permeating the waters and fertilising the land through this supreme application/expression of the feminine principle.

The idea of water as a mysterious and magical force lives in the imagination of children and in the old, rarely visited cave of enchantment and wonder within the human psyche. Who as a child did not throw a coin into a fountain hoping for a wish to be granted? And when we stop at a well or fountain for refreshment, on the surface of things we are seeking its life-giving sustenance, but are we also drawn there by some primeval instinct: are we tapping into something deeper, some ancient and half-remembered connection?

Like the ancient priestesses, so too healer and prophet Michel de Nostredame (Nostradamus) paid attention to the Lady of the Water and allowed her to bring him the answers he sought. He practised hydromancy, or water divining as a particular type of scrying, from his home in France where as a spiritual seeker he sat in a dimly lit room formulating questions and then observing the effects on water in a bowl. As a hydromancer he surrendered to the spirit of water, trusting that this force or power - connected to all things since before time - would communicate in response.

Such communication occurs using old routes or passages that exist within the mind of all humans, but beyond the conscious awareness of humankind. The spirit of water knows these old pathways, and channels messages in the form of telepathy or visions to the one who seeks them. You can activate your imagination and introduce the ancient spiritual practice of water-honouring by placing a wishing well, pond or fountain in the garden. If you are fortunate to have a natural spring on your property, you need only to acknowledge this feature of the landscape for the sacred place that it is.

CHAPTER SEVENTEEN

Shared Offices at the Earth/Physical, Etheric and Galactic Levels

The offices discussed so far belong to individual hierarchies who offer their service to humanity and Earth through the earth/physical and etheric levels of the Spiritual Hierarchy for Earth. The following offices are shared, meaning that multiple hierarchies work together to facilitate the role within the Spiritual Hierarchy for Earth and Ancient Spiritual Family.

The Ancient Spiritual Family is a grand structure consisting of all components of the twelve hierarchies that are the ancient families of this universe, while the Spiritual Hierarchy for Earth consists only of the components of each of the twelve hierarchies that are relevant to the Earth assignment. The Ancient Spiritual Family has been in existence long before Earth was born. Its members may not necessarily be members of the Spiritual Hierarchy for Earth, for the latter are thus because of their interest and role in the Earth assignment.

Because the Spiritual Hierarchy for Earth is a structure with a specific function to serve Earth and all beings who co-exist on

Earth, it consists of offices held by individual hierarchies and jointly held offices and councils. The Office of the Central Sun sits in the core of the structure, and although it is technically part of the Central Sun Hierarchy, its frequencies and facilities are available to all.

The Spiritual Hierarchy for Earth's physical/etheric (third and fourth dimensional) base and core office is in Jerusalem city. It has been so for thousands of years. Like the Jerusalem Hierarchy, Jerusalem city holds the energy for the harmonisation of the Spiritual Hierarchy for Earth. This base will continue to operate until all twelve hierarchies come into balance and harmony with each other. When the frequencies harmonise between the twelve hierarchies, the base will move to the realm of light above the Himalayan mountains. This will become its ascended home and will reflect the ascended consciousness of the twelve hierarchies operating as one functioning structure, the Spiritual Hierarchy for Earth.

Offices within the Spiritual Hierarchy for Earth hold the third, fourth and fifth dimensional frequencies for the beings, human incarnates and frequency bands that they represent. There are thousands of offices within the Spiritual Hierarchy for Earth. The offices most relevant to activating the initiate's memory of the purpose of the Spiritual Hierarchy for Earth are listed below. There are millions of beings and human incarnates who work within and actively assist the offices mentioned below. These beings and human incarnates are recorded within the Spiritual Hierarchy for Earth, but are too numerous to list here. Instead, we have listed the major governing councils and offices.

Council of Arkamusha

The Council of Arkamusha is ancient and vast. Among its many manifestations, it embodies in the seven ancient guardians who live in the deepest parts of the seas and who patrol these depths. They serve as transmitters for ancient frequencies sent to Earth by the Ancient of Ancients.

The Council of the Oceanic Family on Earth

This is a very large council. It includes all creatures, physical and etheric, which utilise the oceans and seas of Earth to travel through or to live within. This includes beings who are not of the Neptunian line. It consists also of the angelic realm beneath the sea, the Council of Arkamusha, and the sea moon. (See The Oceanic Family, Chapter Nineteen).

The Elves

One of the most ancient orders that exist within the elemental kingdom is that of the Elves. The Elves have their own realms, which come together to form the Elven kingdom. This kingdom has its home base in the ancient realm of Arcadia. The Elves have their own names for this realm and home base. Within their kingdom they have several outposts, such as their base on Earth, the planetary realm known as Sirius and a large base within the consciousness of Neptune.

The Elves were present on Earth before the first human being arrived. Their role has been to act as specialised guardians, gatekeepers and protectors. They hold information that will eventually be revealed to humanity as the Human Hierarchy evolves to prove itself worthy of such keys. Many individual human beings are permitted to receive certain keys before the entire Human Hierarchy does because individually they have shown themselves to be committed to the highest path. These ones are 'way-showers' or 'light-workers' of a kind who will come to hold the energy for other humans or actively guide the Human Hierarchy to move into a higher vibrational frequency.

Some humans who have received certain keys from the Elves live simple, humble lives. Their task is not to work actively to bring about change, but to heal and transform humanity's consciousness through their hidden, humble or even silent service. (See also the Elven Family, Chapter Nineteen).

The Overlighters

The Council of the Overlighters for Earth is a fourth and fifth dimensional council that consists of beings of light serving to support the nature realms on Earth. They sit within the Spiritual Hierarchy for Earth and communicate directly with animals, devas of various realms, guardians of sacred places whether they be physically manifested places or etheric vicinities, members of the Children of Earth council and angelic beings. They communicate the needs of the plant species and assist in the maintaining of telepathic communication systems between the plants themselves and other beings and creatures. They maintain harmony within the nature realms and create a symphony of frequencies amongst plants and trees. They regulate life force levels within plants and assist in the telepathic communication between plants and human beings.

The Overlighters are an integral part of the nature and elemental kingdoms. This group of beings are the overlighting and overseeing guardians of plants, trees, lakes, rivers and Earth. Initiates may use their connection to the overlighters to strengthen their spiritual awareness and to aid in the practical task of creating a spiritual garden on Earth. These overlighting guardians are available to all human beings who embrace the role of caretaker, giving their time over to nurture sacred places.

The Tree Beings

A tree being comes into manifestation when an aspect of the tree's Overlighting presence chooses to reside within the tree. This usually occurs when the tree has reached an age where it takes its role as a guardian in the forest or sacred place. Prior to this, the Overlighter is part of the tree as its spirit and essence, however, it is not engaged as a conscious being in residence within the physicality. It may be called upon and is available to communicate with other beings including humans, but it is not physically incarnate. An Overlighter becomes a tree being when it makes the decision to incarnate a substantial amount of itself in the form of a fully developed aspect, into the physical structure of the tree.

Other aspects of the Overlighter remain available to serve the other trees that it is part of and who share its signature frequency.

Not all trees have a tree being in residence. When humans find a tree being, indeed the Overlighter's incarnated essence in the presence of a particular tree, the human being is able to communicate with all other incarnated Overlighter aspects (tree beings) of that signature frequency. For example, if you were to have an oak tree being in your garden and your friend is similarly blessed with having one in their garden, even if it is across the world, you could communicate through the tree being on your property to the tree being on their property. Through the tree being on your friend's property, you could see a great deal of what was occurring in your friend's life and understand much of the energetic environment that surrounds them.

The tree beings will permit this form of 'psychic viewing' and interaction providing the human's intention is aligned to Divine Will. Only a pure, loving and kind heart will gain access to this most advanced technology. This technology has many additional uses and benefits that the spiritual Initiate will discover though interacting with the tree beings.

To communicate with a tree being, lean against a tree that you sense has a 'presence', such as a tree being in residence, and relax. Feel the bark and the firm earth below. Breathe, and allow the mind to settle. Listen. A distant familiar voice may speak inside your mind in a type of telepathic exchange. Messages do not always appear on the first attempt. It can take some time before the channels of communication open completely. The grounding affect of walking in nature and gardening can speed up the process of connecting with the guardians of nature.

Spending time in old forests and other sacred places also raises the vibration in your physical body and energy field. This can significantly strengthen your ability to receive messages from the elemental and nature kingdoms. When you ask permission from the forest guardians to enter, a veil lifts making it possible to hear the trees in the forest as you would hear a small community of people gathered together, as though almost every tree wants to talk, share insights and offer messages.

The Council of Trees

The Council of Trees is a deeply caring community of tree beings. At the 'centre' of this council is the World Tree, a manifestation of the Central Sun. The Council of Trees consists of the overlighters - the signature essence of the trees. Tree beings are ancient, having contributed to many planetary worlds before coming to celebrate Earth by incarnating here. They are recognised by councils across thousands of planets as being Elders and guardians. Many species and beings seek the counsel of tree beings.

The Guardians of the Garden and other Sacred Places

Although Lord and Lady Gaia are the Overlighting spirits of Earth, certain places on Earth have their own particular guardians. Old, established gardens such as a well-loved public botanical garden or large estates may have a council of guardians for the garden and a water guardian for the lake, stream or river on the property. It is worth making the effort to meet the spiritual guardian of your garden or the public garden if you visit regularly. These guardians have many gifts that they are all very willing to share with anyone who seeks their assistance. They are powerful healers and wise counsellors, ready to offer healing and guidance. The guardian of your own garden is able to project thoughts and images into your mind about what the garden needs and how to transform it into a paradise or enchanted realm, or simply how best to enjoy it.

All places in nature are sacred. However, there are certain 'power spots' that attract a great deal of human and 'otherworld' attention. Such places require a spiritual guardian to oversee the vicinity and hold the energy for the vicinity's higher purpose. In England, for example, Stonehenge and Avebury in Wiltshire and the Glastonbury Tor in Somerset, have powerful ancient guardians as spiritual caretakers. The guardian of Glastonbury has protected the land for thousands of years. Before climbing the Glastonbury Tor, ask the guardian for permission to enter. Communicating with the guardian in meditation is a profound way to grasp the deep spiritual purpose of Glastonbury.

Australia also has many sacred sites. The Original People Elders in both human and spirit form oversee 'Uluru' in Australia's Northern Territory. As one would not enter another person's house without knocking first and waiting to be accepted, it is important to ask their permission telepathically through meditation before entering their vicinity. All great mountains, lakes and forests across the world have guardians. It is beneficial to seek their wise counsel. They can talk about Earth's history, or what will unfold in the future – they have access to levels of information that humans do not.

Communicating with the guardians of sacred places intensifies your experience of the vicinity and opens your mind to new thoughts, ideas, realms and dimensions. Communicating with the sacred guardians is not complicated and there is no right or wrong way to do it. As you close your eyes and beckon the guardian, you immediately connect to this higher being. Affirm:

I beckon the energy of divinity that is the guardian of this vicinity for my highest good and will. May our work together serve the highest benefit of all beings.

This useful affirmation will instantly create a bridge to the guardian. We need never feel isolated in nature. All we simply need to do is choose to connect.

The Angelic Council of the Nature Realms

This council of angelic beings oversees the nature kingdom. The council provides the angelic essence of nature. Members of this council include: the angel of water, the angel of air, the angel of earth, the angel of sunlight, and Lord and Lady Gaia. Many angelic beings who are part of the nature realms, such as the sea angels sit on this council. This council also sits in the seventh dimension.

Office of Family

All hierarchies belonging to the Ancient Spiritual Family belong to the Office of Family and contribute their unique frequencies to the office. The office seeks to harmonise the energy between the hierarchies, which in turn helps to harmonise the space between family members on Earth. The office oversees the healing of ancient rifts between the hierarchies of the Ancient Spiritual Family by organising for members of each hierarchy to incarnate into family clusters together. As these human incarnates work through the issues that arise in their human lives, they assist to harmonise the energy and clear karmic debt between members of the Ancient Spiritual Family.

As well as harmonising the energy between existing family frequencies on Earth, the office seeks to integrate higher family frequencies on Earth. For families that choose to accept these higher frequencies, it is possible for all members to ascend together on Earth into the early stages of fifth dimensional experience.

Office of Children

The office of children oversees the development of 'the child' and the experience of 'childhood'. It works closely with the Lemurian Hierarchy, the keeper of the keys to childhood on Earth, and the Central Sun that made a pact many thousands of years ago to remain heavily and intensely incarnated in human bodies until every child experiences peace, and the Innocence of Childhood, as childhood was designed originally to be.

Some souls use childhood to process karmic debt or work through voluntary karma. For these souls, peace and the Innocence of Childhood must still be presented, however fleetingly, so that the soul knows the potential for their highest path and highest truth exists. The Central Sun works tirelessly to ensure its members present these keys, peace, and the Innocence of Childhood, and represent them well, to all children. This is done primarily through human contact, for example a

Central Sun member or an Office of Children representative appears in a child's life for a period of time (teacher, nurse, aid worker etc) or as a permanent figure (community Elder, family member, neighbour, family friend). In cases where an incarnated representative cannot reach a certain child, the child will receive a dream or visitation from a member of the Office of Children or the Central Sun. The Office of Children also uses additional educational means to present its keys to children such as working through its members who are writers and illustrators, to install representations of the keys in children's stories and books.

Office of Youth

The Tansafarie, Central Sun and Mu hierarchies oversee the Office of Youth and work closely with the Atlantis Hierarchy, which holds the keys to adolescence. The adolescent phase acts as a transitional plane from childhood to adulthood, and offers a vital opportunity to grow and expand, and for the soul to seek oneself and find oneself, or to find the path that leads to oneself. The Office of Youth was established to present the key to one's path. Light-workers from this office work in various capacities to present vital keys to adolescents so that they fulfil their highest purpose on Earth by first recognising their own path and choosing to step onto it. These Light-workers may be found in various professions, working as teachers, scout leaders, chaplains, counsellors, coaches and community leaders. They may also serve as biological mothers and fathers, and people who nurture children and young people as their non-biological parents, guardians and caregivers.

This office serves not only the adolescent human on Earth, but the adolescent soul of 'young' hierarchies and young, evolving aspects within all hierarchies. Such aspects may be thousands of years old by human standards and may have experienced multiple incarnations on various planetary worlds. Their evolution is supported and overseen by this office.

Office of Women

Central Sun, Jerusalem, Mu, Bethlehem, Israel and Tansafarie hierarchies oversee the Office of Women, which exists to assist every human incarnated female to reach her highest potential as a woman on Earth. The Office of Women oversees the development and ascension of the feminine energy on Earth, and the integration of higher feminine frequencies into Earth's collective consciousness and emotional body.

Through the collective efforts of the Office of Women and the Office of Men, patriarchal institutions and systems that have disempowered the feminine will be dismantled over the decades to come. This breaking down of the old paradigm so that the offices can shepherd in the new, higher consciousness will occur through a combination of education, activism and a simple 'turning away' from the old way of doing things. As individuals cease to engage in the old paradigm, it loses energy and thus it can no longer maintain itself. When it cannot maintain itself, the structure crumbles and the new era is born.

Through the simple act of turning away from the old paradigm combined with the Office of Women giving birth to the new feminine structures, new structures will rise on Earth that serve to support the individual to honour his/her own path. In this, the individual will feel encouraged to utilise his/her intuition and higher guidance when navigating all aspects of life on Earth. It will become an accepted method of decision making, conflict resolution, planning etc.

Some may say that for this to occur, Earth would need to see massive social change. Social change is already occurring, brought about by a combination of factors that is freeing humankind from many day-to-day struggles. Over time, this in turn will free up an abundance of energy, time and resources that will be able to be redirected into the development of various feminine arts that enhance intuition, telepathy and the receiving of higher communication. As a greater focus is placed upon the development of these attributes, the human race will naturally evolve to ascend into the upper levels of the fourth dimension. From here, humanity will be able to take its seat at the galactic council where all advanced species and societies connect, as a mature and respected member.

Office of Men

As with the Office of Women, the Office of Men consists of the Central Sun, Jerusalem, Mu, Bethlehem, Israel and Tansafarie hierarchies. These hierarchies act as overseers within the council that works closely with the Children of Earth hierarchies to ensure that higher masculine frequencies integrate into the consciousness of mankind.

Overseeing the ascension of male consciousness, the office plans to initiate the rise of men's groups in this next phase. Human representatives of the Office of Men will receive the keys to these groups while in meditation etc and will facilitate these workshops or meetings. These groups provide an opportunity to train men to be the custodians of the new male consciousness anchoring on Earth over these next few decades. Within these groups, there will be the return of specific, empowering, spiritual 'rites of passage' that will aid men to embrace their divine masculine and integrate this into their daily lives. Some of these 'rites of passage' are still used in advanced civilisations beyond Earth and will be gifted to Earth through office of men representatives, to support the training of the current and next generations of males on Earth.

Powerful masculine attributes that have been repressed over the centuries only to rise inappropriately in other ways, will come to the surface to be appropriately integrated and expressed. Humanity will see the rise of true masculine leaders - those who empower the lives of all those who look to them for support. There will develop as the result of the educational work initiated by this office, a growing appreciation of true masculine attributes. Many men have felt the need to apologise for their masculinity. Through misundestanding and out of fear of disempowering the feminine, they have repressed their masculine energy. This shame, uncertainty about how to act and respond, and questions around being male, will be addressed in various formats by human representatives of this office in the decades to come.

Office of Animals

Overseen by Lady Assandra of the Central Sun, and Israel, Mu and Children of the Earth hierarchies, the Office of Animals was responsible for the integration of animal species on Earth. It oversees and records the experiences of the species, how they interact with Earth, how they evolve and in some cases, the office assists species to take their experience and re-integrate back into their own planetary worlds and kingdoms, away from planet Earth.

There are many incarnated representatives of this office on Earth at the moment in human form. They are working to educate humanity about their responsibilities in relation to sharing a planet with other species. Through this, the office is establishing the rights of animals in the physical plane within a legal and ethical framework. The office will anchor the higher dimensional framework for the respect of animals on Earth over these next twenty to thirty years. Many office representatives have positioned this work as their core assignment and reason for incarnating.

In advanced civilisations beyond Earth, animals are recognised as energies of divinity, worthy of love, kindness and respect. Higher dimensional beings do not prey upon the animal kingdom. The office of animal representatives are here to anchor this higher awareness and 'philosophy' of these advanced societies into humanity's consciousness.

Office of the Elements

The Office of the Elements is balanced within its masculine and feminine frequencies. It is a powerful office that balances and coordinates the elements that are the creative building blocks of Earth. The beings that sit upon this council are the energies of divinity that represent the balance of the elements within their own hierarchies. Among many other beings, this office is also held by: Jerusalem - water; Bethlehem- fire; Tansafarie - earth and some metals; Mu - air; Central Sun - light; Gaia - the balance of the elements within the Gaia field of Earth's atmosphere; Pan - wood and metals. Israel - some metals.

Angelic Council for Earth

The Angelic Council for Earth is overseen by many Archangels. Some of the more well known Archangels who sit on this council are: Central Sun – Michael, Jerusalem – Raphael, Mu – Uriel, Israel – Gabriel.

The Children of Earth Council

This council consists of the hierarchies of Gaia, Shiva, Pan, Lemuria and Atlantis. Among other things, the council holds the energy for incarnation to occur on Earth and is responsible for initiating and orchestrating the different stages of Earth's ascension plan.

The Council for the Creation of Planet Earth

The planet called Earth is not one entity or being, nor one hierarchy, but the result of collaboration between the hierarchies. The hierarchies worked together to create a planet that housed and represented all twelve hierarchies equally, all serving and supporting each other.

The title 'Earth' is given to a collective of beings who come together to create the planet.

Fire
Great Fiery Goddess and the fiery core of the Earth (Bethlehem)

Earth (dirt/soil)
Lord and Lady of the Earth, God and Goddess Terra – born of Venus (Tansafarie)

Air
Keepers of the Sky Kingdom of Earth (Mu)

Water
Womb of Earth – Earth's seas, lakes, rivers and streams (Jerusalem/Neptune)

Wood
The Underworld, the fairy kingdom and the Community of the Forest (Pan)

Metals
Tansafarie, Pan, Israel. Israel is the builder of structures for human incarnations and a builder of civilisations both on Earth and off-planet (Israel/Constantinople line). Aside from sharing the platinum group metals with Pan and Tansafarie, Israel hold the keys for some off-planetary metals and materials, some of which came to Earth through meteorites.

Spirit
Angelic spirit of the Earth (Gaia)

Light
The light that lights the Earth, Christ Light of the Earth (Central Sun)

Human
Keepers of the keys of man and woman - Father of Homo sapiens (Israel)

Dragon Spirit
Keeper of the keys to the serpent energy of Earth (Ishtar)

Childhood of Human
Innocence, expression and creative exploration of mankind in its childhood (Lemuria)

Adolescence of Human
The phase of exploration and experimentation of the incarnated man (Atlantis)

Adulthood of Human
Humankind knows itself. The discovered human, having taken its mantle, accepts its role and purpose on Earth (Shiva).

The Office of Communication

There are many ways in which the Spiritual Hierarchy for Earth interacts with, informs and inspires the human family. Mostly, the communications from the Spiritual Hierarchy for Earth come to the human family through individuals who consciously or unconsciously act as conduits for the information. These individuals might anchor the information by writing books, artwork, business ideas, plays, films, community or social initiatives and humanitarian works. Their initiatives then progress to inspire others, sometimes entire countries, to change and evolve.

An individual conscious of his or her higher assignments, mission or purpose on Earth is an extremely valuable asset to the work of the Spiritual Hierarchy on Earth. Through just one person, we can effect great change. When additional human incarnates lend their support to that individual, profound change occurs.

The purpose of change is to initiate a framework that we designed a very long time ago to bring every human incarnate who chooses to allow it to occur to the point where ascension into fifth dimensional consciousness takes place. We cannot force such an ascension on any human being. Our intention is to clear the path so that every human being is able to make a clear, unencumbered choice about his or her own ascension. At present, many incarnates rotate upon the incarnation wheel, making small gains in terms of securing their liberation from the wheel. Through working with awakened human Initiates, we inform and inspire incarnates to utilise the opportunity of their incarnation to free themselves from certain limitations. Each step towards this secures a higher experience for the human incarnate while they remain in the incarnation cycle, or move beyond the cycle.

There are dimensional and planetary experiences beyond Earth's plane that an incarnate is able to choose when sufficient gains have been made in his/her evolutionary progress on Earth. However, the Earth experience is not a punishment for insufficient spiritual progress. Many Initiates voluntarily return to Earth for the joy of physicality or to further assist their spiritual family members long after their Earth assignments are officially complete. Many Initiates love Earth deeply. Their desire to commune with the planet motivates their return.

The Office of Communication is a system of multi-layered avenues that allows for the information to be distributed from various councils within the Spiritual Hierarchy for Earth to the various offices of communication within individual hierarchies. When the information reaches the Office of Communication within an individual hierarchy, it becomes the responsibility of the individual hierarchy to ensure messages reach its own relevant offices and hierarchy members as well as the human incarnates of the hierarchy. In this way, the human incarnate receives information from the Spiritual Hierarchy for Earth through his/her own Office of Communication.

Other ways a human initiate may receive information is through direct interaction with an office or council within the Spiritual Hierarchy for Earth. This usually occurs when a human initiate has a role and position within the office or council. Many human incarnates maintain their responsibilities and commitments to offices or councils even when they come to Earth, working on these higher assignments while their bodies are sleeping. Their etheric body returns to the council or office during the body's sleeping time. Some incarnates have evolved to a level where they are aware of their assignments and work in their councils and offices during their waking state. They are consciously able to fulfil their tasks while operating in their physical lives. This level of awareness usually unfolds in a human incarnate when he/she has reached the vibratory rate of the middle band of the fourth dimension.

The Office of the Law of One

The office of the Law of One supports and oversees the anchoring of the Law of One in all realms, dimensions and planetary worlds that allow it to do so. In vicinities that have not yet aligned to the Law of One, but desire to do so, it helps prepare the soil for the planting of this higher seed.

When the Law of One is anchored, the vicinity becomes automatically aligned to Divine Will. The Law of One becomes its statement of intent and its governing principle. Those aligned to the Law of One are able to reside in the vicinity and those not aligned find that the incompatibility of their frequency with the Law of One makes it impossible for them to remain within the vicinity. They are then faced with a choice – to align with the Law of One or leave.

The Law of One supports free will, but ensures that the free will exercised does not impinge upon the freedoms of another. When one is aligned to the Law of One, one naturally and automatically respects and upholds the rights of others. The Law becomes both a frequency to align with and a code by which to live.

Office of Initiation

Among its many roles, this office oversees the initiation process that allows for human beings to become conscious, active ambassadors for the Spiritual Hierarchy for Earth during their human incarnation. This office overseas the human's initiation journey, which may be directed by a human incarnated teacher who has passed through the same process. Where a human teacher is not present, initiation may be directed by the higher realms through the Initiate's meditations and dream state etc. This office trains a human being to take roles of responsibility within the Spiritual Hierarchy for Earth.

The Shared Assignment of Providing Healing Systems on Earth

All hierarchies have contributed to anchoring healing systems on Earth. Israel, through their Constantinople arm, anchored what is now called modern, Western allopathic medicine and the modern day pharmaceutical industry. Israel also shares keys to Western herbalism with other hierarchies, who each have contributed to 'folk' and/or tribal medicine in their own way. Israel, through their Albion line, holds keys with Pan and Bethlehem to the old Celtic and Druidic herbal lore. Through its Chiron arm, Israel, alongside Atlantis, anchored healing keys into Ancient Greece, while Israel's Chiron and Constantinople arms anchored keys and technology into Ancient Rome.

Tansafarie anchored the first healing keys of the Vikings and the old Scottish clans. The Native American healing system with its herbal medicine, interaction with the Earth and her animals for guidance to promote healing and shamanic healing practices, was brought to Earth by Tansafarie and Mu.

Gaia anchored keys into Russia that brought the awakening of ancient Russian 'folk' medicine and the profound wisdom contained in their ancient, nature-based, earth-medicine way.

The original keys to Chinese medicine and ancient Japanese healing including shiatsu were anchored by Jerusalem. The advanced science of using flower essences to heal humankind were anchored in a joint project by Jerusalem and Gaia, however, other hierarchies have contributed greatly to expanding this field of medicine and healing. Gaia integrated its own version of this advanced science into Earth through many of its members, including Dr Edward Bach who anchored the Bach flower remedies. Gaia also anchored the keys to Tibetan medicine.

Homeopaths belong to various hierarchies and all hierarchies hold keys to understanding homeopathy. Hierarchy representatives who have spent time incarnated on other planetary worlds and into advanced societies have received training in homeopathy or have been exposed to it at some point. Homeopathy is an advanced, non-invasive science used by numerous off-planetary civilisations at various stages of their evolution.

All advanced off-planetary civilisations use non-invasive healing methods, preferring to maintain the integrity of the walls of the energy field. When the layers of the energy field and shield skin are injured through particular invasive procedures, healing takes a significantly longer period of time to occur as the energy fields and shield skin must be rebuilt. An individual uses a great amount of life force in doing this. For this reason and others, advanced civilisations have devoted their resources to evolving their healing methods to become entirely non-invasive.

As a remedy for damaged energy fields and shield skins, Faith Healing and the 'laying on of hands', and Reiki, were anchored by the Central Sun. Healing through touch is understood by all hierarchies. However, the Central Sun has promoted the transfer of love, kindness, healing and life force energy through touch and massage for thousands of years. This is a core principle of nursing and all true nurses know the profound, beneficial results of kindness in touch and when handling a patient.

Keys to nursing in the physical plane are held by Central Sun and Bethlehem hierarchies. Members of these two hierarchies have dedicated themselves to developing methods and systems that promote dignity and compassion in medical facilities. Central Sun members have promoted the anchoring and distribution of keys to do with lifestyle medicine and functional medicine, a form of complementary medicine which seeks to identify the root cause of disease. Much of this wisdom has been shared with humanity by advanced societies beyond Earth via the Central Sun. Central Sun members have been working on a joint project to raise the vibrational frequency of allopathic medicine and its related pharmaceutical industry, and thus bring about its ascension through shining a light on the system itself. Lifestyle and functional medicine forms part of this shining light.

The Ayurvedic healing system, including pre-Ayurvedic wisdom and yoga were anchored and their keys distributed by the Shiva Hierarchy. Shiva also anchored the path of healing through working with the chakras as well as the Pranic healing system. Shiva oversees a variety of ancient healing practices including the Shamanic system co-created by human incarnated shamans and Mother Ayahuasca. As a member of the Children of Earth council, Mother Ayahuasca volunteers as an intermediary between human Initiates, their own higher councils and the other hierarchies within the Children of Earth councils. She provides a platform for deeper soul healing where the damages in a human being are the result of ancient rifts between the Children of Earth hierarchies. She helps repair these damages by encouraging Initiates to seek out and retrieve the lost aspects of themselves and over time, repair their relationships with the Children of Earth hierarchies. Mother Ayahuasca is a neutral member of the council; she is independent and keeps her own counsel. It is for this reason and others, that she is able to perform the role of intermediary and healer of the relationships between the hierarchies.

Pan Hierarchy anchored and distributed the keys to Anthroposophical medicine through their many incarnates who have supported it, including Rudolf Steiner, Ita Wegman and others.

Stem cell research (including other technologies that will soon be revealed to the public) was anchored by Atlantis Hierarchy. Israel Hierarchy holds keys to the ancient, off-planetary wisdom of the microbiome. Although this is old information to numerous civilisations beyond Earth, it is relatively new to humankind in this particular format. Israel Hierarchy is set to 'pioneer' the development of specific therapies using their knowledge of the microbiome and bacteria.

In addition to holding the keys to healing blood disorders,

strengthening and balancing the blood, Bethlehem has anchored across the continents many keys that would now be called 'folk' medicine. Bethlehem members hold keys to old, mystical plant lore, including the use of some psychedelic plants for healing and spiritual/psychic 'travel'. They hold keys to the use of plants in witchcraft for the purpose of healing and expanding awareness. Ishtar and Lemuria hierarchies also hold keys to what would be described as 'folk' medicine or old, antiquated tribal medicine. Still, much wisdom can be found in these old pathways. Alongside Tansafarie, Ishtar and Lemuria hold keys to the Voodoo traditions. Tansafarie anchored the keys to several ancient Shamanic forms of healing.

Mu has also anchored Shamanic healing as well as anchoring the keys belonging to the advanced Pleiadian healers and Sirian high council. Some of these keys were widely distributed in Ancient Egypt and formed part of the Ancient Egyptian healing system. The Central Sun also trained groups of healers in Ancient Egypt to become high priests and priestesses of healing and wisdom. Mu, along with the Lemurian Hierarchy and the crystal representatives of each hierarchy anchored the keys to crystal healing. Mu has dedicated much focus and energy to raising awareness in humanity of the benefits of colour as a healing tool.

Tansafarie has worked in conjunction with other hierarchies to anchor symbols for healing. With the ability to heal damages in the subconscious mind, neural pathways and areas of the mental field that link up to the star core command in a person's own hierarchy, symbol healing is not yet fully understood on Earth. However, it will be revealed as humanity progresses into the next age. The same can be said of sound healing. Although many healers are well aware of the power of sound and music, it will be 'discovered' and accepted by scientific communities into the future. The roots of sound healing, symbol healing and vibrational medicine and healing are ancient and can be traced back to civilisations that still exist on other planetary worlds. These ancient methods will rise in popularity in the decades to come.

Earth healing - the healing of damaged areas of the planet

as well as healing humans, trees, plants and animals through collaborating with the Earth, is of particular importance to the Tansafarie, Gaia, and Pan hierarchies. These hierarchies work together in many shared offices and on numerous joint projects to spread awareness of this important work. Ishtar and Bethlehem alongside Tansafarie, Pan, Gaia and Jerusalem jointly hold the keys to dowsing and share an office and council dedicated to it.

Even though the healing systems were anchored by the particular hierarchies mentioned, other hierarchies have contributed to and expanded upon the original offering by the hierarchy responsible. Chinese medicine is a good example of this. Although its original key was brought down from ancient realms by Jerusalem hierarchy, countless individuals from various hierarchies have contributed greatly to its development in the physical plane. Homeopathy was anchored by Jerusalem and Gaia and yet it was Samuel Hahnemann from Israel who did much to promote its assimilation into human society. Herbalism is another good example. All hierarchies have offices dedicated to the nature realms and specifically, working with the wisdom of plants.

Regardless of the modality that a hierarchy has chosen to develop, each healing system has its place and is embraced equally by the Spiritual Hierarchy for Earth. The chosen healing modality or modalities are delivered to Earth through a hierarchy's own healing offices. These offices may sit in any dimension from the fourth to seventh dimensions. The offices of healing in an individual hierarchy may collaborate with offices of healing from other hierarchies. These healing offices are separate from and in addition to any responsibilities hierarchies may hold in the High Council of Healers (discussed in the next chapter). The High Council of Healers as a separate system has a structure overseen by Lady Mary/Mother Mary. Lady Mary does not oversee or govern the offices of healing belonging to hierarchies other than her own. She may assist as an advisor if called upon.

The Office of Healing at the Earth/ Physical Level of the Hierarchy

These personal offices of healing belong to you and your hierarchy. They are not shared by other hierarchies or other beings. However, aspects or manifestations of you in another form may be present in these offices. These personal offices contain your direct aspects; that is, the higher parts of you personally.

Office of Healing

Every hierarchy has offices of healing. Such offices have the capacity to exist in all dimensions from the earth/physical levels to at least the seventh dimension. At the fifth, sixth and seventh dimensions where healing isn't required in the same way, the offices function to provide keys, technologies, knowledge and wisdom to all other levels within the hierarchy as well as the rest of the spiritual family. The offices exist at the earth/physical levels of the hierarchy when they have incarnated members who are vibrating at this level. By maintaining a presence in the earth/ physical levels of the hierarchy, these offices are able to support the human incarnated members of the hierarchy in their physical, emotional, mental and spiritual health in the third and fourth dimension until they ascend beyond this vibrational frequency.

To reach and maintain a higher vibrational frequency state, a human incarnate benefits from having health on all of these four levels. The offices of healing in a hierarchy have systems of support for all four levels. If physical wellness is lacking, health on the other three levels can do much to compensate for the deficit. However, if mental, emotional or spiritual health is lacking, these deficiencies will eventually drain the life force away from the physical body and undermine physical health. This can be seen where a person's diet is immaculate and their exercise routine perfect, and yet they do not experience complete wellness. By addressing the other three levels, they can truly and wholly benefit from all their efforts in diet and exercise.

It is also true that an eating plan rich in certain nutrients can be healing or corrective in areas of mental, emotional and spiritual/energetic health. In this way, food becomes a medicinal, healing path. The human race is making significant discoveries in this area of health and healing. In time, humans will come to fully understand the role of plants in sharing their life force with humans to restore the human energy field and raise the vibrational frequency of the entire body. Seeds (of true, natural origin) are a good example of this. Even after they are picked, the Initiate will be able to feel the storehouse of wisdom, information and vitality in the seed. When the seeds enter the body they inform the body's vibrational frequency and intelligence. Seeds are a living thing interacting with another living thing - your body. The same can be said of all seeds within fruits and vegetables. These seeds contain vital keys that will be understood by humans in the future.

The Initiate does not need to wait for this advanced knowledge to be 'discovered' or revealed by science. All information contained in every hierarchy's office of healing is open to the seeker and can be received now. Because deficits in the emotional, spiritual and mental bodies will undermine the strength of the physical body in the long term if not addressed, the Initiate's own office of healing is available immediately through meditation to provide support and guidance. The Initiate can connect to this office and anchor its wisdom into the physical plane through calling upon the office in meditation. Through meditation, the Initiate has the ability to interact with the Guardian of the Office of Healing. As a protector and guardian, this being has volunteered to protect its human charge and steer it always towards the path that best serves the Initiates long-term wellness and ascension.

A sub-aspect of one's Master Healer self, the protector guardian functions as a 'security guard' on the boundary of the human energy field. Certain factors can undermine the aspect's ability to function in this role and so if your energy field is easily compromised it is helpful to look at these factors. Firstly, the protector guardian interfaces with the shield skin (see definitions of terms section at the back of the book). The shield skin must be kept strong in order for the guardian to perform its function. Secondly, the protector guardian must be able to interact with its human charge at the very least when the body is sleeping. The mind needs to be as peacefully receptive as possible and this usually means sleeping without being under the influence of artificial stimulants such as substances. It is helpful for the mind to be free of external imagery and thoughts where possible, which generally means allowing some space between watching movies/ television etc and falling asleep. We have observed in these modern times that over-exposure to WIFI has inhibited many protector guardians' abilities to interact with their incarnated human aspect.

Depending upon the hierarchy, the office of healing may also contain healing angels and an ancient herbalist. The healing angel is both a representative of the Angelic Hierarchy and an angelic being from your own hierarchy. This is the angelic aspect of the Master Healer. The ancient herbalist is the aspect of you who has trained in the nature realms with the elemental kingdom, possibly fairies, flower spirits and tree beings and has the capacity to receive telepathic instruction from the plants and trees. The ancient herbalist is a sub-aspect of the Master Healer aspect of you who works through this office.

Another facet of the Master Healer is the shamanic aspect of you who also works from this office. This is the aspect of you trained to journey through many planes of existence to reclaim lost parts of yourself. This type of journeying is vital to healing, as a lost part of yourself can deplete the strength of your physical body, and disrupt your mental and emotional state. It can also create a weakness in your energy field as it can lead to a siphon causing the energy field to lose qi- vital energy or life force. Pure, primordial qi flows from the universal level of your hierarchy (see hierarchy diagram) as well as that which lies beyond your hierarchy. It flows through every office, level and aspect, and down into you, the human representative of your hierarchy on Earth. A lost aspect of yourself creates a 'leak in the bucket'. Where your qi or life force would otherwise be sealed in your body and energy fields, it 'runs out' towards the lost aspect in an effort to sustain the aspect. When all aspects are home with you, your qi is also home with you.

The Aspects of Your Master Healer Self Diagram

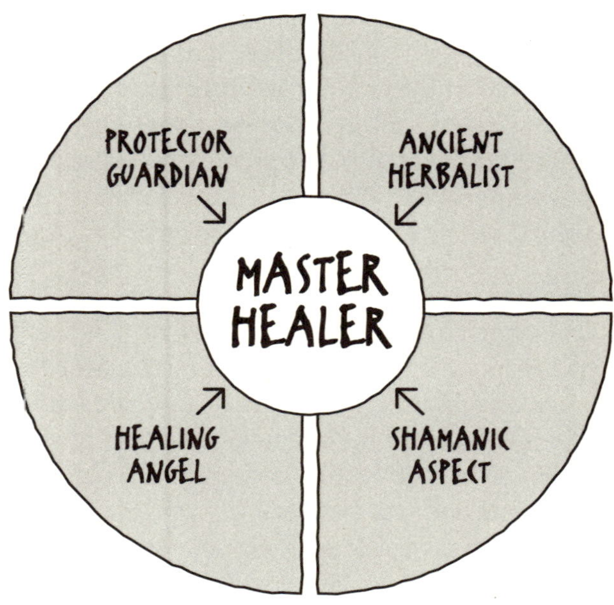

CHAPTER EIGHTEEN

The Fifth Dimensional levels of the Spiritual Hierarchy for Earth

As discussed at the beginning of Chapter Two, every human incarnate is automatically connected to the Cosmic Hierarchy. The Cosmic Hierarchy consists of all things within this our universe including the planets of this solar system. The Spiritual Hierarchy for Earth was designed by the Cosmic Hierarchy as a structure that pooled all of the resources together so that planet Earth could be created and maintained. It is important that the two structures are not confused, for although all incarnations on Earth are connected to the Cosmic Hierarchy by way of their being part of creation in our universe, not all Cosmic Hierarchy members belong to the Spiritual Hierarchy for Earth for not all are part of the Earth assignment.

The Spiritual Hierarchy for Earth is an extension of Christ's House whose origins are not of Earth (as mentioned earlier in the text, the term 'Christ' is used here not to make a religious statement, but to refer to that frequency of the Central Sun Hierarchy, which for ease of understanding is labeled 'the Christ').

Christ's House is an extension of the Central Sun and forms part of the tactical arm of support for the healing mission on Earth. The Christ frequency developed this tactical arm within the fifth dimension to support the mission (and also created the fifth dimension itself). Mother Mary developed the High Council of Healers to lead the healing arm of the mission and present opportunities for the healing of the All. The fifth dimension is the working base of the High Council of Healers and is also a place of rest for all members of the mission and Christ's household, or indeed, the family of Christ. There are many other beings of light who contribute to the mission in ways that draw on their ancient skills and experience. These beings bring technical support and the agreement to strengthen the healing mission by incorporating the frequencies and keys that they hold into the mission's toolbox. They are friends of the mission and are ancient brothers and sisters and family members of the Central Sun.

The Spiritual Hierarchy for Earth was created to create Earth and to house beings who wished to ascend collectively and individually over the course of many billions of years. It has seen many dark days and many days of celebration. When the fifth dimension was created by the Central Sun, it allowed for a safe realm where the Law of One, created by that which is Pure and One, would be lived by and adhered to and understood to be Truth and Law of the highest kind. This fifth dimension is a place of rest for beings who have come from higher planes well beyond the fifth dimension, to be in service to the Spiritual Hierarchy for Earth and humanity and Earth, by serving in the Spiritual Hierarchy for Earth in a human body on Earth. These beings, although unconditional in their love for man, requested a place of rest where the Truth would be known and no duality resided. Thus is the fifth dimension a gift of gratitude to them for their divine service and their incarnation into the lower worlds so that the lower worlds and all that inhabits them could be freed from their pain, suffering and isolation.

Your interest in this book suggests that your contribution to the mission is either through your being a member of the Christ household, indeed one of the Central Sun's direct creations and manifestations, or a part of the Central Sun's extended family as a brother or sister hierarchy or a family member hierarchy. Remembering your hierarchy's role plays an integral part in your initiation as a healer and may be helpful in understanding the role your multidimensional self plays in the mission to return humanity to grace.

Meditations can assist you to reclaim all of your memory banks as they can assist you to piece together the puzzle so that your ancient history is known to you and you are able to draw upon this information when approaching the history of the Cosmic Hierarchy as a whole. Meditation can assist you to understand at an experiential level, what your mission is and where to place your focus to ensure that your mission is fulfilled to the highest degree. For this to occur, set an intention in your mind and heart for it to be so. Close your eyes in meditation and call Christ to you. Allow this energy of divinity to lead you, to teach you and to show you your highest path home to the full realisation of who you truly are. Your light will grow and expand through this process, the vibrational frequency of your energy field will rise, and each time you interact with Christ in this way you will have different experiences, all designed to raise you up and return you home.

In addition to Christ's House, The Spiritual Hierarchy for Earth has contained within it, a structure that houses many sub-councils that come together to form the High Council of Healers. This high council has members who, throughout history, have been sent to incarnate on Earth. Primarily, the members sit in the fifth dimension, however, there are human incarnated members who also sit in the fourth dimension and many Initiates in training in human and other forms also sitting in the fourth dimension.

Divine Will oversees this High Council and it is automatically aligned to the Law of One. Mother Mary is the overseeing guardian of the council and she is instructed by her highest self, the Divine Spirit, the Invisible Virgin Spirit.

The High Council of Healers is explained in detail below so that you, the Initiate, will come to locate your current place in the High Council of Healers and examine yourself in relation to your assignment on Earth. As an Initiate, you will come to know your place of rest in this life as the fifth dimension, and through your meditations you reinforce your commitment to return here as often as possible with the intention of ascending to live in this realm while maintaining a human body simultaneously.

The High Council of Healers and Your Potential Healing Assignment

The High Council of Healers existed before human beings began populating Earth in any great number, before human beings came to Earth to establish tribes, colonies and civilisations. The council's primary residence was in the fifth dimensional communities in the planetary realm known as Sirius.

The High Council of Healers consists of advanced beings with technological expertise, angelic beings within the celestial frequencies and archangels of the nature kingdoms and sea realms. Indeed, the council is made up of a diverse range of beings from many spiritual families, realms and frequency bands. All of the knowledge, wisdom and technology required to correct any imbalance within any human or animal vehicle, is contained in the High Council of Healers.

While on Earth, the council works directly with the nature and sea realms. Many potent medicines able to restore human beings' immune systems are found in nature and in the seas. The council directs physically incarnated human healers to seek out these cures found within their own environments as a way of holistically restoring balance to the entire person – the emotional, physical and etheric bodies of a human, as well as his mind.

This approach enables a human to make his peace with Earth and create harmonious connections between his body and the waves of energy emanating from him, and the Earth kingdoms. This is essential for true and lasting healing to occur. The awareness of a human being's interconnectedness with its environment is a key that all competent healers possess.

The High Council of Healers is organised within a structure that allows for the competent orchestration of the Assignment of Healers on Earth. The Assignment of Healers is, in its most basic description, a blueprint for the complete healing of the Earth, humans, and all realms and creatures connected to the Earth. This assignment has been in operation for thousands of years and will continue to unfold until all things connected to the Earth are restored to their rightful balance that allows for the safe and clear path of natural evolution to present and be made available to all creation.

Ancient Healers

Ancient Healers are the Shambhala Council Elders who work within the Human Hierarchy to restore balance between this hierarchy and other species. The Human Hierarchy has billions of members, each connected to their own spiritual hierarchy. The ancient healers do not work with humans through direct service to them individually, but serve the human hierarchy as a whole. They oversee the ascension of the human hierarchy from a higher or overlighting perspective rather than from a 'hands on' or active participating level.

The ancient healers plan and alter the blueprint of the Human Hierarchy drawing from the perspective they gain through seeing the overview of human existence on Earth. Through observing the progress of the human species throughout humanity's entire existence, their perspective is highly regarded and extremely useful within the High Council of Healers and the Spiritual Hierarchy for Earth. The ancient healers also advise councils and offices within the galactic levels of individual hierarchies and within the universal councils that organise many facets of the manifested universe.

In order to preserve their detached and overseeing state,

those serving on the council of ancient healers are generally not permitted to incarnate: to incarnate would see a significant change in their vibrational frequency as these ones are primarily sixth dimensional.

Universal Healers

Universal healers are called to many realms and dimensions within the universe that intend to lift their civilisation or planetary world or realm to seventh dimensional consciousness. Their role is highly technical and advanced. Universal healers deal with raising the vibrational frequency of beings, species and physical vicinities into the seventh dimension and assist them to apply their new experience and manifestation in a practical way in their realm, world, dimension etc.

This path and the universal healers who orchestrate it will not be needed on Earth to serve humanity in general for quite some time. However, individual aspirants may call upon these divine beings to guide them in their transition to seventh dimensional experience and practical living.

Galactic Healers

The galactic level of one's hierarchy exists in the etheric and vibrates within the frequency range of the fourth dimension. It is not until the upper galactic level that the etheric realm becomes fifth dimensional. There are many councils that operate from this level in the hierarchy, including the galactic councils, planetary councils, the council of the Mothership, and one's own Council of Twelve (the 'twelve' being the major extensions of one's soul and can be seen as the twelve elders of one's hierarchy).

It is in the core galactic council that all hierarchies, including one's own, congregate for the purpose of communicating in a structured and unified way. Many of the decisions affecting the spiritual hierarchy for Earth and other hierarchies in the galaxy are made in these councils. Mandatory council meetings are held regularly in the galactic council level where one's hierarchy meets with other hierarchies. Before and after a major crisis on Earth, all hierarchies are required to meet at the galactic council level to discuss matters. This is a responsibility each hierarchy has as being part of the Ancient Spiritual Family and Spiritual Hierarchy for Earth.

Being consciously connected to one's own galactic council has many benefits in assisting the human self to understand the various occurrences on Earth. It is from this council that the human self receives the overview or higher perspective on the unfolding of events on Earth. Human incarnates consciously connected to this council receive an understanding of the Earth's blueprint and how they individually contribute to Earth's highest good.

Not all human incarnates connected to their own galactic councils will be galactic healers in the defined role of assisting other hierarchies to heal their own galactic councils or by promoting the work of the galactic councils in the physical plane. Those who carry the role and title 'galactic healer' work actively to assist the higher purpose of the council in the physical plane of Earth. In this way, they are engaged with the council's agenda and identify opportunities to further the council's work on Earth.

Galactic healers are concerned with the galactic levels within individual hierarchies and the Spiritual Hierarchy for Earth. They may hold their roles for a short period of time while balancing and resolving the galactic level councils and offices within their own hierarchies and may hold this role as well as holding the role as 'Earth Healer' or even 'Pleiadian Healer' in a human body in the Earth's physical plane. When actively holding the galactic healer role and title, they live and work from the galactic levels of their own hierarchy.

They generally hold an advanced level of understanding of spiritual technology, such as symbols, holograms, heliography, and universal symbols and languages that are recognised throughout the galaxy and not just on Earth.

In the physical plane, incarnated galactic healers may channel this information through their artwork, designs and possibly their music or sound healing investigations. They will seek knowledge of the healing benefits of coded drawings and designs, and sounds. They are interested in this because innately they know that the spiritual technology serves to heal the galactic levels. Galactic healers may be called upon to produce artwork either through traditional mediums or computerised mediums, which act as triggers or activators of dormant memory banks in others. These artworks include sacred and sometimes secret 'codes', which are read by the technology contained in the blueprints of human beings that begin to activate as the human awakens and ascends.

Galactic healers may be called upon by their higher councils to perform 'hands on healing' sessions or 'sound therapy' sessions when working with human beings who require assistance in connecting with their own galactic levels and councils. In such instances, a galactic healer may channel through the information required for connection to occur and the channelling may take the form of 'toning' (bringing through the frequencies that will serve connection by using one's voice to make healing and connecting sounds), as well as simply channelling energy through the crown, through the hands and body, to be anchored to the Earth through the feet.

Planetary Healers

Planetary healers work to support Earth and surrounding planets as Earth ascends at this time. They do not usually incarnate into human bodies to fulfil their tasks as planetary healers although they may have had experience in human bodies. This is primarily because they are more effective in bodies that allow them to travel freely between planetary worlds. A human body is more restricting and at present does not allow for interplanetary travel.

Planetary healers exist in all dimensions from fourth to seventh and may be of Sirian, Pleiadian, Neptunian, Venetian/ Venusian, Martian or of other origins. They usually call one planetary world home although they may have experience in various planetary worlds. Their role allows them to oversee the balancing ascension and overall evolution of planetary worlds individually and as part of a planetary family.

Earth Healers

Earth Healers are involved directly with the physical plane and require incarnation on Earth in some form in order to facilitate interaction between the frequencies they hold and the frequencies of the Earth plane. They require a physical vehicle and may choose the body of a human being or an animal. Generally, if an animal's body is chosen, it will be one that is able to interact with human beings in some way to inspire a human or a group of humans to be the source of change and healing in the world. Examples are: a dog or cat which enters the home of a human family; an animal which requires rescuing and in so doing, inspires the coming together and community participation of a group of humans; a horse who teaches a human to surrender his/her pain and return to the Divine Rhythm of all things.

If a human body is chosen, the human being will undergo a series of challenges and lessons to provide adequate opportunity for the key requirements needed for healing to develop. Key requirements that a healer on Earth must cultivate in order to be effective as a healer are: discernment, empathy and compassion, the ability to hear the universal sound, and the ability to observe.

The universal sound is an eternal frequency. It exists throughout all time and place, has always existed, and will always exist. A healer who attunes to this universal sound is reminded regularly of the universal laws and truth. This prevents illusions or false belief systems from developing. The only requirement for hearing the universal sound is the willingness in the Initiate to surrender the world as he/she currently experiences and perceives it and allow the universal sound to begin a process of re-educating and fine-tuning the body and mind. This is a process that cannot be easily mapped out as to provide a formula or list of expected experiences or instructions.

The universal sound is a great force in its own right and a great master teacher. It takes each Initiate on an individual case-by-case level and re-educates the individual according to his own unique needs and manifestation in the human experience. This process unfolds differently for each Initiate because of the variations in every individual Initiate. The universal sound underpins all creation.

Experience the universal sound through attaining silence in the mind, surrendering attachment and beliefs about the physical world, allowing the breath – its gentle rhythm – to bring stillness to body and mind, and/or achieve this experience while being in nature. When done with conscious intent, it is possible with complete surrender to achieve connection. An exhilarating experience such as riding a wave, being in the middle of a storm without fear, and swimming in water provides an opportunity to connect with the universal sound. An Initiate may also connect to the universal sound and unify with it upon leaving the body at the time of death or while giving birth to a child. When a baby enters the birth canal, this can signal a point of release in the mother's body and trigger the level of surrender required to connect her with the universal sound.

Pleiadian Healers

There is a smaller group of healers that must be mentioned as a very small number of readers will require the keys below. This group is known as the Pleiadian Healers. There are several thousand incarnated on Earth at the moment, indeed not as many as there will be. As Earth ascends, more Pleiadian healers of fifth dimensional consciousness will return the Earth. Up until this time, many Pleiadian healers have incarnated on Earth to resolve personal karma, the collective karma of the Pleiadians, and lay the foundation for complete human and Earth healing by releasing keys into Earth and into the consciousness of humankind. These keys will provide the building blocks for Pleiadian healers incarnating in the future to create a structure of advanced healing Earth and humans alike.

These future Pleiadian healers will be the doctors, surgeons, scientists and energetic healers of human and Earth. They will 'discover' advanced technologies, reveal mysteries, and provide answers that will lift the scientific world to a new level of understanding, simply by locating the ancient memory banks and keys within them and decoding and interpreting the keys left by the past Pleiadian healers incarnated on Earth.

Originally, prior to the first human incarnation of a Pleiadian healer, the Pleiadian healers resided in the Pleiades and used their advanced genetic technology to 'seed' other planetary worlds. Their information allowed for the creation of species in various planetary worlds and then for the evolution of these species in their own natural way, according to and influenced by the energetic and environmental conditions of the planetary world in question. This expression of genetic exploration by the Pleiadians allowed for the great expansion of the All That Is.

When the Pleiadians began to express their need for genetic exploration within the physical perimeters of Earth, many other beings who also had an interest in Earth, but who were not Pleiadian, began negotiating terms with the Pleiadians. This led to tension and the restricting of information by the Pleiadians with other beings and vice versa. There were various councils who attempted to mediate these negotiations. The realm of Earth became embroiled in a competition for territory in which to conduct and explore the outcomes of genetic experiments. From this, a karmic cycle was set in motion that is still revealing itself to this day. The karmic wheel is still turning for the majority of humans who were involved in or affected by the decisions made at that time in Earth's history. Only right action and compassion will allow the cycle to close and the wheel to stop turning.

Many thousands of years ago, and in response to this conflict and karmic cycle, many Pleiadians who held the appropriate qualities coordinated their abilities and formed the Council of Pleiadian Healers. This council continues to operate at many levels and in many planetary worlds, including Earth. The council recognises the need for the ancient wisdom of the Pleiadians to balance the Pleiadians' immense power, and form ethical boundaries within the colonies and civilisations of its genetic offspring. In short, the council seeks to implement the Law of One within all planetary worlds where its genetic offspring reside.

As the ancient elders, indeed the genetic ancestors of many species within many planetary worlds, the Pleiadians recognise the responsibility to establish opportunities for species to be educated in the harmonising benefits of aligning to universal law (the Law of One). The Law of One ensures that creation is permitted and able to evolve without the risk of enslavement by an opportunistic or malevolent species. Such species would seek to take advantage of younger species or species that had not yet become aware of existence beyond the third dimensional plane. This precise scenario has occurred on Earth on numerous occasions, but most intensely at the time humans of various cultures consider the 'fall from grace'; that is, at the time when the 'gods' and/or the ancient ancestors of humans became involved in competition which resulted in that first turn of the karmic wheel on Earth. Thus, in the case of the Pleiadians and the situation outlined above, they and their genetic offspring were joined through pain and confusion in a way that had never before occurred so directly in any other planetary world that they had seeded.

The forming of the Council of Pleiadian Healers became an essential component of the healing of human and Pleiadian, and the many Pleiadians who subsequently became human through the necessary incarnation process designed to eventually free them of their karmic responsibility to Earth and their earth-based genetic offspring. (Please note that although the Israel Hierarchy created the first human being, the Pleiadians contributed significant DNA and genetic technology to the human vehicle). By accepting a human body, it was understood that Pleiadians would develop sufficient compassion for the human race and that their compassion would serve as part of a healing force to correct past mistakes. The ancients knew that the root key to all healing is deep compassion. In order for healing to occur, the conditions need to be correct. Deep compassion and/or the willingness to surrender to deep compassion are the correct conditions. One may also require patience without fear, which may be defined as simply, trust. These conditions form the foundation that allows for deep healing and form part of the keys offered by the Council of Pleiadian Healers. The council's work is to promote the establishment of these conditions on Earth and in the human consciousness. The new Pleiadian healers who will incarnate in the future will carry these keys as have all incarnated Pleiadian healers, and will have greater scope to integrate them into the modern human world.

The several thousand Pleiadian healers on Earth currently are for the most part, aware of their assignments and agreements. They work in the healing field either from a scientific or spiritual perspective, or both. They recognise their individual work in contributing to the greater work of the Pleiadian task force of Earth and the Council of Pleiadian Healers which exists in the upper fourth and fifth dimensions.

Of the current physically incarnated Pleiadian healers, most are aware of their status as healers and their assignments as human beings on Earth. The remainder will awaken within the next ten years. These ones are either newly incarnated and are currently experiencing their childhoods or adolescences, or are adults entering the initial phase of awakening right now. Those who are aware of their status as Pleiadian healers are either working in their right assignments or will transition onto their higher path over the next five to ten years. This is in accordance to the divine blueprint of the Council of Pleiadian Healers.

Their assignments will require them to be involved in the healing of individuals, groups, and Earth. The primary focus of all Pleiadian healers is and will be healing and to plant keys that aid in establishing the conditions that allow for healing to occur. The Pleiadian healers are trained extensively in their higher council prior to incarnation on Earth. Their training once they arrive on Earth is not in learning new things, but in remembering their ancient connection to the Pleiades and the power and wisdom in themselves. Thus, the most important training is the inner exploration required to remember these things. Inner exploration consists primarily of inner reflection, meditation, and opening one's channels and memory banks so that full awakening and remembering occurs.

Central Sun as the Guardian of the Spiritual Hierarchy for Earth

As you will observe through the diagram, the Spiritual Hierarchy for Earth is supported by the two 'arms' above it, the High Council of Healers arm, described in detail above, and Christ's House arm. Above Christ's House is the Office of the Central Sun, which begins the section of the structure under Central Sun hierarchy jurisdiction. Within this section, we find councils and offices such as the Council of Balance and Justice and the High Council of the Law of One, overseen by a Divine Will office.

You may wonder why these offices are under Central Sun hierarchy jurisdiction. The Spiritual Hierarchy for Earth has had a colourful history. Over the course of many millions of years, various individual hierarchies that come together to make up the Spiritual Hierarchy for Earth have experimented with their own paths and potential. At times these experiments may have appeared in conflict with the general harmony of other hierarchies. Always, these conflicts remained at the third and fourth dimensional levels and never at the fifth dimensional levels and above.

The Central Sun Hierarchy has always maintained its alignment to Divine Will and has never deviated from this for the purpose of experimentation etc. During times when the Spiritual Hierarchy for Earth has had some of its founding hierarchies in conflict, the Central Sun Hierarchy has provided a clear and divinely aligned focus from which to navigate the direction of the entire structure. In addition to this, the offices it holds in its jurisdiction on behalf of the Spiritual Hierarchy for Earth remain fifth dimensional and have thus never encountered

Central Sun as Guardian of the Spiritual Hierarchy for Earth Diagram

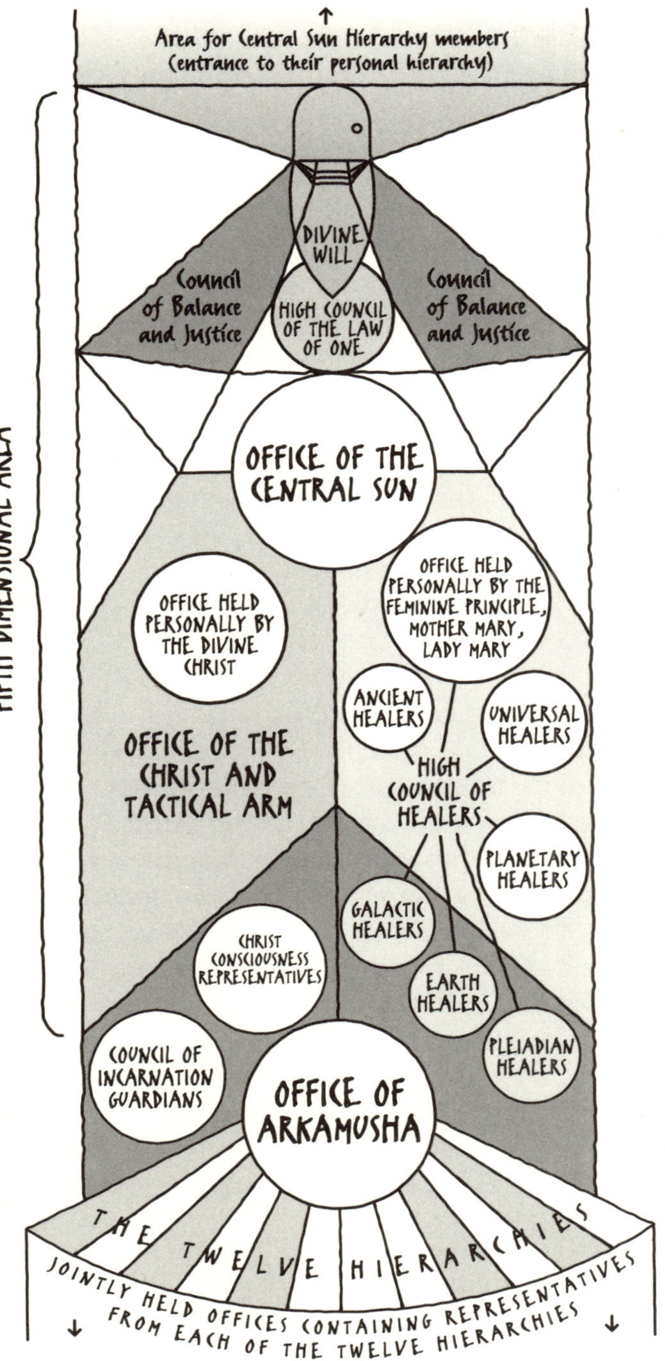

infiltration from any of the experiments of other hierarchies. For these reasons and others, it has been essential to ensure the main governing offices are within the protective band of the Central Sun's jurisdiction, thus maintaining their integrity and divine alignment.

As the guardian of the Spiritual Hierarchy for Earth, the Central Sun has embraced the role of raising the vibrational frequency of the entire structure. In order to do this on the earthly plane, it has sent large numbers of aspects to incarnate into human form and has equipped them with extensive gifts, tools and abilities (see chapter on the Central Sun Hierarchy). In the higher levels, it supports the entire Ancient Spiritual Family and Spiritual Hierarchy for Earth through appointing a council of beings who act as the structure's guardian. This council sits in the Office of the Central Sun. The will of this council is governed by the Office of Christ, which provides the tactical support to fulfil the directions of the guardian council.

The Council of Balance and Justice for the Spiritual Hierarchy for Earth

The Council of Balance and Justice for the Spiritual Hierarchy for Earth functions in the same way as the Council of Balance and Justice within a person's own hierarchy. It acts as a grounding frequency for all offices, becoming their 'true north' or point of alignment. All twelve hierarchies that make up the Spiritual Hierarchy for Earth are able to seek the wise council of this section of the structure and use the guidance received to steer their own aspects, offices and councils. This council works in conjunction with the High Council of the Law of One, which provides support to all councils to make decisions that are aligned to the Law of One. The Law declares that: *When all are allowed to be within their frequencies, all shall come into peace and harmony.*

Council of Christ Consciousness Companions

Every human incarnate has a Christ Consciousness Companion assigned to their spiritual path. It is an individual's choice whether or not to make use of this opportunity during their lifetime. This being works as a guide, instructing you in the principles of compassion, trust, allowing and integrity. The Council of Christ Consciousness Companions sits at the fifth dimensional levels of the Spiritual Hierarchy for Earth.

This council serves the mission of Christ's House through trained Christ Consciousness Companions. Christ Consciousness Companions are Masters initiated through specialised training with Christ and have attained Christ Consciousness. The training process can be likened to an apprenticeship whereby the apprentice must demonstrate a commitment to the principles that define Christ Consciousness. Such principles include compassion, trust, allowing all things to be and flow as they need to, and integrity.

Once a Master has been initiated, the Master is then assigned to an individual who wishes to attain Christ Consciousness this lifetime, and live these principles within his/her daily life. Christ Consciousness Companions work from the Sun Level of the Initiate's own hierarchy and act as a bridge between the Initiate in the physical plane of Earth and their own Sun Level vibration.

The Companion remains very close to his/her human apprentice and has an active role in their physical life, often 'living' in or close to their apprentice's energy field. The Companion observes their apprentice during the day and then teaches them when they sleep at night. Such teachings include learning how to strengthen Christ energies and principles in daily life and relationships with others. The Christ Consciousness Companion Council focuses a great deal on thought vibration and emotion, training Initiates to adopt higher frequency thought forms and strengthen these through the use of beneficial feelings, which are sent into the higher, selected thoughts to further energise them.

Fifth Dimensional Realms in Service to the Spiritual Hierarchy for Earth

Arcadia

Arcadia was created by Jerusalem and Central Sun hierarchies. It holds fifth dimensional frequencies as well as the frequencies of higher dimensions. Lady Mary who is the Lady of the Flowers created the original rose in Arcadia, and she blooms there still. Arcadia is also the birth place of the Rosaceae species and home to the flower spirits of the Rosaceae species. Many species have evolved from the cradle that is Arcadia. It is a sanctuary and a place of awe-inspiring beauty.

Avalon

Birthed by the Bethlehem Hierarchy, Avalon sits primarily in the fifth dimension. As a transportable realm, it has the ability to move its location. Currently, it resides above Glastonbury in England as it has for thousands of years.

Entry into Avalon is by invitation only. The Initiate must have either integrated fifth dimensional frequencies or demonstrate an intention to do so before an invitation is issued. Occasionally 'friends of Avalon'- Initiates who have supported or served Avalon during its many centuries stationed on Earth or who have been ordained as priests and priestesses of the Order of Avalon, but who are not of the Bethlehem Hierarchy, will receive open invitations whereby they are permitted to come and go from the realm as they please. The Guardians of Avalon, who are fully enlightened members of the Bethlehem Hierarchy, oversee entry into this realm.

Avalon holds the energy for the return of the divine feminine on Earth. Within this assignment, Avalon recognises the importance of the divine masculine also, and holds the energy for the balancing of the two energies on Earth as they anchor and integrate into future societies.

Many hierarchies have contributed to Avalon by way of sharing keys with this sacred vicinity. For example, Pan Hierarchy contributes the frequency of the Bard and the sacred music and sounds to the realm. Jerusalem Hierarchy contributes the holy apple trees to the realm. Through the office of the Lady of the Lake, Jerusalem Hierarchy provides essential support to the work of the realm in the physical world.

Kunlun

Kunlun is a fifth dimensional realm with an active, accessible fourth dimensional bridge that allows for upper fourth dimensional humans to communicate and interact with its residents. Because Kunlun has the capacity to hold both upper fourth and fifth dimensional frequencies, it can accept Initiates who are close to attaining degrees of enlightenment and immortality and who require assistance from those who have previously attained the level themselves.

Like Avalon, Kunlun exists to hold the energy for the ascension of humanity and also as a dwelling place for higher beings. Although it once interacted more closely with humanity, like Avalon it has withdrawn from such close association. However, human seekers with genuine benevolent intention to connect with Kunlun's inhabitants and share in its keys may be granted access in meditation or dream.

Shambhala

The Council of Elders, who are ninth to twelfth dimensional beings, sits also on the Council of Shambhala, which is capable of operating in the fifth and sixth dimensions simultaneously. This council is overseen by the Honourable Sanat Kumara, the Ancient of Days, of Tansafarie. Ancient Mother Bethlehem manifests herself as the council fire in the centre of the council as well as a member of the Council of Elders and the Council of Shambhala.

This council and its realm provide keys of the highest frequency to the All That Is. This realm has a presence on Earth, but its presence is considered only a small outpost in comparison to the expanse that is Shambhala. Shambhala can be considered one of many homes of the Gods. It is a sanctuary for the Ancient Mothers and Ancient Fathers of this universe and many other universes. Its majestic terrain stretches across galaxies and cannot be fully fathomed by the human mind at this time. However, some humans have glimpsed the possibilities, having been gifted this experience by the Council itself.

The presence of the small outpost on Earth, and more specifically, *in* Earth is a gift of divine compassion by the Elders of the universe. It serves as inspiration and motivation for all Initiates to continue their efforts to reconnect and remember the truth of who they are. Shambhala emits frequencies and radiations of higher thought forms and codes. These codes are often read by the templates within Initiates who have reached certain stages of awakening and may serve to awaken dormant, ancient memories. The codes activate keys in the energetic structures of the Initiate that assist in clearing, ascension and reconnection.

Shambhala is of the greatest assistance to Initiates who have already moved beyond the middle band of the fourth dimension and are requiring additional support to navigate the final bands before the gates of the fifth dimension. This support may come while the Initiate is still in human form, but it most often comes upon the release of the Initiate from the physical body as the spirit is seeking to reach the highest vibrational frequency possible during this important transit. Many Initiates have reached the Ascended Master Level through the support of this realm and council.

Overseeing Offices within the Spiritual Hierarchy for Earth in the Fifth Dimension

Council of Incarnation Guardians

The Council of Incarnation Guardians provides support to the individual incarnation teams and incarnation councils of the twelve hierarchies. This council does not facilitate the mechanics of incarnation such as readying the blueprints and organising the incarnating aspect's support teams, but acts within the boundaries of its advisory role. Occasionally it will be called upon to mediate between hierarchies where the plans of one hierarchy to incarnate one of their aspects affect the incarnation plans for an aspect of a different hierarchy.

Council of Arkamusha

The title 'Arkamusha' is the umbrella name given to the twelve hierarchies that come together to form our Ancient Spiritual Family. The Council of Arkamusha is the overseeing and guardian council of the Ancient Spiritual Family. It supports the twelve hierarchies by offering wise counsel, mediation, and access to an extensive treasure chest of keys, gifts, tools and abilities. The Council of Arkamusha consists of fifth dimensional and higher representatives of each of the twelve hierarchies. These representatives are generally ancient masculine and feminine beings who sit within the governing councils of their own hierarchies and are very often titled as the 'grandmother' and 'grandfather' or 'elder' aspects of their hierarchies.

Keys as part of a Hierarchy's Assignment within the Spiritual Hierarchy for Earth

Keys are energetic constructs that act as 'openers' into specific frequencies. Without them, these specific frequencies are inaccessible. Each hierarchy is responsible for being a caretaker of a ring of keys. Some of the keys on this ring are for the hierarchy's own use and cannot be accessed by other hierarchies. These types of keys relate to the intimate functioning of the hierarchy and there are many such keys, too numerous to elaborate here.

The remaining keys on the ring are part of that hierarchy's contribution to the All That Is, and although held by the contributing hierarchy, may be utilised by other hierarchies under certain conditions. Where the keys are regulated or made accessible to the All That Is through an overseeing or governing council made up of representatives from other hierarchies, all members of the council have direct access to the keys.

In any situation where council members are privileged with the responsibility of representing keys, they will contribute their own abilities and frequencies to magnifying the unique characteristics and essence of the keys through the realms and frequencies of which they form a part. The council member from another hierarchy brings with her by way of her membership in the council, the keys to her own realms and frequencies.

By collaborating through its keys with other hierarchies, a hierarchy expands itself and creates for itself its purpose. Likewise, when a human being identifies his unique skill and shares this or works with others to distribute his gifts throughout the family/community/society/the world, he creates for himself his purpose and this in turn enriches his understanding of the meaning of his life or reason for his incarnation. This understanding will eventually lead him to the discovery in the physical plane of his hierarchy's keys – his hierarchy's unique contribution to the All That Is.

Through a vocational path, one can often find clues to discovering one's hierarchy's keys, but this can be said equally of those who, outside their occupation, pursue an interest that engages them on a lifelong quest. For those who have recognised the need to seek beyond formal work structures to satisfy their deepest yearnings and fortunate enough to be able to engage in such a quest, this life's work and service becomes a physical manifestation of their hierarchy's keys in the Earth's plane.

CHAPTER NINETEEN

Seven Structures Collaborating with the Spiritual Hierarchy for Earth

As we have already discussed, there are twelve hierarchies in the Ancient Spiritual Family that are stationed here, fulfilling the Earth assignment at these moments in time. In the All That Is, there are also seven structures that function as hierarchies, collaborating with the Spiritual Hierarchy for Earth. These seven structures are different from the twelve. The twelve are formed by and based upon the twelve signature frequencies created by our Divine Father and Divine Mother. The seven structures are made up of many representatives from all of the twelve hierarchies. These representatives carry the signature frequency of their respective hierarchies as well as the specific frequency code of the structures they serve. They may belong to more than one of the seven structures listed below.

The Angelic Family

The first of the seven structures is the angelic family hierarchy. All members within this structure belong to their own hierarchies, but also carry an angelic frequency. They were born through their own hierarchy in collaboration with the angelic family structure.

For example, Archangel Raphael belongs to the angelic family structure, but he also belongs to his own Jerusalem Hierarchy, which is his signature frequency. He is one of many angelic representatives of the Jerusalem hierarchy. Archangel Michael belongs to the Central Sun Hierarchy and he also serves the angelic family structure as a member. The Central Sun Hierarchy is present at the birth of all angelic beings.

The Elemental Family

The second structure is the elemental family hierarchy, which houses beings from the nature realms. Such beings include: the dwarves, fairies, elves; all manner of sprites from the woodland to the water sprites, guardians of sacred places and angelic beings of the nature realms (who also sit in the angelic structure).

This elemental structure is used to populate planets that are in themselves collaborations made up of the contributions from many hierarchies. The structure anchors itself on the planet and then its organisational arm moves about establishing the nature realms upon that planet. Once the nature realms are established, the structure maintains the realms over billions of years. Beings who make up the elemental family structure come from different hierarchies and maintain their core connection to their respective hierarchies even when sent on assignment by the Elemental Hierarchy.

Beings are not birthed in collaboration with this hierarchy. They come from their own hierarchies and join this one in addition to their own for the purpose of facilitating complex assignments on various planetary worlds in an organised and coherent way.

The Sirian Family

The third structure is the Sirian family hierarchy. This structure was born out of the Mu Hierarchy and is, in essence, an arm of Mu. Mu invited other hierarchies to incarnate aspects of themselves into Mu/Sirian genetics to expand and evolve the race and also as a gift for the other hierarchies to expand themselves. Like the human incarnation process, when a being incarnates into a Sirian body on Sirius, the essence of that being returns home to its own hierarchy when it is ready to leave the incarnation (some Sirians have remained alive since their original incarnations and have not 'died').

Within the Sirian family structure is the Sirian royal line. This royal line consists of the beings, Lord and Lady Sirius, and all of their personal aspects and creations. The royal line is Lord and Lady Sirius' own 'hierarchy' contained within the structure of the Sirian family hierarchy structure. This royal line is of the Mu Hierarchy signature frequency. The Sirian office of Lord and Lady Sirius (the 'Lord' and 'Lady' simply means the masculine and feminine frequencies of the Sirian royal lineage) is the overseeing office of the entire Sirian race. This overseeing office can only ever be held by the Lord and Lady Sirius of the Mu Hierarchy.

The Sirian High Council is made up of Lord and Lady Sirius' Council of Twelve as well as representatives from other arms of the Mu Hierarchy with Sirian aspects. At times, Sirian aspects from other hierarchies have also served on the council.

The Human Family

The Human Hierarchy works in exactly the same way. The original blueprint for the human body prototype was created by Israel Hierarchy. Other hierarchies collaborated with the project when it was decided that the human prototype would incarnate through the Earth's frequencies. Israel sought agreement with the other eleven hierarchies to bring its prototype to Earth, which was then and continues to be a realm shared equally between the twelve.

Reaching this agreement was essential before Israel could initiate its plan for the prototype to be brought to Earth. This is due to all of the twelve hierarchies being equally involved in the creation of Earth and her realms and are thus equally, the guardians of the Earth. Through this agreement, it can be said that in a sense, all twelve hierarchies 'birthed' this human prototype, which, after it incarnated on Earth, came to be known through the galaxies as the Terran (the Earth human).

In this way, the Human Hierarchy is unlike the core of the Sirian family structure, known as the Sirian royal line, which was birthed only by Mu. Within the human family structure there is no royal line or core. The power, responsibilities, gifts and blessings are shared equally among the twelve hierarchies that make up the human family structure.

The Elven Family

The fifth structure, the Elven family has been developing for billions of years. It is made up of Elven colonies and races from various planetary worlds and realms. The original Elven frequency was birthed by the Central Sun, and so in all Elven births, the Central Sun is always the father. In ancient times, hierarchies requested the opportunity to birth their own Elven lines. This was permitted as long as the Central Sun remained the father of all Elven lines. This means that in order for a hierarchy to birth an Elven race, it must secure collaboration with the Central Sun.

The signature frequency of an Elven being comes from its mother hierarchy. Like the angelic hierarchy, it holds the additional frequency codes from its father, the Central Sun, that allow the being to be Elven. For example, in meditation the Elven aspect of you may come forward to introduce itself to you. You may have already identified your own hierarchy as being Mu. Therefore, although your Elven genetics originated from the Central Sun hierarchy, your Elven aspect is still of Mu Hierarchy - it shares the same signature frequency as you do.

The Elven King and the Elven Queen inhabit many realms simultaneously. They act as grandparents of all Elven lineages. They are the first elves and are therefore members of the Central Sun Hierarchy.

Since those ancient times, many Elven lines have been born, such as the Neptunian elves who were born into Neptune and the Neptunian line of the Jerusalem Hierarchy and who inhabit the sacred lakes and mountains of Neptune. Another example, the elves of Sirius are part of the Sirian Arm of the Mu Hierarchy. These Sirian elves have conducted many assignments on Sirius and in other planetary worlds, creating natural worlds of tremendous beauty and magnificence.

The Oceanic Family

The sixth structure is oceanic in frequency. All hierarchies have an oceanic representative, balanced in its masculine and feminine frequencies, residing in its councils. The oceanic aspect belongs to the hierarchy of its signature frequency, but like the angelic hierarchy whose father is the Central Sun, its father lineage is the Neptunian arm of the Jerusalem Hierarchy. All oceanic aspects belong to both their own hierarchies and the oceanic structure, usually called the oceanic family or sea family. Within the oceanic family lives the Council of the Oceanic Family, where all oceanic members meet and collaborate.

Often individuals on Earth deeply resonate with water, the sea and its creatures. This is partly because at a soul level they are reminded of the embryonic realms of the Source from which the Earth's seas originated. There are others whose love goes beyond the love that most humans have for the water. Such a person may be the oceanic representative of his/her own hierarchy. As an oceanic aspect, the person has access to the vast realms within his/her own hierarchy as well as a seat within various oceanic councils.

The Arcturian Family

The seventh structure is the Arcturian family. It is made up of the Arcturian representatives from each of the twelve hierarchies. The Arcturian frequency was originally birthed by Tansafarie, which collaborated with each of the hierarchies to birth indigenous Arcturian beings from the Arcturian prototype. Thus the Arcturian genetic codes belong to Tansafarie. Like the Elven race, the Arcturian beings take their signature frequency from the hierarchy they were born into, the mother hierarchy, while Tansafarie is the father line.

The Arcturians are a shining example of true harmony and collaboration between the hierarchies in a community and planetary setting. The Arcturian planetary settlements maintain very high vibrational family and community environments. For example, for a person to ascend and become an ascended master through the Earth's incarnation process, he/she must attain the fifth dimension. On Arcturus and in the Arcturian settlements, all citizens hold fifth dimensional frequencies and, in order to attain the level of an ascended master, Arcturians must attain the seventh dimension.

The Arcturians have highly developed structures that require a high group frequency in order to operate. Every Arcturian is loved and supported in the lifestyle of their choosing and in the level of energy they wish to contribute to family and/or community. In this support framework is an understanding that every Arcturian will contribute vibrationally to maintaining within their own energy fields, a very high vibration founded in love, peace and kindness.

The Arcturian race watches the developments on Earth closely at this time, poised to offer frequency codes to harmony in family and community when the requests for these are made by humankind. The Arcturian family structure has sent members from Arcturus to Earth to incarnate into human form. These Arcturians in human form went through the same birthing and incarnation process as the Terrans (Earth humans) so that they may transcend the levels of human incarnation and thus help clear the way for the ascending human.

Non-incarnating Arcturians have assisted the human family by interacting through their Arcturian forms with the Earth's frequencies. They have spacecraft that possess the ability to enter Earth's atmospheres. In this way, they have been supporting the human ascension project for many thousands of years and will continue to do so until the project is complete. Their intention has never been to harm humankind nor interfere, but to remain committed to answering the calls of those human incarnates who call upon the assistance of the Arcturians in their ascension journeys.

CHAPTER TWENTY

Your Hierarchy from the Seventh to Twelfth Dimension

When you encounter the seventh, eighth and ninth dimensions within a hierarchy, you begin to understand the hierarchy's full co-creational capacity. You begin to see that the human incarnated aspect, the human being, is a very small, albeit very important, component of the entire structure. In the seventh to twelfth dimensions, the true power of the hierarchy is revealed. In these dimensions, one can fully appreciate the magnificence, beauty and wonderment that every single hierarchy contributes to the All That Is. The love that each hierarchy has for the rest of the Ancient Spiritual Family is the most significant in these dimensions, creating a symphony throughout the All That Is. Angelic beings from all hierarchies contribute to this symphony, their pure love flowing always into the 'space' that unifies us all.

Although we will discuss 'aspects' in this chapter, understand that at these levels of a hierarchy, the aspects are more 'shards' of consciousness, vast beings often taking the form of massive rays of light. When we discuss ninth dimensional levels, heading upward toward the twelfth dimension, we refer to vast bodies of consciousness moving through entire galaxies, which may still manifest in more individualised forms when desiring to do so. We may also be referring to entire planets.

It is important to note that from the seventh dimension upwards, the forms are fluid and are not subject to the same incarnation limitations of birth and death like an incarnated aspect on Earth, although some forms of incarnation are still open to them. The Arcturians are a good example of this. When they reach their Ascended Master level, they come to live in the seventh dimension. From here, they may choose to remain in their Arcturian form while maintaining their seventh dimensional vibratory rate. The option to maintain their specific form is still open to them.

Even within these higher levels, every hierarchy has a masculine and feminine balance. This balance is always exact and perfect although it may appear to lead from one or the other, or may appear androgynous. One is never superior or inferior to the other, regardless whether it is the masculine or the feminine leading. In some instances, it is more appropriate for the feminine to lead. For example, the feminine side will lead at the Ancient Goddess Council, and yet within that feminine manifestation, she sits balanced internally within both her feminine and masculine aspect.

As discussed in the previous chapter, every hierarchy has an oceanic aspect which serves as the representative of the water element within their own structure. This connects automatically with the universal water, the waters of the All That Is and the Lord and Lady of the Sacred Waters of Life. The water element representative holds offices in the seventh, eighth and ninth dimensions simultaneously, as well as the lower dimensions, and is perfectly balanced in its masculine and feminine aspect. At the ninth dimensional level, the oceanic aspect of a hierarchy may manifest as the waters of an entire planet, it may be the oceans and rivers of a world not yet revealed to humanity. It may be the creation of the blueprint for an entire species of oceanic creature, such as the dolphin family of the Lemurian Hierarchy. For in the Lemurian Hierarchy at the ninth dimensional level, the oceanic aspect holds the creator frequency and group consciousness of the dolphin species. At the third, fourth and fifth dimension, the oceanic aspect may physically manifest as a dolphin.

Every hierarchy has an elemental aspect who serves as the nature and earth element within their own structure. This elemental aspect manifests itself as the nature realms of the hierarchy's own creation. For example, a hierarchy may create a seventh dimensional realm. Their own elemental aspect will preside over the creation of the nature realms that are to be part of this seventh dimensional realm. The hierarchy may also invite the elemental aspects of other hierarchies to provide diversity within the said nature realm.

In the seventh to ninth dimensions, we find the crystal representative of the hierarchy and every hierarchy has one or more of these beings. This is the essence and 'higher self' of a type of crystal, metal or related substance in various physical planes across many planets. These beings are the overlighters and the higher guardian aspects of the physical substance - they are the essence of the crystal/metal itself. The signature frequency of the crystal comes from the hierarchy to which the representative belongs. Again, we use the terms 'lord' and 'lady' below and when we do so, we use them to refer to the masculine and feminine aspect of the essence of the crystal/metal/related substance.

The crystal representative is the consciousness of the crystal/metal. There are people incarnated on Earth now who are the human embodiment of their crystal essence. Such people are crystal representatives of their hierarchy in the physical plane. They have come in human form at this time to heal the last of the damage to their frequencies. Much of this damage occurred in the mid to final phase of Atlantis. When individuals attempt to misuse crystal technology this harms the being for whom the physical crystal is a manifestation. This misuse is being healed now.

The Crystal Representatives for Each Hierarchy

Central Sun

The substance of physical gold and its higher self, Lord and Lady Gold. Rose quartz is an aspect of Lady Nada within the feminine aspect of the Central Sun. Onyx and lapis are also creations of this hierarchy.

Jerusalem

Lord and Lady Amethyst, Lord and Lady of the Pearl, the physical substance that is coral and shell. Like many crystal beings, they have a presence on Earth, but also on other planets.

Israel

Lord and Lady Copper, Moldavite, Mercury and Lead.

Mu

The diamond energy in all its manifestations. Lord and Lady Diamond. The pink diamond is a direct manifestation of Lady Mu. Uranium.

Tansafarie

Lord and Lady Turquoise.

Bethlehem

Lord and Lady Silver, the blue sapphire and Lord and Lady Sapphire. Moonstone manifested from Bethlehem.

Ishtar

Jade - the Jade Lady, Lord and Lady Ruby.

Shiva

The Lord and Lady of the sacred Shiva Lingam.

Gaia

Lord and Lady Emerald.

Pan

Lord and Lady Amber.

Tansafarie, Israel and Pan

Share the platinum group metals.

Lemuria

Lord and Lady of the Aquamarine stone.

Atlantis

Black obsidian, Lord and Lady Obsidian.

Some crystals, metals and substances not listed here may be 'Council manifestations' where they are the result of the collaboration between various hierarchies. We have not listed every crystal or substance here, but have endeavoured to provide a brief overview.

The Golden Line

Every hierarchy has an angelic aspect serving as the angelic light of the hierarchy. Many hierarchies have a council of angelic beings who support the work of the hierarchy in the creation and maintenance of all of its planetary worlds, realms and dimensions. Connected to and supported by the angelic councils, the Golden Line lives in and flows through all hierarchies and is part of their spiritual anatomy. The Golden Line carries the Christ frequency into the hierarchy and is embodied by the masculine and feminine Christ Consciousness representative within each hierarchy. The office of the Golden Line is found in the ninth dimension within each hierarchy. However, the Golden Line's origins stretch up further than the ninth dimension. Having the line's office in the ninth dimension allows the Golden Line frequency to manifest itself in as many planetary worlds, realms and co-creations as possible and so the ninth dimensional office becomes the line's 'working base'.

The Golden Line can be considered a gift to the Ancient Spiritual Family from the Central Sun. In the Central Sun, the Golden Line is part of its core frequency and is manifested by its every aspect and lineage. The Christ Light lineage, Christ's House, is the operational arm of the Golden Line for the Central Sun.

All aspects within a hierarchy are able to carry this Golden Line, which is responsible for linking the ninth and higher dimensions to Earth's frequency for future generations. Each hierarchy has a line that embodies this cause and becomes its 'operational arm'.

For example, the Maitreya line is the Golden Line of Gaia. Gaia trained a lineage of Initiates within the Maitreya frequency so that these Initiates could travel the portals and pathways between Earth and the ninth dimension, linking Earth with its future and higher potential. In Israel, the Albion lineage carries the Golden Line, manifesting in the physical plane as the ancient god of Briton, Albion, and then in the Arthurian frequency.

Although considered by some to be a myth, Arthur's 'Camelot' is currently the idea, the ideal or unmanifested higher potential, of the Golden Line of Israel. The essence of the line, demonstrated in the idea of Camelot, has been anchored on Earth as a key of potential to lead human incarnates towards a higher and happier future by following their own Grail Quest.

When a hierarchy anchors such a frequency in the physical plane through the planting of a seed in the form of an idea, this seed, watered over many generations, can begin to germinate. When many incarnates allow the germination of such an idea, their combined co-creational 'will' draws the forces together to bring about the physical manifestation of the idea. This is why the Golden Line of every hierarchy is so important to humanity's future; it holds the potential of a peaceful and free future for Earth and all her inhabitants; it consistently anchors ninth dimensional frequencies into the Earth's frequency, and it propels the ascension process for Earth and humanity. It is determined in its intention to see humanity ascend and it focuses this intention continuously on the Earth's outer atmosphere as a way of illuminating the path for those awakening now and for already awakened Initiates.

The Spiritual Hierarchy for Earth at the Seventh to Twelfth Dimension

Seventh Dimensional Angelic Realm beneath the Sea

The angelic realm beneath the sea consists of: archangels and angelic beings who are of a celestial oceanic frequency; sea angels; sea mothers and sea fathers who are angelic beings serving as guardians of the sea realms. Sea mothers and fathers are 'foster parents' of the new Children of Earth beings who are being born into the Earth's plane. They travel through the spiritual embryonic fluid that is the sea and is the womb of mothers-to-be on Earth.

All sea angels are able to live in the seas of Earth while remaining conduits for the finer celestial frequencies to travel through and interact with the Earth's frequencies. They are Neptunian in origin and are part of the chorus of beings who stand as the Ancient Guardians of Neptune. Archangels who serve as the Ancient Guardians of Neptune as well as hold other offices and titles within the angelic realm beneath the sea include, Archangel Coriel and Archangel Raphael, along with Ascended Master Tobias. Although these beings are able to interact in the fourth and fifth dimensions, their home frequency base is in the seventh dimensions and beyond.

Seventh Dimensional Council of Fairies

Fairies are a specific frequency, different from the flower spirits and water sprites, although they share similar tasks. Fairies hold a specific signature frequency, birthed by the Pan Hierarchy, that sets them apart 'genetically' and through their signature frequency from other species of the nature realms. Fairies have the ability to exist in all dimensions, however, there are highly evolved fairies who hold council in the seventh dimension and consider this dimension their home base. Like human beings, not all fairies resonate at the same vibrational frequency and live in the same dimension as each other. Fairies, like humans, are at different stages of evolution. While groups of fairies live in the fourth dimension, other groups have ascended beyond these levels and have become the ascended masters of their own race and species. (It is important to note that fourth dimensional fairies are not 'less than' their fifth, sixth or seventh dimensional cousins. Many fourth dimensional fairies volunteered to remain in this manifestation to shepherd the Earth community through the many levels of their ascension. They have agreed to this as part of their own higher assignments).

The Seventh Dimensional Council of Fairies consists of the ascended masters of the fairy kingdom. This council collaborates with similar councils in the fourth, fifth and sixth dimensions. This higher dimensional council acts as an overseeing body and spiritual guide for all members of the fairy community who choose to accept such assistance. Fairies, like humans, have a choice whether to accept the assistance of the higher realms. Where one fairy may embrace guidance from more highly evolved levels of its own species, another fairy may reject assistance. Human beings exercise their free will rights in much the same way.

Council of Crystal Representatives

All crystal representatives belong to this council. Nearly all members of this council have brought themselves into human incarnations at this time in Earth's history. This is primarily to rectify the misuse of crystal power that culminated in Atlantis. Many crystal representatives are also here in human form to forgive those who misused their crystal technology in Atlantis. The council will also initiate a new wave of education on the true power and correct use of crystals, metals and related substances into the future.

Council of Elders

The Council of Elders are the wise ones who are the founders and apostles of the Ancient Spiritual family. Twelve feminine and twelve masculine members sit upon this council. Although this may be technically considered a council of twenty-four members, we consider it the Council of Twelve for the Ancient Spiritual Family as the masculine and feminine representatives of each hierarchy are 'two that are One'. The Council of Elders contain aspects that are ninth to twelfth dimensional. Each Elder aspect is in direct communication with the divine mother and divine father its own hierarchy. The Elder aspect may be a sub-aspect or direct manifestation of the divine mother/divine father level, which sits at the twelfth dimension.

CHAPTER TWENTY-ONE

Understanding Incarnation

How You Were Chosen to Represent Your Hierarchy on Earth Now

Many want to come to Earth right now to synchronise their ascension with the ascension of the Earth. They recognise this as an opportunity to advance swiftly by benefitting from the shared energy created by a multitude of beings ascending simultaneously. With each new ascension cycle, the Spiritual Hierarchy for Earth takes more and more Initiates through to the upper levels of the fourth dimension where they can begin the final stage of their ascension training.

The length of time this training takes varies from person to person and depends upon the development of all of the person's aspects throughout all her incarnations. Although there will always be variations in the vibrational frequency of a hierarchy's aspects due to their individual experiences and stages of evolution, the state of each aspect contributes to the overall current vibrational frequency of all aspects combined. This is very useful when one aspect of the hierarchy has attained a level of enlightenment in a previous incarnation. Such a high level of attainment is of tremendous support to the hierarchy's next

Initiate readying himself to ascend. This next Initiate benefits vibrationally from the past work of the previously incarnated and ascended aspect of his own hierarchy. The ascended member of the hierarchy may even return as a spiritual guide or guardian to advise this next member of the hierarchy as she prepares for her ascension. In a sense, on our ascension journey we are following in the footsteps of our own higher aspects - the ascended masters of our own hierarchies.

The length of time that the training takes is also determined by our willingness to dissolve the lower levels and ascend - essentially 'our heart must be in it'. Earthly life offers many tempting distractions and while these may at times be used wisely to enhance one's spiritual path (and some may argue are part of the path itself), one must maintain a moderate path, enjoying life while keeping a gentle and consistent focus on home, however one perceives this home - God, the Source, the Tao, the Great Mother, Christ, one's own heart, the Buddha, the Divine Mind, enlightenment etc. In this, our graceful, aligned focus positions us to allow for the natural way to unfold in all situations and moments - and this 'allowing' fast tracks our ascension exponentially. We currently have record numbers on Earth with this focus, vibrating at this frequency and consciously working their way through their carefully planned and orchestrated training programs. Every facet of their incarnations has been designed by their higher selves and incarnation councils to lead them to this point.

In order to understand your incarnation and how it has been developed to support your ascension plan, it is necessary to understand the different areas that your hierarchy's incarnation council considers before your physical life begins. First, your higher council chooses the aspect of itself that will incarnate. This is generally done within the Ray Being level of the hierarchy. The aspect will be chosen according to what the hierarchy requires in order to evolve and expand. It may need to heal sections of the hierarchy and so the aspect may be taken from those sections in need of healing. Your higher council may have chosen to be of spiritual service on Earth and thus will choose an aspect of your hierarchy capable of fulfilling this role.

It may send an aspect into incarnation with higher spiritual attributes and yet with a mixture of other aspects of the hierarchy needing healing. This usually manifests as a life plan that sees the human incarnate having some challenges earlier on in life, overcoming these, and then spiritually awakening during midlife (sometimes earlier depending on the individual assignment).

Generally, evolved aspects who have awakened in one or more earlier incarnations are capable of taking many aspects of the hierarchy with them into human incarnation for the purpose of healing, evolving the aspects and transmuting multiple layers of karmic debt simultaneously. This is one reason why it is important not to judge another's life situation. For these evolved aspects may appear to the untrained eye as changing their direction often in their early years, seeming unable to settle, making 'mistakes', living unconventionally and having lots of karmic debt, but in actual fact they have volunteered to take on the karma of many aspects of their hierarchy to ascend entire sections of their hierarchy. When one is clearing multiple aspects, life doesn't generally present as being perfect in the conventional sense and may even appear temporarily chaotic. This is because in order to clear the karma of multiple aspects, the human incarnate temporarily experiences the karma. Through experiencing it and then making a higher choice while in it they transcend the karma and thus evolve the aspect/s that were once trapped by the karma.

When the hierarchy sends an aspect to incarnate, the hierarchy will address unresolved issues or incomplete assignments with other members of the Ancient Spiritual Family and the aspect will thus incarnate into the most appropriate representation of these areas needing completion. The aspect of the hierarchy will live with the other incarnated aspects of the Ancient Spiritual Family for the purpose of completing these assignments. This is generally done through co-existing with other incarnated aspects in a discrete family life.

When choosing a family to incarnate into, the hierarchy will look for incarnated members of its Ancient Spiritual Family within the physical family lineages. It is not looking for specific individuals, but rather the signature frequencies of hierarchies with which it has agreements or incomplete assignments. In this instance, it does not matter who the physical family members are on Earth, in their human personalities. It only matters from which hierarchy they originate.

In the case of karma, a hierarchy and its incarnating aspect does not have karma with a particular person, but with the hierarchy of that person (it is also possible to have karma with another line within your own hierarchy). It does not matter if the incarnating aspect clears the karma with one or more representations of the hierarchy with which it shares karma as long as it is cleared. This is very useful in the case of an aspect of another hierarchy reneging on completing its assignment with you. Another representation of the hierarchy can be activated to step in and take its place.

This is seen where one may have 'issues with' a certain type of person. It is not always the characteristics of the person you have issues with, but the manifestation of certain frequencies carried by a particular hierarchy in the physical plane. When you heal this emotion towards these certain frequencies and the hierarchy that carries them, your issue with 'certain types of people' will begin to diminish and resolve. In short, it is rarely one individual that disturbs you, it is the frequencies that they carry that you find disruptive to your harmony. Looking beyond the individual to the hierarchy they belong to, will give you greater clarity. You may then proceed to a deeper level by communicating to your higher self and higher council, requesting your liberation from this difficulty and stating your desire to return to your original harmony and peace where the other hierarchy is concerned. In some cases, you may even communicate with the higher council of the other hierarchy to cement your decision to restore peace within yourself. It is not important for you to identify precisely the other hierarchy involved here; it is your intention to be healed that will itself achieve the result you desire.

In deciding your incarnation, your hierarchy will choose a family in the physical plane which resides in an environment or vicinity that your healing plan needs in order to thrive. When your healing plan needs a change in vicinity or environment in order to keep thriving, this is arranged by the Divine Orchestrators of your assignment on Earth. Some Initiates who have incarnated into hostile or difficult environmental conditions may wonder how their home vicinity is beneficial to the thriving of their healing plans. Here, the incarnated aspect must search for the key within to unlock the purpose of this in terms of its ability to deliver the healing of themselves and their hierarchies. Generally, their answer will not lie in this life, but will be found through searching the past incarnations of their hierarchy's aspects. One modality that may facilitate this process is kinesiology where the practitioner asks your body direct questions through muscle testing. Self-directed meditation can also be an efficient way of tapping into answers for yourself.

At various stages of our lives we all experience events that are challenging or find ourselves in circumstances where the path forward seems blocked or unclear. In the meditation below, you are taken to a safe place - the Great Hall that is a fifth dimensional meeting ground for the Ancient Spiritual Family, where you will call forth the aspect of you that may provide the answers you seek. You may also call forth your higher self or your entire higher council to help explain the reason for events unfolding in your life the way they have.

Meditation for Retrieving Past Life Information to Assist Your Understanding of This Life

Visualise your spirit slowly lifting up and out of your body. From its new viewpoint, your spirit can see the whole room that your body is lying in.

Your spirit floats up to the ceiling, through the roof, and to a height where you can see the rooftops of any local buildings.

Moving higher up now, you begin to see not only your area, but also neighbouring suburbs or surrounding countryside.

As you float higher and higher, you begin to feel as though you are moving out of the Earth's atmosphere.

You can see Earth below as you move further out into the galaxy.

You can feel the velvety blackness of the galaxy all around you.

Up ahead you can see the shimmering lights of distant stars and worlds, however you are not going there today, you are going somewhere else that is also safe...

In the soft velvety blackness of the galaxy, you can see not far from you, an outline of a door.

You can tell it is a door against the inkiness of the galaxy as the light from the realm on the other side of the door shines through it.

Float over to the door and place your hand on the door handle.

Gently open the door and step onto the lush green lawn of the realm you are now connecting to.

Shut the door behind you and walk across the lawn.

Above you, you can feel the blueness of the sky, the warm sunshine on your face and ahead of you, the gentle spray of mist from the water features that grace the garden.

As you look ahead, beyond the water features, you see the magnificent and massive, 'Great White Hall'. From the hall extends a fan of white marble steps.

Allow yourself to walk towards the Great White Hall,

drinking in its beauty and strength.

As you walk closer to the hall, you notice that its two massive entrance doors are opening slightly.

A beautiful Being of Light steps out and stands on the marble steps.

This being is to be your guide and support in all that we are about to do.

Sit down with this Being of Light on a sun couch positioned at the top of the marble steps.

From this new position you can feel the sunshine on your face and see over the whole garden.

Connect with the Being of Light that is with you. Feel safe with this energy of divinity by feeling its love and support for you.

Put your intention forward that you would now like to understand any past life situation or aspect that has led to your experiencing the circumstances of your current life.

In the distance you can sense that there is a part of you desiring to reconnect with you. It may be a higher aspect, your higher council, or it may be a part of you from a different time.

As this aspect/higher self/higher council nears, you begin to sense certain characteristics it has. If it is a past life aspect, you may sense its age, gender and possibly cultural distinctions. Study the aspect of you to gather as much information as possible.

If it is an aspect, invite it to now stand in front of you. Ask the aspect why it has come. What would it like to tell you? Communicate openly with the aspect in order to understand the whole story. The aspect may show you visions of where it has come from as a way of explaining itself. If your aspect shows you a scene of its past life experience, stay with it for as long as it takes to understand the issue and then invite the aspect back to the Great Hall for healing.

When you have finished communicating, if the aspect is in need of healing and resolution, invite the aspect to be guided by the Being of Light beside you into a cylinder of white light. This cylinder waits patiently to take the aspect up into the heavens for healing. The aspect has been released to the Higher Realms when you can no longer see the cylinder.

If it is your higher self or higher council presenting, ask this being or body of light to reveal to you elements of your divine plan and blueprint so that you might better understand your life circumstances in this incarnation.

When you have gathered as much information as you can handle at this time, make your way back across the lawn and toward the entry into this special realm.

Thank the beings of light for their support as you step into the galaxy and shut the door behind you.

Feel yourself floating down through the galaxy and closer into the earth's atmosphere. Move towards the building where your body lies.

Connect once again with your body and ground completely into it.

Gently move your hands and toes and reconnect with Earth's floor again.

Take a deep breath and when you are ready slowly open your eyes.

You may need to document any information you have received or make note of any additional clearing work to be done.

CHAPTER TWENTY-TWO

Beyond the Hierarchies

Try and penetrate with our limited means the secrets of nature and you will find that, behind all the discernible laws and connections, there remains something subtle, intangible and inexplicable. Veneration for this force beyond anything that we can comprehend is my religion...

Albert Einstein

Your signature frequency, or the signature frequency that is you, lives at the very core of your being. It does not matter what body or form you take in any realm or world, this signature frequency remains the same and remains at the core of who you are. Your hierarchy is the extension of your signature frequency. This signature cannot be altered, influenced or affected in any way. You cannot swap from your signature frequency, it is beyond your earthly control, far beyond your personality and is the ultimate essence of who you are.

The Great Father/ Great Mother/ the Oneness/ the Tao

- however you wish to perceive this Source, is instinctively venerated and revered by all creation because He/She/It is the unconditionally loving keeper and creator of the signature frequencies and these signature frequencies are ultimately of this Source. This Source holds the keys to these frequencies and only the Source has access to them.

The signature frequencies are incorruptible by external or self-initiated forces. Regardless of whether a human lives as a perfect angel or villain, the signature frequency of that person remains the same. The signature frequencies of us all although different are created equally.

We like to believe that we evolve, that we are 'striving towards something' and in a sense we are; we are working to return home to who we truly are. However, we must remind ourselves that we are not really becoming something and nor do we need to make ourselves into something worthy. We already are that which we are trying to become. We already are and have always been, our signature frequency. At some point we all return to this. But, how do we return to it, even though at the absolute level, we are already there?

As we return in stages to our own hierarchies, so too do we return to our original Source. The ultimate homecoming cannot be achieved by striving for it, but through yielding we connect back into that place within us where we are already home. We find Her, our original mother, in the quietness, in the non-doing, when we momentarily pause in our lives and watch the subtle movement of the wind through the leaves of a tree branch.

Our original mother and our ultimate home is beyond the hierarchies as well as being intrinsically linked to every part of every hierarchy.

In acknowledging the origins of all hierarchies, we thus acknowledge the essential oneness of creation - the All That Is. The Source doesn't differentiate between 'good' and 'bad' as we do on Earth; that something or someone could ever be excluded from the Oneness. A hierarchy may house a manifestation that people view as negative, while people may consider other manifestations worthy. In the earthly plane, at a very basic level this could easily correlate to the upstanding citizen being considered a treasure, but the person who doesn't comply being considered an outcast. In the higher dimensions every aspect of creation and action is understood. Not only does it have its place, it is part of the great balance. And, from the perspective of the signature frequencies, actions are external forces, unable to penetrate the frequency's original purity and are therefore ultimately irrelevant.

In accepting and understanding all twelve hierarchies and all of their manifestations and choices, we have the opportunity to connect to the Source and put an end to the internal tension that judgement and a belief in separation create. Once this is achieved, we realise that all of the hierarchies are connected, they are all part of the Source. Through the Source that is above it all, but also *is* it all, we are all linked. And, ultimately, we are also the Source. At the highest level of your hierarchy, you are one of the twelve gods and goddesses of light, one of the foundation stones of creation and ultimately, you are also the all-encompassing light. Beyond this, the 'you' yields entirely and returns to its essence, and the source of its signature frequency.

As part of a natural universal law of harmony, the way of the Source is to flow as spontaneously as water. Through this natural flow, the divine balance between all energies is maintained. The in-breath balances the out-breath, the day balances the night, as masculine and feminine balance each other.

In this context, the way is reflected through the Law of One: *When all are allowed to be within their frequencies, all shall come into peace and harmony*, which is naturally adhered to by the Spiritual Hierarchy for Earth by way of its alignment to Divine Will. This 'allowing' principle is the essential key in the Law of One - when all are *allowed*. In the words of the late Alan Watts: "Because of the mutual interdependence of all beings, they will harmonise if left alone and not forced into conformity with some arbitrary, artificial and abstract notion of order, and this harmony will emerge *tzu-jan,* of itself, without external compulsion."[1] In allowing the way of the Source to rise and reveal itself in all aspects of your life, harmonious conditions naturally arise - the Source transforms confusion into clarity, difficulty into ease and fear into understanding and peace.

It is in this acceptance and the essential balance that naturally arises from it, that the Initiate can begin to experience something of what lies beyond the hierarchies. While there remains an internal battle between the little mind/lower emotional body and the way of the Source, the Initiate will stay in the third dimensional levels of the hierarchy. However, when the Initiate yields to the way of the Source and thus becomes flexible and graceful, like water, as it were, the Initiate's natural internal balance is restored and the doors to the higher levels of the hierarchy and beyond open.

This yielding is not a new principle. Ancient Initiates and mystics who became masters did so because of their willingness to yield, and some documented their journeys. Through the ancient paths and their related writings we encounter human beings who walked before us, clearing the way so that we could see and remember the truth of who we are.

The key to experiencing that which lies beyond the hierarchies is found through yielding. While it is true that there is a time for warrior-like determination upon one's spiritual path, the time for yielding must also be recognised. In this modern world where 'pushing ahead' and 'slaving away' until the goal is attained is highly valued, the idea of letting go of the struggle, perhaps even letting go of the goal altogether, seems counterintuitive. And yet, letting go is what is required in order to break though that final barrier between yourself and the ultimate realisation of who you truly are - letting go of the barriers around your heart, letting go of the beliefs in your mind, letting go of controlling how you think your 'return home' should be. This relates also and most importantly to everyday life. Learning to let go of control in our

---

1 Alan Watts: Tao, The Watercourse Way. Pantheon Books, New York, 1975, p.44

daily concerns and identifying when it is appropriate to surrender does take spiritual education and discipline - a willingness to acknowledge when we are 'pushing up stream' and the courage to let go of our agenda. Remembering that our signature frequency, our Divine Perfection, already 'is', will surely make this easier.

Here, we see that dance again between the masculine aspects of ourselves moving us forward and the feminine aspects compelling us to let go. The tide rolls in and the tide retreats - there is a time for both. On the spiritual path, one learns earnestly by reading, studying, listening, practising, and then one is guided to go out into the garden and do nothing at all. Through the deepest yielding, in itself very often a lifelong journey, that which is beyond the hierarchies will reveal itself. Just as other forms of investment can yield handsome returns, so your deep yielding here may bring rewards in ways beyond imagining.

Through being reunited with your hierarchy, the wisdom, experience and intelligence of this ancient structure is able to propel you on this journey and guide your steps along the way to your ultimate homecoming. Let your hierarchy take you by the hand and show you the way.

Definition of Terms

All That Is

All That Is, was and ever will be manifest, suffused with the energy of the Source or Creator who manifests as any and all of creation, so that Creator and Creation are One in reality and in divinity.

Ancient Spiritual Family

The Ancient Spiritual Family is a grand structure consisting of the twelve hierarchies which are the ancient families of this universe. The Office of the Central Sun sits in the core of the structure, and although it is technically part of the Central Sun Hierarchy, its frequencies and facilities are available to all.

Arcturians

Higher dimensional beings living in the fifth dimension and upwards. The Arcturians have formed advanced social and community structures that are in service to the Christ consciousness assignment of the Great Ascension. These communities are presently assisting the ascension of Earth and humanity as well as other planetary worlds also undergoing deep changes at this time.

The Arcturian genetic codes and incarnation councils have an 'open incarnation' policy where incarnates from other hierarchies within the Ancient Spiritual Family have the opportunity to incarnate into Arcturian genetics and frequencies. Such incarnates must be aligned to the higher universal laws within the All That Is, for example, the 'Law of One', and have attained at a minimum fifth dimensional consciousness. The original genetic codes, keys and frequencies of Arcturius and the Arcturians are of the Venetian/Venusian lineage of the Tansafarie Hierarchy.

Arkamusha

One of the family names given to the Ancient Spiritual Family after Mu's birth. It means the ark for Mu, the cradle that holds everything that was birthed from Mu's parents as well as everything birthed after Mu and by Mu.

Aspects

Internal characters or parts of oneself. If the soul is a small pool of water, the aspects are each drop of water that makes up the pool. Each drop of water is as important as the other as each drop comes together to make the whole. Likewise, it is essential to the overall well-being of the 'pool' that each drop of water is as clear as possible. Any pollution in a single drop of water will pull down the vibration of the whole pool.

Aspects are not limited to the human form. You can have aspects for yourself living in other planetary worlds, realms and dimensions. Here, they may be in other forms such as animals, birds or other species.

Channels

Channels live within a person's crown chakra, feet and hands. All chakras of the body contain channels. These channels allow for information and energy to flow throughout the human system. Channel systems are also found in the etheric realms above and below a person. These etheric channels create the link to higher dimensions, and to the Earth and sea. There are channel systems in the heart chakra to connect humanity together and to bridge humanity with nature and animals.

Channel systems

A channel system can be likened to a complex matrix of millions of optic fibres. Information travels through these 'optic fibres' from one port to another. The feminine aspect of your mind (the lunar mind) receives the information sent through these 'optic fibres' to you. Your lunar mind is best described as a port that is linked to many other ports throughout the galaxy. For example, you may be connected to the port of St Germain. This means that you will receive transmissions from his port that are relevant to you and compatible with your frequency bands. These thousands of optic fibres (the channel system) you are working through 'hook' themselves into your port (lunar mind). Your channels receive the messages and if you are connected to your lunar mind, you receive the messages also. You may have for example, a channel system that is linked to the Council of Ascended Masters. This means that you will be able to receive messages from that council when required.

It is possible to have many channel systems connected to different beings, realms and dimensions running simultaneously. Such connections may include the sea realms, the angelic realm – to the archangels or to specific guides. In order to differentiate the information, the channel system itself has a 'sorting out section' where it files and organises messages. This is why people who channel can often feel as though there is a line up of guides waiting to talk. Information is lined up rather than all assembled together.

A channel system also has the ability to translate information that may have come from different parts of the galaxy or telepathically from people across the other side of the world that do not speak your language. The channel system will automatically convert data to your understanding and language.

Channelling

Channelling is receiving messages or higher information. It is the process of receiving information through the lunar mind (feminine aspect of the mind). Information is generally transmitted from the lunar mind to you through telepathic exchange or intuitive awareness. Channelling can also be received through automatic writing, visions, sounds, drawings, and through sensations and feelings that bring a knowing. A common form of channelling is instant perception where a person instantly understands something as though the clue has been dropped into their mind.

Channelling – 'Walk Throughs'

A less common form of channelling that requires a mention is 'Walk Throughs'. A Walk Through is one who allows another Being of Light to move into their physical body to deliver a message or perform a healing. The being temporarily moves into the physical body of the person channelling. The person may not remember what has been said and may experience going into a different space or state while the message or healing is being transmitted.

Children of the Earth Hierarchies

There are five Hierarchies that are given the Children of the Earth title. They are Gaia, Shiva, Pan, Lemuria, and Atlantis. They are called as such because unlike other Hierarchies, Planet Earth is their home base - they were birthed either as part of Earth's birthing or onto Earth once she was born.

Christ Consciousness

Christ Consciousness is a force and source of Light. It is a consciousness in its own right, but is connected to and part of the eternal Oneness. It is often perceived as golden light as it has an illuminating and brightening effect and is connected to and a part of the Central Sun.

Christ Consciousness and the Central Sun

The Central Sun is a centre of light, healing and ascension for many planets and realms throughout the galaxy. There is a Higher Council within the Central Sun that assists humanity and Mother

Earth regularly. The council is one of many facilitating the shift of Mother Earth and all those on Earth so choosing, to ascend into the dimensions of Love and Light. The Central Sun Higher Council specialises in such things as planetary and individual ascension as well as the transmutation of fear. Calling on Christ Consciousness to enter every cell of your body in meditation and before you fall asleep is a very powerful exercise. By doing this you allow Christ Consciousness to work in your body to transmute fear and lower vibrational frequencies. This higher energy will prepare you for ascension and make your job a lot easier. Christ Consciousness is able to live within each level of you including your Hierarchy. It bases itself within the Sun Level of your Hierarchy, but is designed to extend down into all levels.

Christ Consciousness Higher Council

There are many beings of light that sit on the Christ Consciousness Higher Council. Lord Sananda, an aspect of Lord Jesus the Christ sits on the council alongside Lord Buddha, St Germain, Lady Mary Magdalene, Mother Mary and many others. The Christ Consciousness Higher Council meetings are open to all beings who have attained Christ Consciousness.

Councils

Higher Councils, Councils of Light. Councils are groups of light beings gathered in equality with the intention to assist in governing specific areas of Earth, humanity, and the galaxy for the highest good and will of all.

Dimensions

Realms of vibrational existence.

Divine Will

Divine Will is the manifested intention of the Divine Father/ Divine Mother of the All That Is. There is no presence higher than this.

Etheric body, etheric vision, etheric plane

The etheric body is the energetic body/field around a human body. The etheric body is found outside the auric field. The auric field is closer to Earth and is denser than the etheric field. Aspects of fear and the personality of an individual can be found in the auric field. The etheric body is a light body and a bridge that the higher self uses to connect to the human self. Contained within the etheric body are higher frequencies, colours, sounds, telepathic abilities and the gift of etheric vision. Etheric vision allows the initiate to see on a higher plane whilst travelling in their etheric body. This, and the telepathic ability, is why the etheric body is used in meditation. The etheric plane is the reality where an initiate can communicate with and see the ascended masters. An initiate travels to an etheric plane in the etheric body to receive higher teachings and training from the beings of light. When you do some of the meditations in this book, you are using and strengthening your own etheric tools and abilities.

Etheric realms

Etheric realms are realities that do not have the density and solidity that Earth has. These realms may seem almost transparent and light whereas Earth appears very solid. Because of the lack of density in these realms, beings living in etheric realms do not have the physical restrictions that humans have on Earth. Etheric beings do not require food consumption to the degree of human bodies and do not experience sickness and ageing as a process of deterioration. Some etheric realms co-exist with Earth and can been seen and visited by humans when they enter the meditative or dream state. Humans can experience etheric realms by leaving behind their physical bodies and travelling in their etheric bodies. Some Initiates train to master this ability through their lives and do this by transmuting the density in their physical form. This is achieved through dedication to meditation, releasing of fear and negativity, and caring for their human body.

Frequency

A set vibration of colour, sound and light.

Hierarchy

Every person on Earth belongs to a hierarchy. A human being is a member of one of the twelve hierarchies that forms part of the Spiritual Hierarchy for Earth. Your hierarchy is constructed of geometric light designs and sound, which houses and organises the many parts of your soul that your soul has chosen to send to Earth and other planetary worlds and realms for experience. Your hierarchy, while participating in the grand assignment to restore Earth, is connected to the Spiritual Hierarchy for Earth and the planet Earth herself.

High Council of Healers

The High Council of Healers is a spiritual body of light and consciousness, which sits in the fifth dimension and is overseen by the Divine Mother Mary.

Higher Self

The higher self is the station into which other aspects of your hierarchy connect and then reach down into your physical body on Earth. The higher self is the director of the plan for your physicality and time upon Earth and administers the practical components of the Earth assignment.

Human Initiate or an 'Initiate'

A spiritual being who has incarnated in human form for the purpose of or intention to ascend or spiritually awaken. A person in some form of spiritual training.

Keys

Information banks of higher technology, colour, sound, light and memory. These information banks are encoded into a person's body or places in the Earth. These are released in a person's body or areas on Earth when the individual or area is moving into a new vibration or higher frequency. Contained within the key is often a memory of themselves in a past time or how to do something they couldn't previously do. For example, you may travel to a sacred site on Earth and whilst there, have a key released in you. You may find for the months afterward, memories activate of times that you have spent there in previous incarnations. Abilities you had in that life may return to you and aid you in your personal/spiritual development in this life. You may find that you have new channels available to you and your meditations have shifted into a higher frequency.

Law of One

The Law of One states that: *When all are allowed to be within their own frequencies, all shall come into peace and harmony. It can be considered the practical operating system for the All That Is.*

Light-Worker

A person on Earth who has made a prior agreement before incarnating or enters into a level of training to:

- Awaken to higher levels of awareness and connect to higher frequencies.
- Be of service to the higher development of humanity and/or Earth, nature.
- Use the keys, gifts, tools and abilities with which they incarnated to aid themselves and others for the highest good of all.

A Light-Worker is a being of light who incarnates specifically to reach a higher level of spiritual awareness and aid others to do the same in the process. This may not always look the way one would expect. They are not always the expected 'upstanding citizens', and may at times be the ones going against the current. They may manifest as rebels, activists or appear to be the villains; in fact it may even be their perceived 'wrongdoing' that inspires others to undertake good deeds to counteract the effect of bad action.

Light-Workers work in all different professions and some not necessarily in professions at all. The Spiritual Hierarchy for Earth places light-workers in all places and walks of life. Light-Workers are the shining lights in the darkness, the guiding lights in a family, and the caring ones in the corporate world. They may challenge the status quo in organisations, companies and institutions. They exist on Earth to guide humanity into another way, to show the way into a more loving way of living and being.

Lunar Mind

The feminine aspect of your mind responsible for allowing channelled information to reach you. The lunar mind receives all higher inspiration and divine guidance. Every person on Earth's floor has a lunar mind, which is connected to their hierarchy. Because of these factors, everyone has the ability to channel. A person can choose not to channel by refusing to connect consciously to their lunar mind. A person can also choose not to have conscious awareness of their hierarchy or higher self.

Because the lunar mind is the feminine aspects of the mind, connection can be made by removing yourself from intense logical and analytical exploration into allowing and trust. Allowing and trust is developed through becoming in tune with yourself and your essential nature. Meditation, prayer, writing, sitting in nature and observing nature's natural cycles and rhythms in your daily life are powerful tools to use when developing a connection with your lunar mind. The feminine aspects of your mind are in essence, creative and intuitive. By allowing your creative self to express, you are exercising parts of your lunar mind.

Memory banks

Memory banks are storehouses for memories; feelings, thoughts, experiences and information. These memory banks are found at the cellular level of a person. Data from previous incarnations can be stored in a memory bank. This data can be triggered by the people, places or experiences of this life, thus activating past life recollection in an individual.

Over-lighting Devas

The Over-lighters, or the Over-lighting devas, are an essential part of the nature kingdom. This group of beings are the over-lighting and overseeing spirits of plants, trees, lakes, rivers and the earth itself.

Shield Skin

The shield skin is the outermost layer of the physical skin and the innermost layer of the energy field. Its health is critical to maintaining the strength and vitality of the physical body and the purity of the mental field. Its robustness and integrity allow the human incarnate to live in the emotional body of the higher self, to have divine command over the human emotional condition. The shield skin is weakened by over exposure to WiFi and mobile phones and eroded by toxic chemicals either ingested or placed upon the skin. The shield skin is strengthened by naturally grown fruits, vegetables and herbs, accurately prescribed homeopathy, flower essences, aromatherapy, sunshine and fresh mountain air, forest or sea air. Sunbathing and bathing in the sea or clean lake and stream water may cleanse and rejuvenate the shield skin. Home harvested rain water collected in a clean environment, purified or distilled and then 'recharged' in the sunshine is also beneficial to the shield skin.

It has been the author's personal experience that eating homegrown watercress grown in pure rainwater is profoundly restorative to the shield skin. Anecdotal benefits have been reported by others through treating the physical skin with 'probiotic sponging' in order to build up the shield skin (probiotic sponging is the sponging or spraying of the skin with highly probiotic liquids such as organic raw apple cider vinegar, water/honey solutions etc). As everyone is different, the Initiate would need to ascertain for themselves whether these methods prove effective.

Signature Frequency

The signature frequency is the indestructible essence of a soul - the soul's quintessence that cannot be tainted or altered or removed from the Oneness. The knowledge of signature frequencies exists on a scale and is of an intricacy that cannot be perceived by humankind. It is the Great Mystery, the essence of which remains forever in the safekeeping of the Source.

Spiritual Hierarchy for Earth

The Spiritual Hierarchy for Earth was formed before Earth's creation. It is the governing body of the planet. The Spiritual Hierarchy for Earth consists of twelve founding individual Hierarchies. As Earth developed, interest in her grew and thus the Spiritual Hierarchy for Earth received new individual members from different parts of the galaxy, however, the founding members remain and are the core of the governing body.

Resources Consulted...

My gratitude to the work of:

Lao Tzu: *Tao Te Ching* (various translations).

Sri Swami Satchidananda: *The Living Gita, The Complete Bhagavad Gita* (1988). Virginia USA, Integral Yoga Publications.

Marvin Meyer: *The Nag Hamadi Scriptures* (2007). New York USA, Harper Collins.

Dr. Norma J Milanovich, Cynthia Ploski and Betty Rice: *We, The Arcturians: A True Experience,* (1990). USA, Athena Publishing.

Alan Watts and Al Chung-Laing Huang: *The Watercourse Way* (1975). New York, Pantheon Books.